CW00940378

Forts & Palaces
of India

Forts & Palaces
of India

Amita Baig
Photographs: Joginder Singh

Om Books International

First published in 2010

OM
Om Books International

Corporate & Editorial Office:
A-12, Sector 64, Noida 201 301
Uttar Pradesh, India
Phone: +91 120 477 4100

Sales Office:
4379/4B, Prakash House, Ansari Road
Darya Ganj, New Delhi 110 002, India
Phone: +91 11 2326 3363, 2326 5303
Fax: +91 11 2327 8091
Email: sales@ombooks.com
Website: www.ombooks.com

Copyright © Om Books International 2010

Text: Amita Baig
Photographs: Joginder Singh
Design: Alpana Khare, Sunanda Kashyap, Neeraj Aggarwal and
Supriya Sahai

All rights reserved. No part of this book may be reproduced or
transmitted in any form by any means, electronic or mechanical, including
photocopying and recording, or by any information storage and retrieval
system, except as may be expressly permitted in writing by the publisher.

ISBN: 978-81-87108-47-4

10 9 8 7 6 5 4 3 2 1

Printed in Singapore

Contents

Introduction

In recent years, there has been growing acknowledgement by scholars and specialists of the significance of history as recorded in the oral tradition and in ancient texts. Written, rewritten, and interpreted over centuries, ancient Indian knowledge frequently remained in the realm of folklore, its authenticity always doubted. Today, there is an effort to accept, albeit tentatively, that these 'tales' are the foundation of India, Bharat, Hindustan.

In India, forts dominate the countryside, evoking long-forgotten battles – a rallying point for new alliances, towards a new world order. Often there is little didactic information about ancient forts, but local legend and belief hold many to belong to the period of the Ramayana or Mahabharata. For over 4,000 years, India has withstood social, political and religious turmoil, each era contributing to the spectacle of empire, testimonial of wealth and power, each building a fortification against the enemy. None of these were built in a single generation but what characterises them is the architectural vocabulary which defines them.

The earliest-known settlements like Mohenjodaro were extremely sophisticated but without fortifications or enclosures associated with later periods when empires were established. Pre-Buddhism, the northwest region of the subcontinent was divided into *janapada*s, or counties demarcated by boundaries. The *janapada*s were named after the tribes or the *jana*s who had settled them. These *janapada*s evolved into larger political entities by a process of expansion which eventually led to the formation of kingdoms known in Buddhist tradition as *mahajanapada*s or great republics.

It was after the advent of the Aryans around 1500 BC that kingdoms began to be established, marking a shift from clan-based societies to small fortified kingdoms. At this time, classical texts began to be written and social structures formalised, establishing hierarchies which were to define Indian culture for centuries ahead. By the end of the first millennium, societies of North India had transformed from pastoral clans to territorial units, ruled by a combination of divinity and power.

The first recorded empire was Magadha. Its capital, Rajgriha, was surrounded by five hills, so it had a natural defence of mountains and rivers. These are the most recognisable remains of ancient India, with traces of walls and bastions still in evidence. The ancient kingdom of Magadha is written about in the Ramayana, Mahabharata, and the *Puranas,* as well as in Buddhist and Jain texts. Magadha was also the first attempt at significant development of an empire as it expanded to include eastern Uttar Pradesh, most of Bihar, and Bengal. Around 500 BC, a fortification was built at Pataligrama on the River Ganga. The region fulfilled the basic requirements for a sustainable fort – water, agricultural lands, extensive forests, and access to trade. It later became the famed Pataliputra. The *Arthashastra* vividly describes the fortified city of Pataliputra, and although archaeologists have subsequently verified its existence and scale, there are no visible remains.

In the early records of military warfare in Magadha, a *mahashila-kantaka*, or large catapult was used for hurling rocks; the *rathamushala*, a chariot fitted with a mace, was used to drive through enemy ranks and, *agni curna*, a compound of saltpetre, sulphur and charcoal, was perhaps the first form of gunpowder to be used. The Nandas, successors to the Magadha lineage, developed the empire so well that its army, as recounted by Alexander's commanders, stood at 200,000 cavalry, 200,000 infantry, and at least 3,000 elephants.

Chandragupta Maurya succeeded the Nandas of Magadha in 321 BC. Kautilya, Maurya's Brahmin advisor, was renowned for his treatise on matters of the state, good governance and military strategy. In the *Arthashastra* he describes how settlements were to be located and fortified, and prescribed six major types of forts: The *mahi durg* or mud fort, the *jala durg* or water fort, the *vana durg* or the forest fort, the *giri durg* or hill fort and the *nara durg* or the one protected by the most able men. Most crucially, it identified availability of water as the essential element in a fort. The layout within the fort was also carefully detailed. At the centre should be the temple, built according to the canonical texts. Its architecture and layout are described in great depth and are still adhered to. Centuries later when many of the forts have fallen into disuse and decay, often the temples are still in worship. Within the fort, the king's palaces were secluded and surrounded by residences of courtiers and trusted nobles, layers which established hierarchies that have never really changed.

Megasthenes, Alexander's ambassador to Chandragupta's court described the capital Pataliputra as *"33.8 km in circumference, perhaps the largest city in the world at that time …eighty stadia in length and fifteen in breadth. It is the shape of a parallelogram and is girded with a wooden wall pierced with loopholes for the discharge of arrows. It has a ditch in front for defence and for receiving the sewage of the city within."* It had 570 towers and 64 gates, a sumptuous palace set within gardens, and contained a series of *apadana*s with columns decorated in gold and silver. The *prasadam* or *apadana* is the precursor to the *baradari* as we know it today and was the basic structure for a palace, often made of wood or less durable material than the fortifications. This was the first attempt at establishing a systematic kingdom with a local government, efficient administration, and large armies.

The Mauryan Empire extended as far south as present-day Karnataka. It reached its zenith under Emperor Ashoka, who adopted the Buddhist philosophy for the state, building monasteries or *vihara*s, and universities, leaving behind a legacy of religious instruction more enduring than that of empire-building. Following Ashoka's death in 232 BC, the empire declined and threatened to disintegrate and it was only in 310 BC that Chandragupta and his successors re-established their empire. By 413, this was once again flourishing. When Fa Hsien, the Chinese traveller visited, he found *"the people are rich and contented, the kings govern without recourse to capital punishment…"*

Even so, the Indian subcontinent was in continuous turmoil. The Dravidians were driven south following the Aryan power struggles for supremacy in the north. A number of dynasties emerged, giving rise to powerful kingdoms, though they still paid tribute to the ever-expanding Gupta Empire. By the 6th century, the Chalukyas rose to power in the Deccan and gradually extended their control over most of the region, while the Pallavas built an elaborate kingdom across most of the southern tip of India, overcoming the Cholas.

In the north, the 7th and 8th centuries witnessed the emergence of a new clan who came to be known as Rajputs. They became the warrior class in Rajasthan and Central India, with huge armies and bodyguards forming a barrier in Western India.

By the 8th century, incursions from Central Asia continuously challenged the existence of the small western kingdoms. Invasions by Mahmud of Ghazni in the 10th century, in no less than 12 campaigns, obliterated those that survived. He reached as far as Kannauj and Ujjain; and laden with treasures and prisoners, he returned to Ghazni. Tempted by the riches Ghazni had won, Mohammed Ghori came to India. He left Qutb-ud-din Aibak as his commander, irreversibly changing the course of Indian history. Aibak soon established his independence and created an empire. It heralded an era of massive fort and religious construction across India. The Slave kings changed the vocabulary of Indian architecture. They were followed, in the 13th century, by the Khiljis who established control over most of the fertile Gangetic Plain of North India, and then, by the early 14th century, the Tughlaqs had established themselves. Although the Tughlaqs held power for less than a hundred years, they left outstanding architectural legacies, as did the Sayyids and the Lodis, who ruled North India briefly. They adapted Indian materials to their architectural idiom and so developed a unique style. Entire cities lived within the forts with layouts similar to those described in the *Shastra*s, but now with a mosque at the centre.

In the centuries ahead, Delhi and the Gangetic Plain witnessed the bloodiest wars for control and supremacy. What is notable in this period is the emergence of Islamic potentates across the country; all of whom fought bitterly for supremacy, especially in Patan, Ahmedabad, Malwa, the Deccan, and Gaur in the east. Commanders who were left to control possessions in the Deccan broke away to become powerful Sultanates, leaving behind handsome architectural legacies. An ill-conceived scheme to shift the Tughlaq capital to Daulatabad heralded the end of the Tughlaqs. The weakened Tughlaq Empire, retreating from the Deccan, gave rise to the establishment of the Vijayanagara Empire, which became a formidable force in the south, with one of the largest and wealthiest fortified cities.

With the Tughlaq Empire in such disarray, Delhi was vulnerable and finally laid waste to by Timur, ancestor of Babur the Great. It was Babur's conquest of India in the 16th century that laid the foundation of the Mughal Empire. Babur's was a hard-won battle with no time to consolidate his empire. He was succeeded by Humayun, who struggled with failure and even retreat. Finally, with help from the Shah of Persia, Humayun re-established himself in Delhi, bringing with him Persian influences to the court. But it was under his son Akbar, a mere 14-year-old when he ascended the throne, that the Mughal Empire reached its zenith. Akbar's rule was defined by the construction of great forts and cities, most notably Fatehpur Sikri. Fatehpur Sikri was not merely a statement of empire, but also reflected Akbar's vision of a syncretic culture, an attitude that defined his reign.

Akbar's historian Qandahari wrote that: *"…a good name for kings is achieved by means of lofty buildings…"*, while Shah Jahan's historian Kanbo legitimised the emperor's passion for building: *"…such things create esteem in the eyes and augment respect and dignity in the hearts…"*.

Akbar's son Jehangir had the good fortune of consolidating the empire, building pleasure gardens and pavilions in the Himalayas but it was Shah Jahan, without doubt, who was the most celebrated builder. His achievements are exemplified in the Taj Mahal, built as much as a symbol of the love for his queen, as for the grandiose empire he presided over. Consumed by avarice, Shah Jahan's son Aurangzeb killed his elder brother Dara Shikoh and imprisoned his father to secure the throne, and ultimately, his ruthless ambition destroyed the Mughal Empire.

During this period, Rajput courts in Rajasthan and Central India were also building and consolidating their kingdoms. The Rajputs were proud defenders of their lands, and built some of India's most extraordinary forts and palaces. Although many of these forts predate the Mughals, it was during this time that they consolidated their positions. When the Mughals invaded Rajputana, many Rajput kings allied with them, thus contributing to what was one of the biggest pre-colonial empires in Asia.

Meanwhile in Western India, Shivaji, famous for his guerrilla warfare against Mughal emperor Aurangzeb, founded the Maratha state. He established his capital at the fort of Raigarh, building many of the Maratha forts which were considered almost impregnable. For most of the 18th century, the Marathas and the Bundelkhand rajas of Central India were a formidable force against the Mughals, and they account for some of India's highest concentration of forts and palaces, perfectly situated for prolonged sieges. In due course, the Peshwas, their Brahmin prime ministers, became the rulers of the Maratha Empire and they grappled with the growing ambitions of the British East India Company. The emergence of the Sikhs in the plains of the Punjab; heavily armed and fearless as they established themselves across the region, posed a formidable challenge to the Mughals, and later, the British.

In South India, the Deccan Sultans had joined forces to destroy the Deva Rayas of Vijayanagara, decimating the population. The region also saw the emergence of the new kingdoms of Gingee and Vellore; as well as the rise of Asif Jah, a Mughal potentate who grew to control most of the Deccan. This was soon to be vitiated by the emerging power of the infamous Haider Ali, a powerful and fearless soldier who, followed by his son Tipu Sultan, changed the fortunes of South India.

India was a desirable destination for traders, conquerors, and maverick bounty hunters, with its spices, opium, gold, and silks on every merchant's list. The Portuguese, by far the most adventurous seafarers, had already presented themselves at Akbar's court in the 16th century. In return for safe passage for the Mughals by sea, they were permitted to settle on the western coast of India at Diu, the first of many forts they controlled in this region.

Following the Portuguese, the British, Danes, Dutch, and French, all found their way to India to seek their fortunes and this depended on the trading ports they could control. The French first captured, Pondicherry and Karaikal on the east coast from the Raja of Thanjavur and then the tiny port town of Mahé on the west coast. These were small takings considering their aspirations, since they too had presented themselves at the court of Aurangzeb, based on the rumour that fortunes could be made in diamonds from Golconda.

The Portuguese, meantime, had failed to consolidate their presence in Cochin and were vanquished by the Dutch. They then wrested Goa from the Adil Shahis in the 17th century, and built upon his fortifications at Velha Goa – then known as the 'Rome of the East'. It was the acme of their colonising ambitions and the centre of prolific construction – forts, churches, and palaces, controlling much of the trade on west coast.

The 18th century saw the emergence of the British East India Company as the most powerful force in the country. They had built Fort William, consolidating their control of Calcutta and therefore, trade along the River Ganga in the east. In the west, they acquired Bombay from the Portuguese as part of the dowry of Catherine of Braganza when she married Charles II. Wresting control of the South from the French and with a base at Fort St George in Madras, the British East India Company controlled the major ports of India and thus all trade. Following the 1857 'War of Independence', the British Empire was established with Calcutta as its capital. The fundamental difference in European forts built in India is that they were designed to fortify themselves against the people as against earlier forts which were built to provide protection for the people.

By the early 20th century, the British decided to shift their capital from Calcutta back to India's historic capital, Delhi. The culmination of British ambitions was in the building of Lutyen's New Delhi, and here too, as in all of India's forts and palaces, an integration of Indian skills, design, and form was achieved. Around this time, the relatively marginalised, but fabulously wealthy maharajas also chose to leave their forts and orthodox lifestyle and adopt the European lifestyle. They built new palaces outside the forts, and of indescribable proportions, as each sought to outdo the other in scale, embellishment, and extravagance. Forts and palaces as they stand today are a testimony to centuries of cultures absorbed and amalgamated.

Facing page: Courtyard in Madhavendra Bhawan, Nahargarh

Ancient Forts

KALINJAR

The most evocative fort of the Vedic era is certainly Kalinjar, which is mentioned in several texts of this period. Located as it is, almost at the border between Uttar Pradesh and Madhya Pradesh, in a remote corner, it remains virtually unvisited. Built on the last spur of the Vindhya Mountains over a 1,200-feet chasm, it appears towering 800 feet over the plains. Sheer walls of impregnable stone emerge out of the mountain. It was once an inhabited area, the hill covered with numerous structures, temples and shrines.

Many legends are attributed to this historic fort. According to one, Kalinjra, son of King Bharata, is said to be its founder while another claims it to be the abode of Lord Shiva. Apparently its very name was coined to represent Shiva who, after consuming poison churned out of the seas by *devas* and *daityas*, rested here and destroyed Jaran, the time barrier. It thus represents the timelessness of Lord Shiva who, it is believed, still resides here.

There is a mention in the Mahabharata of the Lake of Gods, which has been identified as Budhia ki Talab, an old tank excavated in the rock, with steps and several buildings around it. Legend has it that one of the Chandela kings, Kirtivarman, was cured of his leprosy after bathing in the waters of the spring. In gratitude, he built the steps surrounding the tank and the Neelkantha Mahadeva Temple, which still stands today.

The epic poem *Chand Raisa* by Chand Bardai, court poet to Emperor Prithviraj Chauhan, records how Chauhan defeated the Chandelas, and speaks of their history. The great Chandela warrior Chandra Varman of the Chandravanshi clan, (mortal descendents

of the moon), is recorded on a stone tablet in the fort. Ferishta, the medieval historian names Raja Kedarnath as the builder of the fort in the 7th century AD. Local legend has it that many of the buildings were standing on this hill before the fort was built. Although records of Kalinjar are only available after the 10th century, it has significant oral history, and is considered to be one of the first forts built by the Chandelas around the 1st millennium.

The embodiment of Hindu faith, the fort is built on a huge hill, towering strategically over the countryside, its extensive stone fortifications once the cynosure of all eyes. There are two entrances to the fort: the main one is on the north, towards the town while the second is at the southeast. The first entrance used to be guarded by seven gates approached by a flight of steps. The first of these, Alamgir Darwaza, named after Emperor Aurangzeb, is square, lofty, and plain in construction, though rebuilt at a later date. This is followed by a steep ascent up a flight of stairs to the second – Ganesha Darwaza, and higher up on a bend is Chandi Darwaza. There is then a double gate with four towers known as Chauburji Darwaza or the Gate of Four Towers, with inscriptions alluding to many periods. The most important of these gates is Budhbhadra which possesses only one inscription. The Hanuman Darwaza is so named because of the carving of Hanuman on the hill, while nearby is the reservoir of Hanuman Kund. It is thought that these gates represent the seven known planets, or perhaps, symbols of the ascent to heaven. Many rock carvings representing Kail, Chandika, and Shiva-Parvati distract from a fairly gruelling climb up to the fort. The sixth gate, Lal Darwaza, is almost at the top and has a colossal figure of Bhairav carved into the rock. Opposite, there is a statue of Shiva as destroyer with his eighteen arms holding a skull and sword, and decorated with snake armbands. Further on, there is a carving of two water carriers with their vessels attached to a pole. These sculptures are almost completely meshed with the natural grandeur as water courses over them, the sculptures glistening in the sunlight. At the centre of the fort is the great Neelkantha Mahadeva Temple, which is still profoundly worshipped, pilgrimage today taking much the same form as it did 2,000 years ago. The whole area is dotted with sculptures of the Chandela period; though many are damaged and eroded, occasionally, one can see a perfectly preserved example of the pristine perfection of their art.

Central to the sacred geography of Kalinjar is the Patal Ganga, or underground Ganga, which surfaces in a cave carved with sacred images. Nearby small *tals* or catchments are defined with ghats and are reputed to have curative powers. Beyond the Patal Ganga is the Pandu Kund which is approached through a dark passage.

Above: Rock carvings adjacent to the Neelkantha Mahadeva Temple, Kalinjar Fort

Below: The Venkat Behari Temple inside Kalinjar Fort

Facing page: The Neelkantha Mahadeva Temple is still an important pilgrimage site

According to a legend in the Mahabharata, the Pandavas came here to hide when they were being pursued by Duryodhana. Just outside the cave is a two-foot-high stone statue of a *dwarapala* who has stood guard over the fort for centuries.

No one can be absolutely sure when this fort was built, but legend and folklore breathe life into this desolate monument standing atop a hill, hiding forever within its walls the secrets and mysteries of its construction.

Above: Buddhi Talab, now identified as the Budhia ki Talab which has found mention in the Mahabharata

BANDHAVGARH

Bandhavgarh has been occupied well before recorded history and today, archaeologists are verifying 2nd and 3rd-century inscriptions which were the legends of Bandhavgarh. It was part of the Magadha Empire and later ruled by the Vatakas between the 3rd and 5th centuries. The Sengars ruled from the 5th century and the Kalchuris in the 10th century, when it was known as Haihey Kshetra. The Baghelas, Rajputs from Gujarat, captured Bandhavgarh as late as the 13th century, as they fled the Khilji onslaught in Gujarat and ruled continuously since.

As with many ancient forts of India, there are strong mythological connections which are still valued. The hill itself is believed to be a gift from Lord Rama to his brother Lakshmana. 'Bandhav' means brother, and hence its name. Built on a virtually unscalable mountain top, the fort is over 2,000 years old and has found mention in the *Narad Panch Ratra* and the *Shiva Purana*. The histories of the Baghelas and Bandhavgarh are closely connected,

and the former royal family traces its own lineage back to the first Baghela king, Maharaja Vyghradev Singh Ju Deo, whose life was saved by the goddess Durga. Her *vahan* the tiger still roams not just the forest but also the fort. Apocryphal or otherwise, these legends live on in Bandhavgarh.

Maharaja Vyghradev came to this area in 1178, and first settled in an old fort called Marfa near Kalinjar and made Gahora his capital. When his son Karan Deo got married, Bandhavgarh came as part of an extravagant dowry, and in time went on to become the capital of the southern Gahora kingdom.

In time, Bandhavgarh began to be raided by the Slave kings but despite several attempts, the inhospitable terrain surrounding the fort as well as the sheer height of the hill fort made it almost impossible to conquer. Raja Bhedchandra Deo, in 1494 and again in 1499, invited the wrath of Sikandar Lodi by allying against Mubaraq Khan, the Governor of Jaunpur, appointed by the Lodi Sultans. These attempts to capture Bandhavgarh failed as supplies inside the fort outlasted those of the Lodis' invading forces. In the 16th century, Emperor Akbar conquered Gahora and as a result many of its people fled to Bandhavgarh and sought protection in its remote heights. But the next raja, Vikramaditya Deo shifted his capital to Rewa, leaving the fort to its more hardy residents, the last of whom left in 1935.

The ascent to Bandhavgarh is not for the faint-hearted. A steep path cut into the mountains climbs up a virtual precipice interspersed with acutely angled turns and high gateways. Karan Pol, an 11th-century gate at the top, with studded wooden doors still in place, is so small that not even the smallest elephant could pass through it. Bandhavgarh was and remains a perfect *vana durg*. Many buildings still stand – a parade ground, a jail, and barracks – that are reminders of the infrastructure required in a self-sufficient fort.

The layout of the fort, which is extensive, is significant for the large number of water tanks, obviously once quarries which were later dignified with ghats and platforms. The palace area, the Moti Mahal, with richly carved, pillared verandahs and wonderful views across the Bandhavgarh National Park, lies close to the temple.

Ramnavami and Janmashtami are occasions which attract pilgrims from miles around, drawn to its legend, and sacred heritage of almost two thousand years. The oldest temple in the fort is built in Kalchuri style. Its *garbhagriha*, or sanctum sanctorum, has a *shikhara* which appears stunted but would have been the dominant feature at the top of the hill and for miles around. At the edge of water tank lies an 18th-century temple, square in form, with pillars and a dome.

Above: The statue of reclining Vishnu

The most outstanding legacy of Bandhavgarh are the sculpted *dashavatar* or ten incarnations of Vishnu – monolithic stone sculptures set on the crest of the hill, and on promontories, both exposed to the sky as well as encased in the temple structures. There are wonderful carvings of fish, tortoise, etc., each of which represents a different aspect of the powers of Lord Vishnu, the seventh *avatar* being Lord Rama, to whom this fort is believed to be dedicated.

Halfway down, on a small plateau, is the statue of a reclining Vishnu. The Charanganga, a tributary of the River Son, emerges here, cascading gently over the stone, and is still revered and worshipped.

Bandhavgarh National Park spreads across 448 sq km, surrounding Bandhavgarh Fort. The maharajas of yore ensured no forest land was cultivated and that this was their personal hunting ground. Each maharaja had to have his 'bag of kill' and a bag of less than a hundred would not befit a king. Gulab Singh of Rewa (1918–1946) was credited with having killed 616 tigers. That said, they also pioneered the protection and preservation of this tiger reserve – today the fort and its forest sustain each other.

SISUPALGARH

Sisupalgarh is on the outskirts of the historic Ekamra Kshetra, the sacred core of present day Bhubaneshwar. There is no empirical information about this fort, but ongoing archaeology now provides major clues to its history. The most striking feature is the impressive scale of the mud fortifications that surrounded and protected the old town. Outside the fort wall was a moat filled with water, which provided protection against intruders, but may also have been a node of water harvesting for the citizens within. Sisupalgarh was occupied from the beginning of the 3rd century BC up to the middle of the 4th century and therefore, would have played an important role in the fortunes of the Kalinga Empire.

High mud ramparts, with a massive base, were built around the town. Eight gateways protrude, providing impressive entrances; walls had guardrooms, passages, and watchtowers. The excavated western gateway of Sisupalgarh is interesting as it is a remarkably elaborate edifice in a simple setting. It has an enormous entrance, over 8-metres wide with access through inner and outer gates whose gatehouses are reached through steep stairways.

The township inside appears well planned, more or less in a square with streets in a systematic grid. There are remains of the local houses that had two or three rooms, and a large verandah. It was clearly a well-established city and there is even evidence of cart tracks. In the centre of the fort are the remains of a large, pillared hall, with huge monolithic carved pillars.

There is much debate about the origins of Sisupalgarh; some historians think that it is the same as Tosali mentioned in the inscriptions of Ashoka at Dhauli, located not far from here. Others say Sisupalgarh was Kalinganagara, the ancient capital of a king named Kharavela who probably ruled between the Ist century BC and the Ist century AD. Shrouded in mystery, working against the myths and ravages of time, archaeologists are trying to unravel the links between India's recorded and unrecorded past.

Right: Interior of Rani Mahal, Ranthambore Fort

RANTHAMBORE

At the eastern end of the Mewar Ranas' expanded empire lies Ranthambore. It is still located today, much as it has been for thousands of years, in dense jungle, where the roar of the tiger breaks the silence; the quintessential *vana durg*. Ranthambore Fort is located within a national park. The fort itself is about three miles in circumference and spans one of the highest hills in the meeting point of the rocky Aravalli outcrop and the Vindhya Mountains. It is believed to be among the older forts of India – the construction of the fort is said to have started during the reign of the Chauhan Rajput king Sapaldaksha in AD 944.

The fort was a vital citadel as it stood along one of the major routes of invaders into India and controlled the trade route between Central Asia and the great Indian plains. Given its location, it was one of the most contested forts in the region, and one of the most invincible. Apart from its towering fortifications, there was always a thick jungle around, which provided an additional buffer. After the defeat of Prithviraj Chauhan by Mohammed Ghori in AD 1192, the fortunes of Ranthambore rose and fell as successive invaders fought for control of this strategically placed fort in northern Rajputana. From Iltutmish to Ala-ud-din Khilji and the Sultan of Gujarat, Ranthambore was the focus of the expansionist ambitions of the Slave kings. All these were brief interludes in its history as the Rajput rajas, including Rana Kumbha, fought to retain its control. Finally Emperor Akbar laid siege to the fort and managed to capture it by bribing the Bundi defender, Surjana Raja. With each defeat, the Rajput custom of *jauhar* was performed and the women of the palace were consigned to an 'honourable' death.

The fort passed to the Kacchawahas, maharajas of Jaipur in the 17th century, and the area surrounding the fort became a hunting ground for them. Later it was used as a prison fort where prisoners were executed, having been numbed with opium and then thrown over the fort walls. In an account of this, François Bernier, a traveller of the 17th century wrote: "*Prisoners were kept on an average for two months, before the Governor would have them brought out. They would then be placed on the top of the wall and after having them drink some milk (decoction of the milky juice of the poppy), they would be cast down headlong on the rocks below. The opium was given to the prisoners to make them insensible.*"

The interior of the fort is enormous and there is evidence of palaces, pavilions, mosques, cenotaphs, and temples, and at its peak would have been a luxurious royal court. The Raj Bagh ruins lie between the Raj Bagh tank and the Padma Talav or lotus tank.

The Gupt Ganga is a series of steps cut into rock until they arrive at a perennial stream – an essential feature of a *vana durg*. Although it is in ruins, it is still possible to see how magnificent it must have been, even as the buildings are gradually being enveloped by nature.

The fort is approached by an extremely steep flight of stairs, hewn into the rock face and within the crenellated bastions. There are four gates at different levels, which act as guardians; each one placed at a sharp angle to the path in a system that ensured that no advancing army could proceed unimpeded. The last gate is heavily spiked and can still be closed. Ranthambore echoes the past, its silence broken, not only by the endless stream of tourists to the national park below, but also to the Ganesha Temple inside. At the summit and within the protective fort walls is a Ganesha Temple. It is believed that this most auspicious Ganesha gives blessings to married couples and today, the postman carries to the temple, wedding invitations from across the country to seek his blessings.

Above: Padma Talav inside Ranthambore Fort

Left: Massive gateways at different levels protect the fort

BHATINDA

Bhatinda Fort, located in southern Punjab is perhaps one of the most impressive forts of the region. The fort is curiously shaped like a schooner, a shape determined by the land formation on which it is situated. As it was built at the edge of the Thar Desert, it was designed to withstand the harsh environment. There are a large number of historical events that are linked with this fort, given its strategic location on the trade route from Central Asia to India. The Scythians otherwise known as the Sakas, who swept across the plains of India, are said to be the earliest to pass through. Over the centuries, it has been a heavily contested fort that has played an important role in the defence of India.

The history of Bhatinda Fort dates back some 1,900 years, to the 2nd century AD. With the establishment of the Kushan Empire over the northwest of India, the kings set about consolidating and building their empire. The fort is believed to have been built by Raja Dab along with Emperor Kaniska. Some sources trace it even further back, to the Harappan era, but that seems more the realm of legend.

Rao Bhatti founded the town of Bhatinda in the Lakhi jungle area in the 3rd century. The Bhattis were an ancient Rajput tribe who dominated the region at the time. In AD 965, Bala Rao Bhatti occupied the fort and gave it its name. It has also been known as 'Bhattian da Kot' or 'Bhattian da Adda', meaning the Fort of the Bhattis or the Abode of the Bhattis. In AD 1004, Mahmud of

Ghazni besieged the fort and this was followed by the invasion of Mohammed Ghori, who also annexed Bhatinda and appointed his trusted general, Qutub-ud-din Aibak as Governor of Bhatinda Fort. It was Prithviraj Chauhan, the strongest king at that time, who managed to recover the fort after thirteen months of fierce battle. Clearly Bhatinda Fort defended against access into the Gangetic Plain.

Razia Sultan succeeded her father Iltutmish as sultan of Delhi, and was the first woman to be appointed sultan. It was, however, a short-lived position – her brother Feroz Shah usurped her throne and Razia was imprisoned in Bhatinda. One of the legends of Bhatinda Fort is that she attempted to jump the bastions in an unsuccessful attempt to reclaim her throne in Delhi.

Later Brar, a Jat king and a known marauder and warrior, captured Bhatinda. Bhatinda's position was strengthened after that as it was visited by several Sikh gurus – Guru Nanak Dev in AD 1515 and then Guru Tegh Bahadur and Guru Gobind Singh.

In AD 1754, Maharaja Ala Singh of Patiala captured Bhatinda and it became part of the state of Patiala. Maharaja Karam Singh of Patiala later renamed it Gobindgarh to commemorate the visit of Guru Gobind Singh. The fort houses two *gurudwara*s, one in memory of Guru Gobind Singh and the other for the Sikh survivors of World War I. The Nishaan Sahib, a tall pole with a sword on the top, dominates the skyline.

The fort is constructed of large bricks that were particular to this region at the time. An immense structure, it has four large bastions, one at each corner, and 32 smaller ones, in absolute symmetry – the largest with a circumference of 290 feet at the top. The walls of the citadel, which slope from the base upwards, are of extraordinary scale and strength – they are as wide as 53 feet at the base and taper to around 35 feet at the top. The fort walls tower a hundred feet over the surrounding countryside. The bastion tower or *burj* is 120 feet above ground level, and is the remarkable feature of the fort. It is one of the most impressive forts of Punjab.

Top: Stairway to the fortifications and ramparts

Below: View of the main entrance from the gurudwara

Left: Gurudwara *dedicated to the tenth Sikh guru, Guru Gobind Singh inside Bhatinda Fort*

Rajput Forts

Mewar

CHITTORGARH

India's largest fort and Rajputana's proudest bastion, Chittorgarh is the iconic symbol of the valour and sacrifice of Mewar's Sisodia kings and their armies who relentlessly fought invaders.

Chittorgarh is built on a formidable, isolated rocky plateau rising steeply from the rugged plains. Once known as Chitra Durga or Chitrakuta, there is little authenticated history of the origins of this fort. The earliest written accounts say it was taken from the Mori kings by Bappa Rawal, founder of the royal Mewar lineage, in AD 734. Chittorgarh quickly became the most powerful seat of power in Rajputana, and remained the Mewar capital for 834 years. Several attacks and sieges were fought off in this period, but the fort fell thrice: first to Ala-ud-din Khilji, the second time to Bahadur Shah of Gujarat in the mid-16th century, and shortly after that, to Akbar.

The legendary story of Rani Padmini is inseparable from Ala-ud-din Khilji's conquest of Chittorgarh. Besotted by the beautiful Padmini, Ala-ud-din is said to have asked for a glimpse of the queen in return for lifting the siege. The rani's palace stood at the edge of a water tank, and Ala-ud-din was shown her reflection in the water. This only whetted his lust and he ambushed her husband Rana Bhim Singh, demanding that Padmini be sent to him if the Mewar king was to be freed. The rani rose to the occasion and went to the Khilji camp in a cavalcade of palanquins filled with warriors. When she escaped with the rana, an enraged Ala-ud-din stormed Chittorgarh. With the invading armies at the gate and defeat imminent, according to James Todd "…*the funeral pyre was lighted within a great subterranean retreat in chambers impervious to light of day, the defenders of Chittor beheld in procession the queens, their own wives and daughters, to the number of several thousands. The fair Padmini closed the throng …they were conveyed to the cavern and the opening closed upon them*".

Sultan Mahmud of Malwa was quick to try and capture Chittorgarh once Timur began his forays into India to obliterate the last of the Tughlaqs. Rana Kumbha forged together all the

Facing page above:
Detail of stone carvings
from a Jain temple
inside the fort

Facing page below:
Vijay Stambha or
the Victory Tower

Below: View of
Chittorgarh Fort

might of the Rajput rulers and took into war more than 100,000 archers, and cavalry, and over 1,400 elephants against the sultan.

The second invasion of Chittorgarh occurred in 1535 under Bahadur Shah of Gujarat. Bahadur Shah's army plundered the fort while hundreds of women again performed *jauhar*. The third attack, by Akbar in 1567–68, involved a siege of several months, and Maharana Udai Singh II eventually abandoned the fort and retreated to what would later become Udaipur.

Mullah Ahmad described Chittorgarh in Akbar's time: *"The castle is situated in the midst of a level plain, which has no other hills. The mountain is 12 miles round at the base, and nearly 6 miles at the summit. On the east and north, it is faced with hard stone, and the garrison had no fears on those sides, nor could guns, swivels, stone-slings, or mangonels do much damage on the other sides, if they managed to reach them. Travellers do not mention any fortress like this in all the world. The whole summit was crowded with buildings, some several storeys high, and the battlements were strongly guarded and the magazines full."*

PLAN OF CHITTORGARH FORT

1. BADAL DARWAZA
2-5. DARWAZAS
6. RAM POL
7. SALINDHESHWARA TEMPLE
8. KIRTI STAMBHA
9. RANA KUMBHA'S PALACE
10. KUMBHASHYAMA TEMPLE
11. VIJAY STAMBHA
12. SAMIDHESHWARA TEMPLE
13. GAUMUKH TANK
14. HOUSE OF JAIMAL AND PATTA
15. KALIKAMATA TEMPLE
16. RATAN SINGH'S PALACE

Chittorgarh was completely abandoned after Akbar's invasion, and Udaipur became Mewar's new capital, though Udai Singh's son, Maharana Pratap, spent all his life fighting a guerrilla war against the Mughals to recapture Chittorgarh.

The scale of this celebrated fort is such that it almost appears to bestride the landscape for miles around. Its crenellated walls seem to be hewn from the hill itself. The fortifications are largely intact, and the fort is approached through a series of gates on the western side, up a steep and winding route. Seven huge gateways straddle the path, Badal, Bhairon, Hanuman, Ganesha, Jarlan, Lakhama, and, at the top, the magnificent Ram Pol, the last to be built, in 1459. The ascent to Chittorgarh records the heroism of its great warriors with memorial stones at each gateway.

The fort's ability to withstand long sieges was because it had 84 water bodies, of which 22 still survive. Built on the southwestern edge of the Thar Desert, the fort had been planned in such a way that catchment areas, ponds, and stepwells were interconnected and stored enough water to last extended dry periods. The *kund*s (tanks) and stepwells represent a highly sophisticated system of water harvesting and management.

The 15th-century king Rana Kumbha was a prolific builder. Chittorgarh's most iconic symbol, the Vijay Stambh or Victory Tower, was built by Kumbha in 1448 to mark his victory over the Sultan of Malwa. Built on a 10-foot high base and made of red sandstone and white marble, the tower is elaborately carved with religious images and numerous inscriptions. Within the tower is a *mandapa*, a sacred space, and a staircase that at each level, opens into elaborately carved piers. An inscription on the uppermost storey gives a detailed chronological account of the lives and

achievements of the rulers of Chittor by Rana Kumbha's court scribe Atri. The names of the architects of the tower, Sutradhar Jaita and his three sons Napa, Puja, and Poma, are inscribed on the fifth storey.

Another notable tower is the Kirti Stambha, or Tower of Glory, a 70-foot high structure built by a Jain merchant in the 12th century. Rising up to seven storeys, it is also heavily carved in the Solanki style of Gujarat. The tower is distinctive as it tapers towards the top; and is dedicated to the Jain spiritual teacher Adinath, whose life-size statue is housed within.

Of the many temples in the fort, the Kumbhashyama is the most important. Originally dedicated to Varaha, Lord Vishnu's incarnation as a boar, this temple was built in the 8th century AD and then almost completely rebuilt by Rana Kumbha. It is heavily adorned with carvings, as is the Samidheshwara Temple at the edge of the Gaumukh Kund. Towards its north is a small shrine known as Meera Mandir, dedicated to Meera Bai, the famous Bhakti poet who lived at Chittor. The Salindheshwara Temple nearby has a colossal image of a three-faced Shiva with a massive carved surface. The Sat Bis Deori is a complex of 27 Jain temples.

The complex of the king's palaces consists of a series of buildings with pillared verandahs around courtyards. The Rana Kumbha Palace is entered through the Tripolia Pol, an elaborate, elongated gateway that has rooms within. Kanwar Pada, or the Palace of the Princes, was built in 1450 and some of the blue tile work still remains. The Padmini Palace lies at the edge of the infamous Padmini Talav. A three-storeyed pleasure pavilion known as Jal Mahal stands in the centre of the tank, evidence of what would have undoubtedly been a very lavish court.

Above: Palace of Rana Kumbha

Facing page:
Sculpted Digambaras *on the Kirti Stambha dedicated to the first Jain Tirthankara,* Adinath

KUMBHALGARH

The mighty walls of Kumbhalgarh have, for centuries, awed king and commoner alike. Built to a gargantuan length of 36 km, the walls seem to extend to the horizon. This is one of India's largest and most legendary forts, built by the famed Mewar king and Rajput hero Rana Kumbha between AD 1443 and 1458. Kumbha was a great builder of forts, and is reputed to have built more than 32 forts. Kumbhalgarh is undoubtedly the most substantial in scale and influence, even before it was enlarged in the 19th century by Maharana Fateh Singh. The rana built this greatest of his forts on a hill 3,000-feet high, with a grand aspect across the countryside. From here, Kumbha's kingdom of Mewar spread to Ranthambore and Gwalior in the west. In 1568, Kumbhalgarh fell to the combined forces of Mughal emperor Akbar, Raja Man Singh of Amber and Raja Udai Singh of Marwar, after the fort ran out of water and had to be abandoned.

Encircled by 13 hills, the fort is self-contained and was designed to withstand long sieges. The fortification, extending across the topmost ridges of the hills, is the longest in India, and broad enough for eight horsemen to ride abreast. Massive bastions with soaring watch towers reinforce the crenellated walls, making it virtually unassailable. Its fortifications include seven enormous gates and seven layers of ramparts enveloped around each other. Tara Burj is a superbly situated lookout, and invading armies had to run the gauntlet of these seven gates. Aret Pol is positioned at an acute angle, so that mirror signals could be flashed, warning those above. Akbar's armies were stalled at the second gate Hulla Pol, and to this day, the gate is marked with his artillery. Above lies Hanuman Pol, which was brought to this fort after the siege of Nagaur, and then

the Ram Pol and Bhairon Pol. An extremely steep pathway leads to Paghra Pol. At the summit of this torturous ascent is Topkhana Pol or the artillery gateway, and Nimboo Pol further along opens into lemon orchards.

Rana Kumbha's Palace is at the summit of the hill, where he spent much of his time devoted to the arts, often writing devotional poetry. The palace is a two-storey structure with the Zenana Mahal and the Mardana Mahal interconnected. This palace is profusely decorated with wall paintings. The Zenana Mahal has carved stone screens through which the queens could watch the proceedings of the *durbar*.

The beautiful princess of Jhalawar, whom Kumbha abducted from the palace of her future husband in Mandor, was ensconced at Badal Mahal, or Palace of Clouds, so called because in the monsoon it was often swathed in clouds. It was said that after the rains, when the clouds lifted, Badal Mahal could be seen even from Mandor, much to the chagrin of its prince who had his bride-to-be stolen. Near Badal Mahal, on higher ground, are a series of courts and pavilions with their frescoed interiors perfectly preserved.

It was at Badal Mahal that Rana Kumbha was murdered by his son Udai Singh. Almost a century later, another Udai Singh, founder of the city of Udaipur and father of the famous Mewar king Maharana Pratap, was given a new lease of life here. Udai Singh was the posthumous son of Rana Sanga, the Mewar king who at that time was ruling from Chittorgarh. Legend has it that the infant Udai was saved from being killed by his uncle by his nursemaid Panna Dai, who placed her own son in the royal cradle and escaped with Udai to Kumbhalgarh. Panna Dai's son was killed, but Udai survived and was crowned king of Mewar at Kumbhalgarh. He shifted

Above: View of Kumbhalgarh Fort

Facing page top: Wall painting inside the Zenana Mahal

Facing page left: Doorway inside the Mardana Mahal

Facing page right: View of the fortifications and temples situated inside Kumbhalgarh Fort

Mewar's capital to Udaipur after Chittorgarh fell to Akbar in 1568. Maharana Pratap, who ascended the Mewar throne in 1572, was born in Kumbhalgarh.

Within Kumbhalgarh Fort lies Kartargarh, a fortified palace largely rebuilt in the 19th century by Maharana Fateh Singh. Kartargarh is the heart of the fort and contains an astounding 365 temples, including one with a huge *Shivling*. The temple at the gate is dedicated to the goddess Chamunda. The octagonal Vedi Temple was built by Kumbha, while the Mamdeo Temple has inscriptions about the fort's history. The Neelkantha Mahadeo Temple is *sarvtobhadra*, or with entrances from the four cardinal directions, a unique architectural feature. Jain temples abound here; the Bawan Devi Temple alone has 52 shrines. The major temples are still in worship, and the ring of temple bells continues to reverberate as a life force amid the vast ruins of Kumbhalgarh.

THE CITY PALACE

Indisputably the most beautiful and scenic of Rajputana's forts, and now arguably the plushest heritage hotel in Rajasthan, Udaipur Fort was the third and last citadel of the great kingdom of Mewar. The Sisodia kings of Mewar, who assumed the title 'Rana', were widely held to be the vanguards of Rajputana, the bluest-blooded Rajputs. As such, they took the mantle for the longest and stiffest resistance against the imperial Mughals. But the great Mughal emperor Akbar rose to their challenge and, in 1568, took Chittorgarh after a long and sustained siege, forced the then king Rana Udai Singh to abandon the fort and retreat to the countryside. It was here, at the southwestern end of Rajputana, where the land was more fertile and the climate less harsh, that Udai Singh began work on a fort within which the new Mewar capital would be founded. Thus the city of Udaipur was established and Udaipur Fort soon grew to be another redoubtable Sisodia citadel.

Situated 115 km from Chittorgarh and built on the edge of an artificial lake, Udaipur remained a bone of contention between the Mughals and the Sisodias under Maharana Pratap, Udai Singh's son. Rejecting any compromise with the Mughals, Maharana Pratap set about the task of reconquering Chittorgarh but his army was worsted by Akbar and Raja Man Singh's forces in the Battle of Haldighati in 1576. The maharana was badly wounded but managed to escape, and continued to wage a tireless guerrilla campaign against the Mughals. After his death, his son Rana Amar Singh gave in and acknowledged the suzerainty of the Mughal emperor. Peace was finally established and Mewar became one of the strongest pillars of the Mughal empire, so much so that when Prince Khurram, the future Emperor Shah Jahan, led a failed rebellion against his father Jehangir, he escaped to the protection of Udaipur. After Aurangzeb's death in 1707, Udaipur became the target of the Marathas, and the weakened Sisodia kings had to repeatedly petition the British East India Company for protection.

Above: City Palace illuminated at night, Jag Mandir Palace situated in the middle of Lake Pichola

Right: Lake Palace

Facing page: The spectacular Kanch ki Burj, is a 19th-century addition to the palace

The kingdom later acknowledged the British government's supremacy in return for autonomy in its internal affairs. The first British resident at the court of Udaipur was James Todd, whose *Annals and Antiquities of Rajasthan* had a seminal influence on the historiography of Rajasthan.

The City Palace, the royal residence, rises dramatically against the skyline, on the eastern edge of Lake Pichola, an artificial lake which, for centuries, was the city's water source. The palace is entered through a Tripolia, or triple-arched gateway, leading into a ceremonial courtyard to host troops or large public audiences. Beyond this is a complex network of palaces, courtyards, and gardens. Narrow staircases lead up to rooftop terraces that

command a wide view of the beautiful landscape. Amar Vilas, a multi-storey complex near the Tripolia has a garden courtyard at its uppermost level. There are pleasure pavilions and a square pool surrounded by arcades that open into gardens. This building has been constructed to conceal a natural hill behind. The original palace of Rana Udai Singh is in the southernmost part of the palace complex.

The City Palace is renowned for its endless terraces and pavilions, each with a unique character or function. Suraj Chopar is the balcony where the maharanas could be viewed by the people. Chandar Mahal, built above the temple of Nau Choki Dhuni Mata, has sacred importance. Opposite it,

Below: Detail from the Kanch ki Burj

above the treasuries, is Dilkushal Mahal, a suite of four rooms including the Kanch ki Burj, undoubtedly the most striking room in the palace. This room is a 19th-century addition, built in a semi-circle as in a *burj*, with a rotunda. Long strips of glass arranged in a chevron pattern cover every surface, even the domed roof. In a curious hybrid, the room has portraits of the ranas flanked by large European mirrors. Another striking complex is the Badi Chatur Chowk, intricately painted in the Udaipur School: every surface covered with art as well as mosaics of coloured glass, displaying both decorative and figurative motifs. A vast balcony with European tiles protrudes over the edge, with spectacular vistas.

SHIV NIWAS

Towards the end of the 19th century, a royal guest house, Shiv Niwas, was constructed. It is a huge curving structure, built on three levels with extensive suites around an internal courtyard with a marble pool. Each suite of rooms has its own balcony overlooking Lake Pichola, while gardens soften the glare of the white marble surfaces. In the distance, the Jag Mandir Palace glistens in daylight and shimmers on the lake's surface in the evening. Built on a spectacular scale, Shiv Niwas represents the transition from orthodox palace life, secluded from the public eye, to a more robust European style. Each surface within it is decorated; Belgian crystal tables sit alongside chairs in a Rajasthani design, while all the public rooms are exquisitely rendered with glass panels depicting hunting scenes with tigers, lions, and hunting dogs.

JAG MANDIR

The Jag Mandir is the jewel of the palace. Built in 1620, in the midst of the lake and accessible only by boat, it was the ultimate pleasure palace. It was here that Shah Jahan lived when he fled to the safety of Udaipur after rebelling against his father. The Jag Mandir has a perfect little marble pavilion, Gul Mahal, which is said to have inspired Shah Jahan's Taj Mahal. The three-storeyed

marble pavilion, with a domed central chamber, all done in marble with polychrome, is offset by three smaller pavilions with arcades, pleasure gardens, and sculptures. The formal garden, with water channels and fountains, is said to be a later addition.

LAKE PALACE

Jag Niwas, or the Lake Palace as it is known, was built in the 17th century as another pleasure palace amid Lake Pichola. Replete with pavilions, arcaded passages, and formal gardens, it has a central pool that lent itself to court entertainment. In fact, it was a series of garden pavilions with interconnected waterways. Neglected for many years, it was restored and extended in the 1950s. Encapsulating the idyllic Rajput royal lifestyle, Jag Niwas was converted into a hotel in 1963.

Above: City Palace at dawn

Above left: Bhim Vilas

Above right: A painting of Sajjan Garh

Dungarpur

Above: *Udai Bilas Palace, Dungarpur. The royal family occupies part of the palace and the rest has been converted into a luxury hotel*

Right: *The Durbar Hall in Juna Mahal*

JUNA MAHAL

Juna Mahal is the old palace of the Guhilot Ahara dynasty of Dungarpur, related to the Mewar Ranas. The palace lies at one end of the town and within the fortification around the city. It was, like most palaces in India, built as a continuous process by successive generations of kings from 1282 onwards, and was inhabited until the first half of the 19th century until a new and modern palace, Udai Bilas, was built by the edge of the lake.

Juna Mahal consists of a seven-storey tower supported by two lower levels of barracks and stables. The entrance porch is on the third floor and leads to the Durbar Hall. Large murals cover the walls and ceiling of this hall of public audience. The maharajas are depicted enthroned, riding elephants, hunting, fighting, travelling with their households, and presiding over court. The plastered walls are almost entirely rendered with paintings, inlays of mirror, as well as paintings on paper, and even photographs, framed and embedded into the wall surface. The upper floors of the palace were reserved for private receptions, the maharaja's private chambers, and the *zenana*. Here the rooms are smaller and consequently, the decoration more intimate. Many small paintings arranged in horizontal bands depict mythological themes, mainly the life of Krishna, and cover almost all the surfaces. The simplicity and devotional nature of these paintings are an interesting contrast to the royal iconography of the Durbar Hall.

Sheesh Mahal is a particularly fine hall, intricately and richly embellished with mirrorwork interspersed with paintings. Much of the upper portions of the tower form the *zenana*. It is possible that this area was a later converted to a *zenana* as *jali*s or screens have been retrofitted to block the arcades and balconies, creating private spaces.

The palace was first extended by adding the Durbar Hall to the southeast. The ceiling of this hall is supported by freestanding

Above: *A wall of blue china and richly painted surfaces in Juna Mahal*

Right: *Sheesh Mahal*

Facing page: *Scenes of court life are depicted in the wall paintings*

Following pages (37-39): *Mirror-studded walls in Juna Mahal*

octagonal-shafted columns reminiscent of Chittorgarh. The palace was further extended to the north, effectively creating a small chowk. In the mid-19th century, Maharana Udai Singh added a large audience hall known as the Aam Khas, an attempt to fuse the Diwan-e-Khas and Diwan-e-Aam. Conservative in style, the ceiling is supported by temple columns with huge beams, making it an unusually wide, open space. The wall paintings, as elsewhere, are profuse. Adjacent to this is a small personal chamber, the Hingrat, with every surface covered with glass inlay work.

Throughout the palace, there is architectural and artistic evidence of the affiliation with Udaipur, suggesting not merely close relations of the royal families but also between their craftsmen, creating a distinctive Mewari style.

The paintings in Juna Mahal cover an astonishing variety of subjects: from images of gods and iconography of the maharajas to court scenes and natural environments; there are supposedly erotic paintings done inside a cupboard in the maharaja's bedroom. The mélange of themes, styles, sizes, and techniques have turned the interiors of the palace into a museum of art, similar to post-Renaissance mansions in Italy such as the Palazzo Pitti in Florence. In the private chambers on the upper floors, where the paintings are smaller and express more romantic themes, even a large mural of Lord Shiva seems intimate and reachable.

Jodhpur

Above: *Courtyard within the fort*

Right: *Bastions of Mehrangarh Fort*

Facing page: *Takht Vilas inside the fort*

MEHRANGARH

'Garhon mein garh Mehrangarh', or 'the fort of forts is Mehrangarh', goes a popular saying in Jodhpur, capital of the Marwar kingdom of the Rathore Rajputs. The Rathore rulers carry on their insignia the words *'Rann-banka Rathore'*, or 'Battle-brave Rathore' and Mehrangarh wears with great pride, its record of infallibility, having never fallen to a siege in its entire history. Founded in AD 1459 by Rao Jodha, the founder of Jodhpur, Mehrangarh is one of India's most iconic forts. Towering above the beautiful 'blue city' of Jodhpur, its immense height gives it a stature unparalleled in Rajasthan. Mehrangarh has been the fort and palace of the Marwar rulers since Rao Jodha Singh established his capital here. The hill on which the fort is built is known as Bhaurcheeria, the Mountain of Eagles, but Mehrangarh itself means the Fort of the Sun; *mihir* (sun), the lineage deity of the Rathores, is believed to be of Suryavanshi clan (mortal descendents of the sun).

Along with Bikaner and Jaisalmer, Jodhpur is situated on the ancient silk route that linked Central Asia and North India with the seaports of Gujarat. The city became a major trading centre in the 16th century, but the fort had been built a century earlier, according to some, on the directions of a sage who prophesied Jodhpur's fortunes. Trouble arose for the first time in 1542, when Rao Mahadev ensured a safe passage for the Mughal ruler Humayun, who was escaping the army of Delhi's new king, Sher Shah Suri. Sher Shah didn't like this at all and raided Jodhpur two years later, but couldn't breach Mehrangarh's walls. In the mid-16th century,

the fort was besieged by Akbar, who set about the annihilation of all of Rajputana. The Rathores eventually acknowledged Akbar's supremacy and Raja Udai Singh offered his daughter's hand in marriage to Salim, the future Emperor Jehangir. With this gesture, Udai Singh not only ensured his kingdom's peace, but also became one of Akbar's most trusted aides. His son Raja Sur Singh followed him to the Mughal court and even joined the Mughal army in war. The Mughal-Rathore friendship came under strain when Emperor Aurangzeb sent Raja Jaswant Singh of Jodhpur as Governor to the Afghan border, where he died. There followed a period of instability, with the Rathores' fate closely linked with that of the Mughals. The growing Maratha ambitions after Aurangzeb's death in 1707 brought Jodhpur into their line of fire, but Mehrangarh stood firm. By the late 18th century, Jodhpur once again enjoyed stability and peace.

Meanwhile, the Rathores had built one of the largest and most impressive forts in India, flush with spectacular palaces. Each king added a palace or a garden, and embellishments peculiar to different eras, ultimately creating, over a period of 500 years,

a unique fort. Dominated by massive ramparts and hewn out of the stone hill, Mehrangarh rises a majestic 120 feet, with walls almost 60-feet wide at some places. The view of the city is awesome, extending unbroken to the horizon. There are still numerous cannons mounted on the terrace and ramparts.

The lavish palace complex inside the fort is approached from the north, along a fairly steep ramp and gateways situated at sharp angles. The most famous of these are Jai Pol, built to celebrate the victory over Jaipur in 1806, and Fateh Pol, marking a 1707-victory against the mighty Mughals. The Loha Pol, or the Iron Gate, is at the top and leads into the palace. Sculpted into the palace walls are handprints of the royal women who performed *sati*, self-immolation on the funeral pyre of their husbands.

The palaces are largely attributed to the Maharajas Jaswant Singh I and Ajit Singh. Most buildings were built after the 17th century, under the Mughals. The main public halls of audience are located around the Daulat Khana, a singularly handsome structure. Behind Janki Mahal, the *zenana*, lies Shringar Chowk containing the private royal apartments. Sheesh Mahal is a departure from the traditional mosaics executed with myriad pieces of mica or glass, and has instead, large mirrors of clearly European influence. Phool Mahal, built by Maharaja Takht Singh, has his portrait embedded in the opulently painted dome. This, along with the gilded roofs and richly embellished archways, would have made a chamber of great luxury. Takht Vilas is also heavily ornamented, not just with paintings, but coloured glass designed to capture the sunlight. Glass globes hanging from a wooden ceiling and the original *pankha*, or fan, are some charming features.

Above: Sati handprints on an exterior wall of Mehrangarh Fort

Top: Mehrangarh Fort towering above the blue city of Jodhpur. Jaswant Thada can be seen in the foreground

Facing page: Interior of Phul Mahal

Right: Ceiling detail in the bastion connected to Takht Vilas, Mehrangarh Fort

UMAID BHAWAN

The years between the late 19th and early 20th century saw an enormous change in the lifestyle of the ruling families of the princely states. Effectively denuded of their powers by the British Raj, and influenced by European benchmarks for administration and governance, the Maharaja of Jodhpur too sought a world less exclusive than that of unwieldy forts. Maharaja Umaid Singh inherited from his father Pratap Singh, a progressive state, one which now had an established administration as well as a reasonably polished European veneer, having hosted the Prince of Wales and with the maharaja having played polo in England.

Ascending the throne in 1922, Umaid Singh did not have the most auspicious of starts. A terrible famine swept across Marwar and left the people without food or work. The building of Umaid Bhawan, along with that of an extraordinary water-harvesting system just outside Jodhpur, was part of an ingenious famine relief programme, giving employment to thousands over an extended period, while at the same time raising a monument to the 'new' Marwar. The dynamic young prince chose Henry Lanchester, a famous British architect, to build his new residence. The brief given to Lanchester was that the architecture should have a blend of Hindu and Islamic elements within an overarching European Art Deco style, much in fashion at the time. Built from the famous pink sandstone, or *chittar*, found in Jodhpur, Umaid Bhawan is also known as Chittar Palace.

The building of this huge palace is said to have provided employment to 5,000 men over 15 years, and a train line was especially extended to the site to transport material. The palace occupies 3 acres of a 25-acre area, and is surrounded by sprawling gardens, both formal and informal. Its crowning glory is a massive dome, a 105-feet high rotunda reached by an elliptical staircase. The central domed hall is flanked by a ballroom and banquet hall, with neo-Classical, coffered, barrel-vaulted roofs. The residences are located off the rotunda through a series of symmetrical courtyards, *zenanas* no longer obscured but certainly separated. The design ensured that the temperature inside was significantly cooler than the desert heat outside. The palace had a basement swimming pool, electricity, and modern conveniences such as running hot water. Umaid Bhawan's interior is a perfectly preserved specimen of the Art Deco style, with such novelties as a crystal fountain in a corridor of the private wing. The private Durbar Hall has murals with Hindu iconography painted by the Polish artist Norblin, while the Maharani's Suite has an enormous engraving on glass of the goddess Kali.

Above: Looking down on the circular lobby from under the main dome of Umaid Bhawan Palace

Facing page above: Exterior of Umaid Bhawan Palace

Facing page left: Art Deco bathroom in the Maharani's Suite

Jaisalmer

JAISALMER FORT

In a remote corner of the Thar, the romantic, medieval fort of Jaisalmer rises from the desert like a shimmering city of gold. Visiting Jaisalmer is like walking back in time and discovering a forgotten world of palaces, *havelis*, temples, and bustling bazaars. Unlike most other cities, the town grew to accommodate townspeople threatened by invasions, as well as people from nearby villages. They were settled inside the fort according to their community or clan, often building village-style mud dwellings, in contrast to the fancifully sculpted stone houses. Built of the very same golden-bronze rock on which it stands, and silhouetted against the cloudless desert sky, the fortifications seem like a mirage in the desert. While it was a haven for some, to others it was a menacing outpost that extracted tax from travellers crossing the desert. Today, Jaisalmer is essentially a tourist town, and the local craftwork on sale and the folk dances, music, and acrobatics performed by the fireside at night, lend to it an exotic

Above: The palace complex, Jaisalmer Fort

exclusivity even though modern roads have made access to the city much easier.

Situated strategically on the ancient trade route connecting Kandahar and Delhi with Jodhpur, the fort played an important role in the chequered history of western Rajasthan in general and the Thar Desert in particular, from about the middle of the 12th century. The local name for the Thar Desert – *marusthali* or *marubhoomi* (*maru*, death; *sthali/bhoomi*, land) – is an indicator of the vital role Jaisalmer played in trade across the desert. This roughly triangular hill fort was built by Maharawal Jaisal in 1156, when he shifted to Jaisalmer from his ancient capital in Ludherva, 16 km to the northeast. The city acquired its name from the words, 'Jaisal' (after Maharawal Jaisal) and '*meru*', hillock.

The history of Jaisalmer Fort is unique not only because of its rugged environment, but also because it was ruled continuously by one clan, that of the Bhattis, for over 800 years. An episode in the Mahabharata mentions that after the battle of Kurukshetra,

Lord Krishna roamed the desert with Arjuna and prophesied that one day, a clansman of his Yadav community would establish a kingdom on Trikuta Hill. When Maharawal Jaisal was in search of a more protected location for his kingdom, a passing mendicant narrated this tale to him and suggested that the fort be built on this hill.

Caravans laden with silk, ivory, indigo, dry fruits, and opium provided taxes to the Rawals of Jaisalmer. From the middle of the 12th century, Arabs, Turks, and Afghan merchants were regular traders and contributed to the growing wealth of this fort. Once, in a daring and what would prove to be unwise foray, the Rawal king chose to plunder Ala-ud-din Khilji's caravan. This prompted the Delhi sultan to lay a continuous siege of eight years to Jaisalmer. The Bhatti king, now stranded in his kingdom, led a large group of horsemen, or rather highwaymen, who marauded and plundered the passing caravans, in effect still controlling the desert. Peace was restored gradually and the Bhattis regained their hold on the town.

The city grew rapidly, with a rush of intricately carved buildings constructed within the fort and rich traders building embellished residences outside. Jaisalmer stabilised and prospered further during the Mughal period, with Akbar establishing good relations with the Bhattis and encouraging trade.

The Annapurna Temple, Jaisaloo well and Ganesha Prol are the earliest surviving buildings in the fort. Local legend has it that the Jaisaloo well was created by Lord Krishna striking the ground with his *sudarshan chakra* to unearth water for Arjun, dying of thirst in the desert. More realistically, this was probably the only source of water on the hill, thus sanctified to retain its royal exclusivity. Gadisar Talav was constructed outside the fort to cater to the needs of the larger population.

The outer fortifications, along with the *mori*, the passage between, were constructed a bit later in the 12th century. The royal palaces and the adjoining, ancillary area of Kotdi Pada belong to the same period. The king's palace is connected to the queen's palace

Above: The bastions of Jaisalmer Fort

Facing page:
*Interior of the king's
chamber in Rajmahal,
Jaisalmer Fort*

Right: Jharokha *in
Patwon ki Haveli*

Below: *Recently
restored interiors of
Patwon ki Haveli*

by Hawa Pol, which straddles the entrance to Dussehra Chowk. The palaces that overlook this main square are extraordinarily embellished. A fine tradition of craftsmanship unique to Jaisalmer speaks of the great patronage of the Bhatti kings. These palace complexes were built at the highest point of Trikuta Hill.

By the end of the 14th century, construction of the inner fortification walls also commenced. These provided a second line of defence and huge stone balls placed across bastions could be tilted over the edge to deter intruding armies. Many Jain temples were also built in this period. The Chintamani Parsavnath Jain Mandir is still considered extremely important and houses some of the rarest Jain manuscripts. Akhai Pol, at the base of the fort, was built much later and secured it completely.

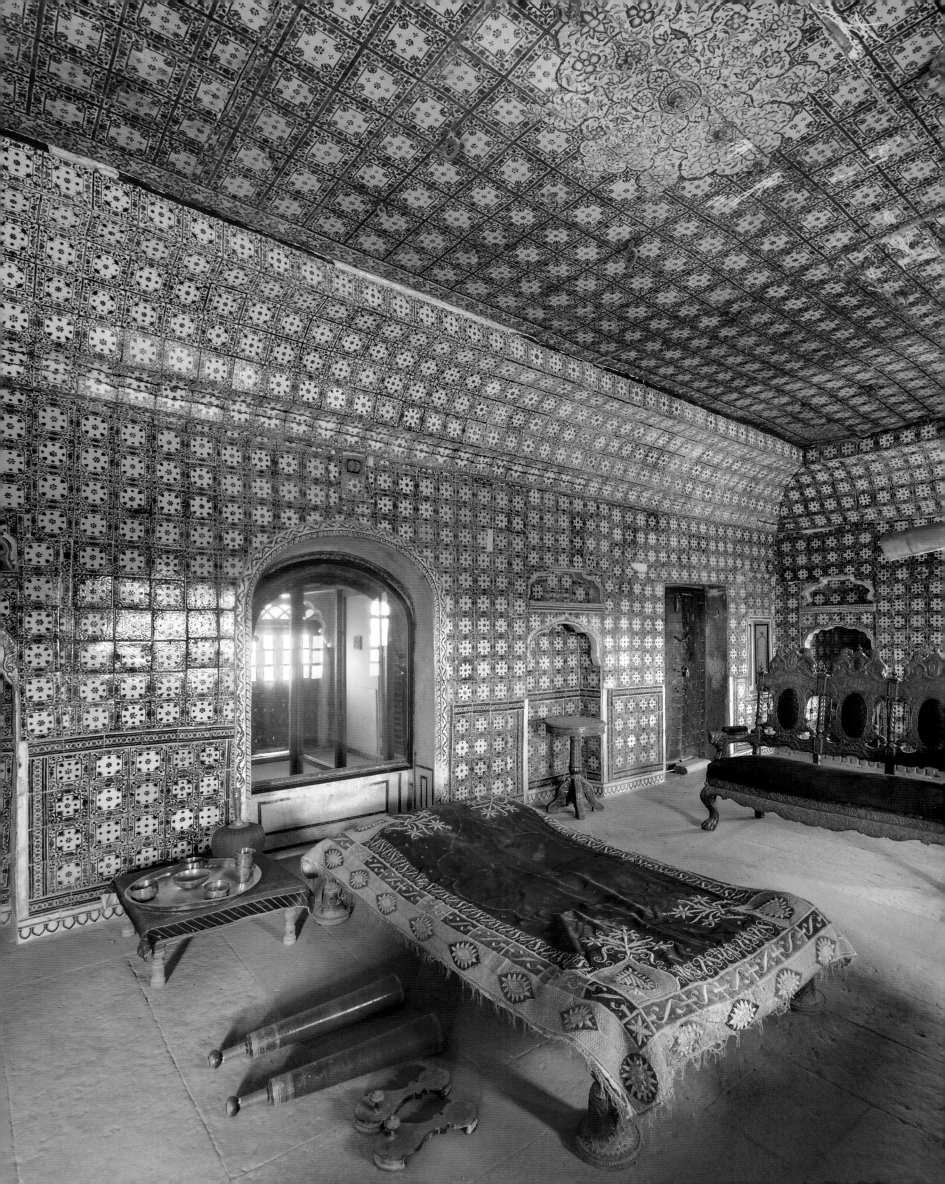

Bikaner

JUNAGADH FORT

Almost at the edge of India and deep in the Thar stands the fort-palace of Junagadh, citadel of the formidable kingdom of Bikaner. Rao Bika, the son of Rao Jodha of Jodhpur, founded Bikaner in AD 1465 The ambitious prince knew he would not inherit the powerful state of Marwar, and so left with a handful of men and founded Bika, the original name of Bikaner, on a remote piece of land, building a mud fort to house his followers. After consolidating here, he tried to reclaim Mehrangarh, Marwar's main fort, a folly that resulted in almost 200 years of war and enmity between Bikaner and Jodhpur. His successor, Raja Jait Singh, was killed by Rao Maldev's

Facing page:
Badal Mahal with a painting of a court scene

Right: Ceiling detail from the Hawa Mahal tower inside Junagadh Fort

Below: Rai Singh's courtyard is the innermost and around which most of the mahals are situated

Marwar army and his territories captured. Jait Singh's son Kalyan Mal allied with Sher Shah to defeat the Mughal emperor Humayun and, as part of Sher Shah's army, sought his revenge against Marwar, laying siege on Mehrangarh and reclaiming Bikaner's lands.

Work on the present Junagadh Fort was started by the sixth raja, Rai Singh, a close ally and general in the army of Akbar. In later years, Bikaner's Raja Karan Singh distinguished himself leading Aurangzeb's attempts to subjugate the Deccan Sultanates. It was his son Anup Singh who finally captured Aurangzeb's most coveted prize, Golconda, in return for which he was given the title of Maharaja. Interestingly, although the rajas of Bikaner were almost continuously at war, mainly against Jodhpur, Junagadh was never captured. Bikaner grew in strength and stature as its territories expanded from Gujarat to Burhanpur, and those influences came to bear on the court. Maharaja Anup Singh ensured that Bikaner flourished in arts and culture.

Junagadh Fort dominates the city with 300-feet high walls, built in 1588, that are surrounded by a wide moat. Originally called Chintamani, the fort has 37 bastions but only two gates, Suraj Pol and Karan Pol, named after the ministers responsible for their construction. Beyond Suraj Pol are a series of courtyards leading to Ganga Niwas, the royal durbar hall built by Raja Ganga Singh in the 20th century. It has huge transverse arches supporting a wooden ceiling, with every inch of wall space intricately carved in stone. Vikram Vilas, the second durbar hall, is comparatively simpler. Anup Mahal, the hall of private audience, opens onto a much smaller inner courtyard. Constructed by Maharaja Anup Singh to mark his successes in the south and his elevated title, Anup Mahal is undoubtedly the most lavishly decorated palace in Junagadh, with gilded plasterwork, an ornamented ceiling, and a Mughal-style niche serving as the Maharaja's throne.

The royal apartments are also spectacularly decorated. Chandra Mahal is ornamented with blue and white tiles, delicately painted ceilings and coloured glass mosaics that create a shimmering interior. The Badal Mahal is painted with monsoon clouds, with the Radha-Krishna narrative depicted on one wall and a portrait of Maharaja Sardar Singh on the other. The Phool Mahal or the Flower Palace is the oldest part of the palace. Its decoration with motifs of vases and rose water sprinkles are typical of the patterns used during the time of Jehangir. The interior is decorated with stucco and glass inlay work. What is most noteworthy about this fort is that almost no surface is left unadorned; each room is carved, stuccoed, painted or inlaid, with successive generations of kings adding to its charm.

Above: Interior of
Anup Mahal

*Facing page
above:* Interior of
Chandra Mahal

Right:
Lalgarh Palace, Bikaner

LALGARH PALACE

In 1901, the Lalgarh Palace was built for the progressive young Maharaja Ganga Singh, educated at the Princes College in Ajmer. Chintamani became Junagadh, or the Old Fort, as the British Resident sought to separate the impressionable young prince from the court intrigue of the old *zenana*. The new palace became the means to bring the maharaja under the direct influence of the Resident. India-based British architect Swinton Jacob designed the palace, and put in modern amenities, European interiors and lavish ornamentation. Even so, the Rajput tradition prevailed, and the palace was built with a delicately carved red sandstone façade, embellished with latticework, screens, balconies and *jharokha*s. The public rooms come first, while the private apartments are arranged around a second courtyard. Swarna Mahal, the reception hall, is decorated in a curious amalgam of western and Rajput styles: a fireplace stands in place of the throne and the ornamentation is without mythological depictions.

Maharaja Ganga Singh was to become Bikaner's most visionary ruler. Even as the maharaja's powers were diminishing under the British, he invested in development and transformed the state's economy by constructing the Ganga Canal, which brought water for irrigation all the way from the River Sutlej in the Himalayan foothills. He had Bikaner connected by railway lines to cities across India, and built hospitals and schools for his people, a legacy that has helped Bikaner become one of the most important cities of Rajasthan.

Bundi

Ruled by the Hada Chauhans of Delhi and Ajmer, Taragarh Fort towers over the small township of Bundi much as it would have when it was built. In AD 1192, when Mohammed Ghori defeated Prithviraj Chauhan, some of the Chauhan nobles took refuge in Mewar, while others established themselves within the protective landscape of the Chambal ravines, suppressing the Bhils and the Meenas to found the state of Bundi. Another account has it that Hada Raj, a Chauhan warrior, fell to Mahmud Ghazni in 1022 when the Afghan was on his way to plunder Somnath in Gujarat. Hada Raj's descendent, Rao Deva, captured Bundi from the Meenas and in time the kingom of Hadoti was established, becoming a formidable force in the area with the help of the Meenas. At its peak, the kingdom of Bundi extended as far as Ranthambore, and fell only to Akbar's forces in the 16th century. In the 17th century, the breakaway state of Kota was formed after the Marathas plundered Bundi for having forged an alliance with the Mughals.

BUNDI PALACE

Overlooking a picturesque lake, Bundi palace is surrounded by the Aravalli Hills on three sides, and bounded by massive walls with four gateways. It stands on the hill beside Taragarh Fort, and served as the royal residence since the early 17th century when Maharaja Rao Rattan Singh shifted here. Rattan Singh was a great patron of painting and Bundi Palace is famed for its lavish frescoes and murals. The palace is approached through the Hathi Pol, a gateway flanked by two enormous sculptures of elephants. The first courtyard has the hall of public audience, a multi-pillared structure with a white marble throne. At the other end, the courtyards open into private chambers that are a treasure trove of paintings. Here, entire surfaces are covered in the most elaborate

Above:
Taragarh Fort, Bundi

Facing page: Interior of the Chitra Shala at Taragarh Fort

Left: Marble throne in the Durbar Hall overlooking the main entrance courtyard, Bundi Palace

Right: *Interior of the palace complex, Taragarh Fort*

Below: *Richly painted interiors, Chitra Shala, Taragarh Fort*

figurative and decorative paintings, later renowned as the Bundi or Hadoti School of miniature painting. The Chitra Shala, Badal Mahal and Chattar Mahal contain the acme of this achievement. The paintings were renewed periodically and there are good chronicles of the Bundi Court over time. Interestingly, the rajas' portraits are part of the narrative themes, with legends of Radha and Krishna, hunting scenes, and decorative motifs coming together in a masterly fusion.

The history of the Hada Rajputs is well recorded in the *Prarara Hadi Rao* and *Vansh Bhaskar*, texts still with the Bundi royal family. Given their strategic alliance with the Mughals, the Hada kings were influenced by the system of Mughal administration and military organisation. Rao Chatar Sal, appointed Governor at the court of Shah Jahan, died in battle leading a unique formation called *gol*, a circular arrangement of soldiers armed to the hilt with spears and lances. This is best described by Todd on his first visit to Bundi: "*…soon the sound of drums, the clangour of trumpets and tramping of steeds became audible. At length, the sadhni aswars announced the*

Raja's presence. As my friend twirled his lance amidst eight hundred cavaliers and fifteen hundred footsoldiers, I thought of his ancestors leading such a gole to maintain their reputation for fealty."

TARAGARH FORT

Taragarh Fort, also known as the Star Fort, is a massive structure, its crenellated walls of immense height, are entered through six gates. A steep, pitched road leads to its main gate, which is flanked by enormous elephant sculptures arranged in an arch. The fort is notable for an enormous bastion, the Bhim Burj, poised over the town. This housed a huge cannon called the Garbh Ganjam, or 'Thunder from the Womb', which is believed to have been cast from the same mould as the massive cannon at Bijapur. Just behind the space for the cannon is a shallow tank, into which the men who lit the cannon jumped to avoid being blown away by the recoil.

A network of tunnels was built to ensure the royal family's escape should the fort be captured. The tunnels lead to the Chattra Mahal down the hill and further into the countryside. The fort has enormous water reservoirs that not only provided against long sieges but also are likely to be the places from where the stone used to build Taragarh was quarried. Most of the palaces within the fort have fallen into decay and there is little evidence of a robust court. There are some memorials to *sati* queens, with the Rani ka Mahal being the most notable building.

Like many other ancient forts, Taragarh is rich in legend. One of these contends that if a Rana of Mewar and a Raja of Bundi met, one inevitably died. This actually happened four times in history, with either Mewar or Bundi's king killing the other with his own hands. Another legend speaks of a treasure of gold, diamonds, rubies and other gems hidden within Taragarh. A member of the royal family could see this treasure only once in his or her lifetime, to select a single piece, but was led blindfolded to it. It is said that the treasure was guarded by an Afghan family of warriors, the last of whom died during World War I, taking the secret of the hidden treasure to his grave.

Above: Ceiling detail from the Chitra Shala
Right: Entrance gateway to the palace complex

Jaipur

AMBER FORT

Amber Fort is unquestionably the culmination of Kacchawaha architectural ambitions. The original fort at this site was built sometime in the 12th century by the Meenas, skilled warriors who lorded over this hilly region and named their fort after the goddess Amba. The Meenas eventually became great allies of the Rajputs.

Amber rose to its height under the patronage of two of its greatest rulers, Man Singh and his nephew Jai Singh. In 1555, a strategic alliance was forged between the Kacchawahas and Mughal emperor Akbar after they acknowledged his suzerainty and married the princess Jodha to Akbar's son Salim, the future emperor Jehangir (though some works mention Jodha to have been Akbar's wife). Man Singh, adopted by the Kacchawaha maharaja, became one of the most powerful generals of the Mughal army as well as a great patron of the arts. He succeeded the throne of Amber and built his palace here. The Kali Temple built by him still remains the royal family's shrine. The temple is heavily carved in green marble and has doors of silver. More interestingly,

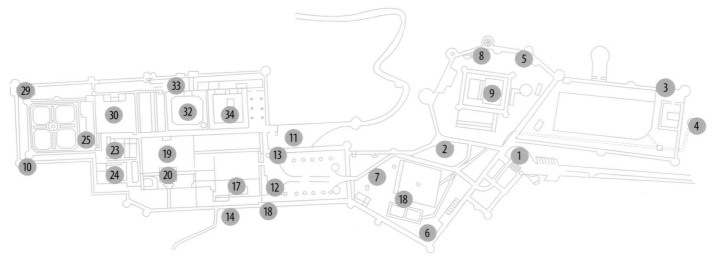

the deity of Kali is part of a meteorite, traditionally revered as Shila Mata, and was brought from Jessore in Bengal.

The ramparts of Amber hug the hillside in a way that it makes them look almost like a geographical feature. Although Man Singh began building the fort in 1592, it was Jai Singh who gave it its present form. Amber represents the finest merging of Hindu and Islamic architecture. The size and scale of its interiors is quite extraordinary. A steep ramp leads to the fort's Jaleb Chowk, or main courtyard, large enough for armies to gather and display the spoils of war. The Diwan-e-Aam is a magnificent structure with double rows of carved columns of sandstone and marble, with elephants carved on capitals supporting the vaulted canopy. The terrace, with views as far as the eye can see, is an architect's delight. Lattice-covered galleries shielded the queens during *durbar*. It is said that Jehangir grew envious of the grandeur of this hall and Jai Singh had the exquisite carvings covered with stucco. The Diwan-e-Khas is painted in the finest Rajput style, with flowers, leafy scrolls, and patterns of lamps and goblets. The Ganesha Pol gate to the south is most intricately decorated with inlaid mosaic and depictions of the Elephant god Ganesha.

The Jai Mandir, or Hall of Victory, is heavily inlaid with mirrorwork, while the Sukh Niwas, 'Abode of Happiness', has doors inlaid with ivory. The Zenana Mahal is around the last courtyard and has spectacular views all around, especially of the exquisite lake garden. Mughal gardens abound, adapted to suit personal tastes, and within the palace complex are a series of water channels designed to cool the private chambers. The walls of the palace buildings are covered with frescoes and paintings depicting scenes from epics, battles, and court life. Amber's finest building, though, is the Sheesh Mahal, the Hall of Mirrors, elaborately decorated with mirrors and excellently preserved. It is a borrowing from Mughal palaces, but remains a perfect specimen of Amber's great wealth and grandeur.

By the 17th century, the buildings of forts began to reach massive scales, not just for military purposes but also expanding the palaces. The expansions also accommodated huge infrastructure, from kitchens and granaries to armouries and temples. The competitiveness among princely states to build grander forts and

Facing page:

Courtyard in Amber Fort

Below: *Amber Fort*

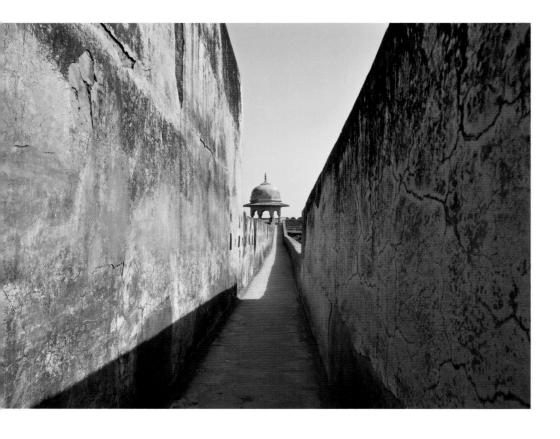

palaces reached its peak in the 'garland forts' of Jaipur: Nahargarh, Jaigarh, and Amber. While the influence of Islamic features, such as the *char bagh*, came to bear on the buildings of this period, the decorative arts also flourished, with walls and ceilings adorned with richly detailed paintings and ornamental work. The three forts of the kingdom of Amber were built in quick succession, each a stronger statement of the imperial power of the Kacchawaha maharajas, as well as one of the great architectural and aesthetic achievements of the age.

NAHARGARH FORT

Nahargarh Fort towers above the now densely populated and huge city of Jaipur, the proud capital of Rajasthan, and its majestic presence still dominates the skyline. Built on a precarious-looking outcrop of the Aravalli Hills by Sawai Jai Singh in 1734, Nahargarh literally means the 'Fort of Tigers', and at the time was probably surrounded by jungle that was undoubtedly tiger territory. Another legend is that it was named after a Nahar Singh whose spirit had cursed its construction. Prayers were held to neutralise this curse, and the fort was named after Nahar Singh to appease his soul. A separate, smaller fortress was built at Purana Ghat for Nahar Singh's spirit and later a shrine was added, where the warrior could be worshipped.

At the centre of Nahargarh is Madhavendra Bhawan, built by Sawai Ram Singh II in the 19th century. It has a unique cluster of 12 identical suites for queens, with the king's apartments at its head. Each of Sawai Ram Singh II's nine wives had a two-storey apartment, set around a rectangular courtyard. These rooms with delicate frescos are linked by corridors and arranged such that the king could visit any queen's room in complete privacy and secrecy from his other wives. In an amusing departure from tradition, it is said that the queens' names were inscribed above the doors.

Sawai Ram Singh II and Sawai Madho Singh II undertook extensive reconstruction and renovation of Nahargarh, and the older buildings soon fell into disrepair. Sawai Madho Singh II was given to a luxurious lifestyle and pleasure retreats, building in 1880 a magnificent Monsoon Mahal for his maharani.

Nahargarh has massive fortifications, in some places as wide as they are high. Much of the original fort now lies in ruin. The cannons ranged across the Hazuri Burj were supposed to protect the fort, but since this fort never faced an attack from either the Mughals or the armies of other Rajput kingdoms, they were usually fired to signal the time to the city people.

JAIGARH

Bulit on top of the Cheel ka Teela, or the Hill of the Eagle, Jaigarh literally means the Victory Fort. It stands between the forts of Nahargarh and Amber, rising above both of them and thus commanding the most strategic position. A deep moat surrounds its fortifications.

Amber and Jaigarh are interconnected with a secret, covered passage. The royal residence was in Amber, on a hill below, and the secret passage ensured a safe escape for the royal family to the much more solid defences of Jaigarh. An austere, functional fort, Jaigarh has none of the pleasure palaces, gardens, and embellishments that mark Amber and Nahargarh. The steep road to the main gate, the Dungar Darwaza, is a deterrent in itself, while the other entrance is through the Awani Darwaza in the east. Jaigarh has several rather unadorned palaces as well as a granary, a well-planned cannon foundry, several temples, and a tall watch tower. The fort used to be the centre of artillery production in the state of Amber.

The highlight of the fort is the massive Jaivan cannon, built in the Jaigarh foundry, and believed to be the largest in Asia, weighing 50 tons and with a trajectory of 20 km. The cannon is delicately engraved and sculpted with an elephant at its jaws. It is said that Jaivan was fired only once, by Sawai Jai Singh in 1720, and the cannon ball landed some 38 km away, leaving a crater so large it formed a lake. Apart from being the main military fortification, Jaigarh was also the storehouse of Amber's treasures.

In its scale and function, Jaigarh was considerably ahead of its time. It has many water channels, part of a carefully designed water-harvesting system, with three underground tanks, the largest of which can store 60,00,000 gallons of water. A 5 km-long canal channels water from the hill into these tanks. At the edge of the desert, adequate water supply was more essential than armoury. Sagar Talav, with octagonal bastions and huge dams, is one of the fort's grand reservoirs.

The core of Jaigarh is Vijaygarh, the fort's foundry. The Mughals and the Rajputs depended on this foundry for their armour. The highest point in Jaigarh is the seven-storey Diya Burj, a turret of lamps designed, possibly, as a beacon. The 10th-century Shri Ram Hari Har Temple houses icons of three gods – Rama, Vishnu and Shiva, and nearby is the 12th-century Kal Bhairava Temple. The palace complex, built by various kings over a period of two centuries, is entered through the Diwan-e-Aam. Beyond this lies the Khilwat Niwas or the military meeting hall, after which is an open, pillared hall called Subhat Niwas, which is charmingly designed with secret passages and large palace-suites for the king and the *zenana*. It has an Aram Mandir, or rest house, while the Vilas Mandir is a pleasure palace for the royal family. The Lakshmi Vilas Palace, surrounded by gardens and courtyards, is richly painted and opens onto a *char bagh*-style courtyard. Remodelled and named by Jai Singh II, this fort was never invaded and remains today, much as it was.

Above: Fortifications that run along the ridges of the hills

Facing page above: Narrow passageway leading to the bastion, Jaigarh

Facing page below: Fortifications with a watch tower overlooking the valley

Chhavi Niwas corridor overlooking the palace
courtyards and Jantar Mantar observatory

PLAN OF THE CITY PALACE

1. CHANDRA MAHAL
   (AND SHEESH MAHAL)
2. PRITAM NIWAS CHOWK
3. RIDDHI SIDDHI POL
4. DIWAN-E- KHAS
5. SILEH KHANA
6. SARHAD KI DEORHI
7. PHOTOGRAPH
   COLLECTION
8. MUBARAK MAHAL
9. CHANDNI CHOWK
10. ISWARI MINAR
    SWARGA SAI
11. ATISH POL
12. HAWA MAHAL
13. TRIPOLIA GATE
14. GAINDA KA DEORHI
15. DIWAN-E-AAM
16. JALEB CHOWK
17. NAQQAR KHANA
18. SIREH DEORHI GATE

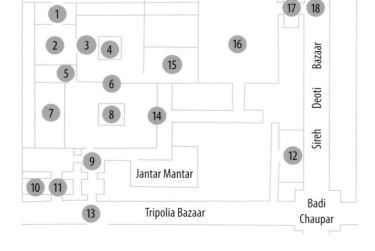

THE CITY PALACE

As the position of the Kacchawahas strengthened in the 18th century, Maharaja Jai Singh's architectural ambitions grew to the extent that he built an entire new city. It was a great planned city, laid out on a *mandala,* of which the city palace occupies two quadrants. Jai Singh II was a great astronomer influenced by Ulugh Begh who had built an observatory at Samarkand. Jantar Mantar was built in 1734 as his personal observatory, and it falls within the palace compound with the Samrat Yantra dominating the skyline.

The City Palace itself was built in 1727, when Jai Singh moved from Amber Fort constructing this enormous complex of palaces, gardens, and temples within a walled city. It was the centre of administration, religious ritual, and patronage of the arts for the state of Jaipur. The walled city was painted pink to celebrate the visit of the Prince of Wales in 1876, and has since earned the cache of 'pink city'. Today, much of the palace is open to public as a museum.

The gates to the palace are a handsome introduction to the splendours within. The royal residence was concealed behind high walls. Monumental arched gateways, with elaborate paintings, lead into the main palace compound. The first courtyard houses Mubarak Mahal, built by Maharaja Madho Singh in the late 19th century, and was designed by Samuel Swinton Jacob. He also designed the magnificent Rajendra Pol, a gateway with a huge brass door leading into the second courtyard. In the middle of this courtyard is the *Sarvatobhadra,* the hall of public audience. Housed here are the large silver urns, made to carry water from the River Ganga to England, for the personal use of Madho Singh. Towering over this courtyard is a 20th-century clock tower.

The third courtyard, Pritam Niwas Chowk has richly painted murals in typical Rajasthani style. Its four doorways are richly embellished with representations of the different seasons; winter has a rose petal design, while summer is symbolised by its peacock feather design.

Chandra Mahal, the seven-storey palace dominates the entire complex and overlooks extensive formal gardens. The gardens are of a grand scale, based on a *char bagh,* divided by water channels and fountains. In the centre is the Govinda Deviji Temple, dedicated to the patron deity of the Kacchawaha maharajas.

Each level of the Chandra Mahal was designed for specific functions. Both the interior and the exterior are richly decorated with paintings by Indian and European artists. Sukh Niwas is at the first level and remains the private apartment of the maharaja. It has walls decorated in the Rajasthani style while its furnishings are completely European. The double-height reception room has provision for women to observe functions from little, screened windows at its upper level. Chhavi Niwas at the fourth level was intended to be a private reception room and is exquisitely painted in blue and white foliate patterns. There are several other palaces such as Pritam Niwas or the Abode of Love which once housed a harem of as many as a thousand women. To the east is Suraj Pol leading directly into the bazaars of the walled city. Nearby the Hawa Mahal, a whimsical façade to a series of terraces, was built to screen the *zenana* as they watched the bustling bazaars outside the palace.

*Left and following
pages (64-65): Interior
of Sukh Niwas*

Below: *Traditional
interior of Shobha Niwas*

Deeg

On an ancient site mentioned as Dirghapura in the *Skanda Purana* and the *Bhagavata Purana*, there emerged in the early 18th century an unlikely challenge to Rajput dominance in the region. As Delhi's power plummeted after Aurangzeb's death, and Rajput states began asserting their independence, the Jats, a mostly agricultural and pastoral people, suddenly became a force to reckon with in the area north and west of Agra. Badan Singh of Sinsini subdued and united rival Jat clans and Raja Jai Singh of Amber awarded him the cities of Thun and Deeg in the hope of containing his ambitions. He was soon declared Raja of Deeg, though as a vassal of Amber. Nevertheless, in the heartland of the Rajputs there had emerged a ruler of significant power who was not one of them.

The foundation of the Deeg Fort as it stands today, was laid by Maharaja Jai Singh of Amber, but it was built largely by Badan Singh as part of his campaign to establish Jat pre-eminence in the region. Deeg was also the place where the later Jat rulers, who established their capital at Bharatpur, constructed their most lavish pleasure palace, the Deeg Palace. Bharatpur already had an impressive citadel and merely needed reinforcement by the Jats. It became one of the most impregnable forts in the region.

The Deeg Palace grew from the modest Purana Mahal of Badan Singh to the flamboyant pleasure pavilions of his brother Suraj Mal (ruled 1733-1767). The most splendid of Suraj Mal's constructions was towards the end of his reign. The Sheesh Mahal is at the centre of the complex of buildings, pavilions and gardens, which in its

Below: *Main living room in Gopal Bhawan*

FORTS & PALACES OF INDIA

day could rival the most extravagant. Situated at right angles to the Purana Mahal, the Sheesh Mahal has octagonal corner towers and a rooftop pavilion with a large *bangladar* dome. It comprises a series of pavilions with waterways linked to large water bodies, Rup Sagar to the east, and the larger Gopal Sagar to the west. The pavilions laid out around Gopal Sagar are not identical but in perfect harmony, rising straight out of the water. Gopal Bhawan to the west is a large central hall with a double-height ceiling flanked by two double-storey wings, Sawan Pavilion and Bhadon Pavilion. Probably used as halls of public audience are Nand and Kishan Bhawans, single-storey rectangular halls, while the eastern pavilion, Keshav Bhawan, is a square, open *baradari*.

Beyond this are the garden complexes. In the southwest corner is the Suraj Bhawan and beyond it is another smaller garden, Hardev Bhawan. This small garden echoes the larger one, with axial waterways and a central octagonal pool. Together with the surrounding buildings, it forms an adjunct to the main complex. Hardev Bhawan has perfectly wrought *jali* screens suggesting it was used as the *zenana*.

Above: *Indian-style dining room with an elliptical marble platform in Gopal Bhawan*

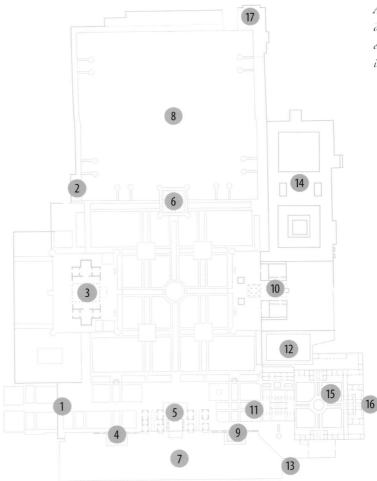

PLAN OF DEEG PALACE

1. SINGH POL
   (MAIN ENTRANCE)
2. TEMPLE
3. NAND BHAWAN
4. SAWAN PAVILION
5. GOPAL BHAWAN
6. KESHAV BHAWAN
7. GOPAL SAGAR TANK
8. RUP SAGAR
9. BHADON PAVILION
10. KISHAN BHAWAN
11. SURAJ POL
12. SURAJ GATE
13. PURANA MAHAL
14. CHAR BAGH
15. SHEESH MAHAL

Right: Sawan Pavilion
reflected in the talav

Below left:
Interior of Suraj Bhawan

Below right:
Crystal-handled
doors of the Gopal
Bhawan living room

Facing page:
Marble fountain in
the main living room
in Gopal Bhawan

Bundelkhand Forts

Chanderi

Chanderi stands on the banks of the River Betwa, on the main route historically connecting North and South India, known to travellers from around the world and even chronicled by Ibn Batuta, the 14th-century traveller from Morocco. It was the northeastern gateway to the Malwa Plateau and the Deccan, and for trade through India. Chanderi was a major transit point, and a humming township, where trade flourished, inns were in plenty, and for centuries, the control of this town was crucial.

In AD 1528, Chanderi was at the helm of the Rajput defence against Babur, founder of the Mughal Empire. The Rajputs had been defeated in Mewar and had incurred heavy losses. Chanderi, under the command of Medini Rao, believing in the might of the Rajputs, allied with Mewar, and held out against Babur, refusing to negotiate a settlement. Babur laid siege to the mighty walls of the fort and in less than a month, it was breached. According to Babur's records of this encounter, "…the fort walls being entirely of stone, were extremely strong…the pagans…put many of our men to flight; they made them fly over the ramparts; some they cut down and killed…they put all their ladies and beauties to death, then, looking themselves to die, came naked out to fight…a pillar of pagan heads was ordered set up."

Chanderi had been the seat of the Pratiharas from the 10th century. Its artificial lake to the east, Kirtisagar, is attributed to Kirtipala, and the fort itself is still locally known as Kirtidurg. The area under Chanderi at its peak stretched from Bundelkhand to the Malwa Plateau. However, from the 13th century onwards, it was assaulted, first by the sultans of Delhi and then the Malwa sultans. Chanderi's rajas were steadfast and mobilised more than 200,000 troops and 5,000 horseman to defend themselves but ultimately they were defeated. Chanderi's location on the route to the Deccan made it vulnerable and it was captured by Ala-ud-din Khilji's army on their long march to Warangal. Later as Malwa grew in importance during the height of the Delhi Sultanates, this region again became independent.

Its outer fortifications and ramparts extend a mile north to south and are of an amazing depth, at some places said to be almost three quarters of a mile. It has many gates: Khooni Darwaza is from where prisoners were thrown to death; Delhi Gate is a majestic structure in its outer fortification with carved *shardul*s, mythical, horse-like creatures seen more often as temple art. Chanderi's architecture reflects the different periods of its history. The longest reign was that of Mahmud Khilji, who, over thirty years of his reign, built some of its finest buildings. The lower fort or Bala Quila has a hollow corridor built into its bastion walls. Within the Qila is the Badal Mahal, one of Chanderi's finest gateways. It is

distinctive as a free-standing arch with tall tapering bastions, and is akin to a minaret, it is spanned by two arches, one above the other, connected at the top with a filigree *jali*; and at the lower archway it is spanned by an arch with heavily carved friezes reminiscent of temple *toran*s. It is thought to have been built by Mahmud as a commemorative arch, or perhaps as an entrance archway to *mahal*s that no longer exist.

Mahmud also built the seven-storeyed Kushak Mahal in 1445. Its lofty, arched passageways, high walls lit by clerestory windows, and impressive interiors are noteworthy. The architecture here is distinctly Gujarati in its execution and it is believed that workmen captured in Gujarat would have been transported here to build these simple yet impressive sandstone buildings. Nearby, Pathani Darwaza is similar to Badal Mahal, but is more heavily ornamented. Jami Masjid is Persian in design, similar to that in Mandu, with domed arcades and a significant façade punctuated by large bays and arches. The curve of the arches supporting the eaves reflects the fusion of Hindu craftsmanship in an Islamic building.

An interesting feature in Chanderi are its huge carved stone panels depicting *Shahi Ghore*, or royal horses. According to local lore, these huge carvings mark the graves of the royal horses. Near the breach in the fortification, there are three standing Jain images and three lotus *Teerthankara*s.

Mahmud's son Ghiyas-ud-din Tughlaq controlled Chanderi through a Governor, Sher Khan who built Kati Ghati, an engineering feat of its time cut into the hillside. Kati Ghati served many, from the armies of Daulat Rao Scindia to the British much later.

The 15th-century Raja and Rani Mahal remain prominent buildings in the citadel, linked by underground passages and with a *baoli*, or stepwell underneath, the palaces were self-sufficient. The Rani Mahal is a more delicately carved structure with rooms leading off series of courtyards and gardens. The upper levels have carved *jali*s and *jharokha*s, similar to those at Orchha. It also has a *hamam* or bathing pavilion alongside. The Raja Mahal has the Chaubisi Temple on one side and the Kunwar Sahib ki Haveli, or Prince's House on the other.

Chanderi's history was fraught with uncertainty. While it prospered under Akbar and Jehangir, once again assuming its role as a centre of trade and producer of gossamer fabric which were famous in the royal courts. With the decline of the Mughals and the rise of Maratha power, Chanderi was without moorings. It fell to Malhar Rao Holkar of Indore. Its last ruler Ramchandra retired to Ayodhya and in this vacuum the Scindias occupied Chanderi. As part of the re-alignment imposed by the British, the astute Scindias ironically transferred Chanderi and its fort to them.

Top: Chanderi Fort

Facing page:
Main façade of
Kushak Mahal

Orchha

Above:
Raja Mahal, illuminated

Facing page: *Interior of Jehangir Mahal*

Through the 16th and 17th centuries, the relatively small kingdom of Orchha produced the most extraordinary architecture and art in the Bundelkhand region. Not far from Jhansi and Datia, Orchha was the capital of the Bundelkhand states from 1531 to 1738, established after the fall of Garkhunder to the Tughlaq armies. During a hunting expedition, the Bundela Raja Rudra Pratap came across a spot near the River Betwa and was so charmed by it that he shifted his capital from Kundar to Orchha, 'The Hidden Place'. Although he was killed fairly soon after starting the fort construction, not in war but while rescuing a cow from the clutches of a tiger, his sons completed building what was to become one of India's most picturesque forts.

Raja Bharti Chand built the citadel at the time when Emperor Akbar's forces were expanding territories across Central India. A hostile terrain reinforced Orchha's defences and the Mughals had to seek support from the Kacchawahas of Narwar to reach Orchha. Eventually, the Raja of Orchha had to secede to Mughal power. However, it was his brother Madhukar Shah who upheld the dignity of the court, refusing to join the imperial army on its southern campaigns, and appearing before the emperor wearing a *tilak*, a mark forbidden by Akbar but which ultimately earned him the emperor's respect.

Then followed a period of internecine wars, which were finally resolved by Jehangir, who appointed Raja Bir Singh as Raja of Orchha, essentially as compensation for murdering Abul Fazl,

Akbar's confidante and court chronicler. It is said that not only did Bir Singh murder Abul Fazl, but he also severed his head and dispatched it to Allahabad Fort as an exhibit to Prince Salim, the future Emperor Jehangir. But Orchha was to pay the price during the reign of Shah Jahan, who was determined to avenge Bir Singh's lack of fealty during his revolt against his father, Jehangir.

Raja Jhujar Singh fled from Orchha when the emperor-in-waiting, Prince Khurram (Shah Jahan), stormed Orchha, but he was soon killed by the Gonds. This left Khurram with a free hand to install Devi Singh of Chanderi, a more loyal subject, as Raja of Orchha in 1634. Inspired by the Maratha consolidations in Central India, Jhujar Singh's brother returned to the throne at Orchha and sided with the Marathas at a time when Mughal fortunes were declining.

Raja Bir Singh was a prodigious builder and has to his credit more than 52 forts and palaces, including the Narsingh Dev Fort in Datia and the citadel at Jhansi. He built much of Orchha's incredible palaces, most notably the Raja Mahal and the Jehangir Mahal. The Mughal influence on these palaces is visible, as they are executed in an almost seamless union of local architecture and decorative arts derived from the Mughals.

The fortifications of Orchha were constructed along the river so that it almost forms an island, accessed only by a bridge. Resting on massive piers of granite, the bridge has high parapets with small niches and pavilions overlooking the river, an architectural feat in itself. Orchha's palaces lie within the fort walls and are set around a

courtyard, the principal palaces being Raja Mahal, Jehangir Mahal and Rai Parveen Mahal.

Jehangir Mahal, built in honour of Emperor Jehangir's visit to Orchha, is the most outstanding. The huge palace, built around a courtyard, has a heavily carved façade, arcades, fluted domes, and sandstone walls; with every surface richly decorated. The imposing entry is through a cusped archway flanked by sculpted elephant brackets holding up the cornices, and leads into the courtyard. Overlooking the River Betwa, five storeys of profusely decorated chambers taper as they rise. On the riverside, the palace is screened by latticework windows, causing a play of sunlight against the shining lime plaster. Pavilions and *chattri*s at the top are as delicately carved as lace. Each wall is painted, each lintel is carved. The Raas Lila, the mythical dance of Krishna with Radha and the *gopi*s, is illustrated along the walls of a courtyard that has a fountain at the centre. Mughal-style gardens have water channels gushing through them. Near the Phool Bagh, the flower garden, is a *baradari* leading to the *zenana*, which also has a complex network of water channels flowing through the buildings, keeping the interiors relatively cool in the summer.

Raja Rudra Pratap started the construction of Raja Mahal, but died in 1531, while the work was still in progress. Raja Madhukar Shah, one of Orchha's most prominent rulers, completed the building and infused it with a great extravagance. The palace is across the main courtyard and set in the form of a square with

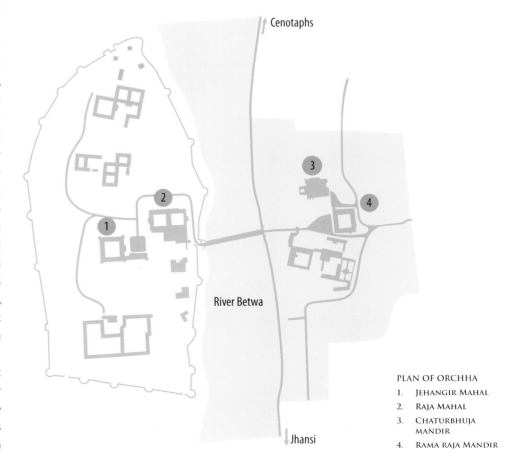

PLAN OF ORCHHA

1. JEHANGIR MAHAL
2. RAJA MAHAL
3. CHATURBHUJA MANDIR
4. RAMA RAJA MANDIR

two courtyards and three and five-storeyed buildings around it. It has a simple façade and housed the administrative secretariats and the Diwan Khana. Inside are the Durbar-e-Khas and the Diwan-i-Aam. The Durbar-e-Khas, for private audience, is on the first floor and well defended by high battlement walls, above which musket embrasures ensure further protection. The Diwan-i-Aam has massive pillars and a heavily decorated ceiling, and has three tiers, with the king presiding from the highest.

The wall paintings, which cover almost every surface of this enormous palace, are largely religious, depicting mythology and legends, including the *dashavatar* of Vishnu, *apsaras* and mythological scenes from the text *Anantsayi Vishnu*, and Vishnu rescuing the earth in his *varaha* incarnation. The paintings are distinguished by their rich colours, which brighten the otherwise dark interiors. The Bundelkhand rajas were great patrons of culture: the noted Brahman poet Keshavdas lived here and wrote the influential *Ram Chandrika*; his *Kavi Priya* was dedicated to one of Bundelkhand's legendary courtesans, Priya Rai.

On the other side of the courtyard is Rai Praveen Mahal, also known as Anand Mahal, which has a charming garden with whimsical topiary. It was built in honour of the great courtesan

of Orchha, Rai Praveen, whose famed beauty led her to being summoned to Akbar's court. She was accompanied to the court by Keshavdas and though she performed there, Akbar could not entice her to remain there. The paintings on the second floor of Praveen Mahal depict *Nritya Mudra*, or Indian dance poses.

Madhukar Shah was a devotee of Krishna, and built some imposing temples in the fort. The Rama Raja Temple is one of the most interesting. Madhukar Shah originally built this as a palace for his wife, Rani Ganesh, around 1558. She had undertaken a pilgrimage to Ayodhya and after a year of devotions, had a vision of Lord Rama telling her to return to Orchha on foot, a distance of 250 miles, with an image of the god that had to be installed in a place befitting a king. Work on the Chaturbhuja Temple was started to house the image, which was temporarily housed in the queen's palace. It is said that when the Chaturbhuja Temple was ready, the image refused to move, and so it remained here and the palace became the Rama Raja Temple, where Lord Rama is worshipped as a king. The temple is now a major pilgrimage destination.

The Chaturbhuja Temple is cruciform in plan and as large as a European cathedral, its four *shikhara*s rising high above the complex. Further ahead is the Laxminarayan Temple, built as much like a fort as a temple, and wondrously painted with Hindu iconography and mythological scenes in a rainbow palette of colours. Once the capital of Bundelkhand shifted to Tikamgarh, Orchha and all its glory collapsed, and the dense forest closed in on much of the abandoned kingdom.

Above and Facing page above: Ceiling in the Laxminarayan Temple

Facing page below: Cenotaphs across the River Betwa

Below: Main façade of Raja Mahal

Following pages (78-79): Jehangir Mahal

Datia

Raja Bir Singh is said to have built Datia, one of the prettiest fort-palaces in Central India, from the spoils of war against Abul Fazl's army. Bir Singh ambushed Akbar's most trusted courtier on his way back from his Deccan campaigns, laden with bounty for his emperor. Abul Fazl was beheaded and his head notoriously dispatched to be presented at the court of Jehangir, then Prince Salim. His son Bhagwan Rao was rewarded for assisting Jehangir when he was captured en route to Kabul, by carving out Datia as a separate state, from Orchha. Bhagwan Rao continued his father's tradition of unwavering loyalty to the Mughal emperors and spent most of his time fighting their battles: against the rebellious Khan Jehan Lodi, against Bijapur, and leading the Mughal forces against the rebellious Lahore Governor. Bhagwan Rao died in 1656, and his *chattri* (tomb) is a significant building in the fort.

Bhagwan Rao's sons also followed the path of war and, allying with the Mughals, had illustrious careers. Most notable was Subha Karan, who sided with Aurangzeb when he fought a bloody battle for succession against his four brothers. Subha Karan also fought alongside the Mughal emperor against the invading Maratha armies and although he died in 1679, his son Dalpat Rai continued this legacy. Dalpat Rai's greatest achievement was the successful siege of Gingee and Aurangzeb presented him with two massive gates, which were installed at Phool Bagh in Datia. Dalpat Rai died around the same time as Aurangzeb, and the next generation of Bundelas was virtually slaughtered by the Marathas. Bundelkhand went into decline as the rajas constantly shifted allegiances and struggled to retain their lands. Finally, General Peron, leading the Scindia armies, killed the Datia raja, Shatrujit, in 1801. His son Parichat sided with the British against the Marathas, which led to a period of relative peace for Datia. Parichat developed Datia and built its walls and gates. The gates are named after the cities they face: Richhara, Lashkar, Bhander, and Jhansi. Datia remained submissive to the British: when the Rani of Jhansi rose in revolt, her father, Moropant Tambe, was captured by the Datia army and handed over to the British. For this, the Datia king was richly rewarded and given the title of 'Maharaja'.

The royal palace at Datia was originally built by Bir Singh in a single grand plan. Unlike many of its counterparts in the region, Datia has a unity of design and execution. In his book *India and its Native Princes* (1882), Rousselet noted: "*Everything about this palace is somber and massive, and one can easily discern the traces of the great genius of King Bir Singh Deo, and of* the notorious *Boundela, whose name has become legendary. Its enormous proportions render it unfit for habitation; the small court of Duttiah, indeed, would be lost in this immense labyrinth, and thus it is abandoned to the bats and owls."*

Its location on a rocky hill amid a vast plain makes the palace appear more majestic than its 130-feet height. Its plan is square, with four squares within, akin to a *char bagh*, and the palaces are arranged around these courtyards. The palace buildings are dominated by elegant *chattri*-style domes, with wide eaves and overhanging balconies defining the five floors. At the base of the main palace is an elegant entrance with five floors of balconies rising above it. Lattice screens shield the royal inhabitants from the public eye. The interior has richly carved ornate ceilings, ribbed domes, and octagonal towers at the corners. The exterior is elaborate, decorated with brackets, arches, and fenestrations. The ornamentation and colour were not embellished by subsequent kings, which gives the entire complex a rare, pristine quality. Although protected by the British government, the small kingdom of Datia failed to survive, its assets unviable and rulers incapable, and the Datia Palace was abandoned to nature.

Left: *Multi-level walkways and courtyards in Bir Singh Mahal*

Facing page: *Corridor connecting the outer periphery to the inner square*

Below: *Ceiling detail, Bir Singh Mahal*

Samthar

Samthar is undoubtedly one of the more ambitious fortifications built in the 17th century. It was an independent Gujar kingdom that rose to power and fame at the time when the Mughal Empire was disintegrating and the Marathas were gaining control of Central India. During the initial Mughal invasions of India around AD 1526, one of Babur's commanders Shamsher built a small fort or *garhi* here. The terrain around is level or *samthal,* from which its current name is derived. The Gujars themselves have a hoary history, as they are associated with the arrival of the Hun invaders in the 5th century and later they fought alongside Prithviraj Chauhan against Mohammed Ghori.

The independent state of Samthar, India's only Gujar kingdom, was carved out of Datia in the 17th and 18th centuries by Chandrabhan Bar Gujar who was keen on increasing his influence in Datia and gaining the confidence of the Datia rulers. But it was his great grandson Madan Singh who supported the Maratha invasions into Central India and was finally given Shamsher Garhi along with a *jagir* of five villages and the title 'Rajdhar' as his reward. In order to survive, he also had to sign allegiance with the expanding British Empire in the 19th century, along similar lines as Maharaja Ranjit Singh II in Punjab and Datia next door. Samthar's fortunes were dependent on their shifting allegiances; they sided with the British when the Rani of Jhansi revolted against them, but they also helped the rani by providing her with a change of horses, under the instructions from the then rani of Samthar, Rani Lallan Ju.

The priority of this young state was to build a fort befitting its stature. It was constructed around the same time as Patiala and has much the same form. The *nara durg,* or fort protected by brave men, is surrounded by a huge moat with three distinct and separate tiers of bastions and fortifications. It is entered through an extremely large and winding entrance into a series of spacious courtyards. At the centre of this mammoth construction, and with another layer of more modest fortification, is the palace, and then the complex of temples and on the outside are the administrative buildings, along with several structures designed to host foreign visitors.

The palace is the most commanding building. An Italian, known locally as Tonton sahib, is supposed to have designed and built the seven-storeyed palace complex. And in a departure from traditional fort design, it dwarfs all the other buildings for miles around, but most notably the temples, even Raj Mandir which

Right: The rajwada in Samthar, an interesting blend of Indian and Italian architecture

houses the family deities. Pleasure gardens, halls of audience and *zenanas*, as well as elephant stables are all built on an almost disproportionate scale. Samthar functioned largely for ceremony and not for war. The Dussehra procession of elephants, lances, spears, and carriages, and fireworks was legendary. This, and other accoutrements of 19th-century princes – horse-riding, tennis, and *shikar* occupied their energies. Their battles were fought in British administrative centres mostly for recognition on par with the Rajput states, the gaiety of their court marred by perceived

slights in gun salutes and protocol issues. But this was a war well fought, as in 1877, the Samthar royal family were accorded the title of 'Maharaja'. However they still coveted the desired gun salute in order to pursue a dignified life of royal pleasure.

Samthar is an overwhelming construction, in almost pristine condition. The family still lives here, served by more than 200 *karimdars*, resident *pujaris* and more often than not, the fort is still lit with *battis* (lamps) as development has not galloped to this fort.

Ajaigarh

Above and Facing page above: *Rock carvings*

Facing page left and right: *Rang Mahal or Dance Pavilion, now mostly in ruins*

Replete with legends and tales of war and valour, Ajaigarh is significant for being the last bastion of the once-mighty Chandela rajas. Rising above the vast undulating landscape of Central India and clearly visible from Kalinjar, the history of this fort is rich with the history of the Chandelas of Bundelkhand. The Chandelas came to power after they overthrew the Pratiharas and acquired this 9th-century fort. Its name is said to be derived from Ajaipala, a sage who lived on its hill, Kedar Parvat. The Chandela seat of power was at Kalinjar and Mahoba forts and this huge fort augmented the Chandela strength in Bundelkhand. After Mahoba was captured by Prithviraj Chauhan in the 12th century from Raja Parmadideva, the Chandelas were forced to strengthen their position in Ajaigarh. The great defeat of the Chandelas was the loss of Kalinjar to Qutb-ud-din Aibak in the 13th century, after which they retreated to Ajaigarh and for over a century, Ajaigarh was the seat of power in Bundelkhand. The rule of the Chandelas at Ajaigarh Fort continued till Emperor Akbar conquered the region and took the fort, then

under a Gond *kiledar*, or fort custodian. Abul Fazl, Akbar's chronicler, refers to Ajaigarh in his records as the headquarters of a *mahal* in the Kalinjar administration. The Mughals continued to rule here until Champat Rai emerged as a force to reckon with, during the time of Aurangzeb's war of succession. He assisted Aurangzeb by guiding his armies through this hostile and impassable terrain. Ajaigarh's fortune changed thereafter, but it remained contested, and over the ensuing years it faced many invasions, the last being that of the British in AD 1809 when Ajaigarh refused to submit to their supremacy. They laid siege for more than a month, not from the gorges below, but advantageously from an adjacent hill from where they could destroy the gates of Ajaigarh.

Its battlements barely visible, it rises from the rough terrain and dense forest surrounding it. The ideal *vana durg*, it is more than 800-feet high and nearly three miles of battlements surround the triangular hilltop. Huge bastions with reinforced corners remain as evidence of its military might. All along the steep ascent there are

relics of Hindu iconography etched into the rock face alongside innumerable *sati* handprints and rock inscriptions from the 12th century till the late 13th century, mostly dating to the reign of Raja Viravarman. At the summit is the Kalinjar Gate that faces Kalinjar, both forts mirror images of the immense power of the Chandelas. Inside, Ajaigarh is strewn with the remains of flourishing cultures. Today, its sacred heritage is more clearly visible than its palaces. A dancing Ganesha, lies almost buried in the sand, images of Durga and Kali and an ancient black stone statue of Vishnu lie strewn alongside a colossal Jain image of Shantinath. Near the Tarhaoni Gate is a panel depicting the *sapta-matrika*s or seven mother-goddesses, and Veerbhadra, a form of Shiva. Two huge caves known as Ganga and Yamuna provide perennial underground water and the Padmardideva Talav, the queen's bathing tank still evokes the spirit of better days. At the heart of the fort lies Ajaipal Talav, where the worlds of the king, the priest, and the public converged. The fort resonates with the stories of the Chandela bards – of the many loves of Parmadi, the heroism of his two Banaphar warriors, Alha and Udal – and folk songs from the 'Alha Khand'.

Inevitably, as in many of the forts conquered by the Mughals, temples were demolished to make way for the new order, their richly carved stone was reused even to reinforce the ramparts. The British Army captain, Pogson's description is as relevant now as it was in 1809: *"The ruins of the magnificent Hindoo temples, built of stones, laid without cement, but most nicely fitted to each other, and adorned within and without, with sculpture, of chaste design and exquisite workmanship. The era of these venerable buildings is lost in antiquity but they are evidently much older than the fortress."*

Sultanate Forts

Tughlaqabad

Above: *Fortifications, now in partial ruin*

Right: *Corridor inside the Ghiyas-ud-din Tughlaq tomb complex*

The Tughlaqs followed the Khiljis in dynastic succession, when the last Khilji was murdered by his chief minister. They were amongst the first great builders of forts and cities on an unprecedented scale. Even though their rule was brief, lasting a mere hundred years, their construction was prolific, as cities, stepwells, *serais*, bridges, and other civic structures burgeoned around Delhi. They brought with them engineering skills, and introduced India to complex architectural domes, vaults, and arches.

Of the eleven Tughlaq rulers, the first three were prolific builders and each built a capital city, the first of which, Tughlaqabad was built by Ghazi Malik, or Ghiyas-ud-din Tughlaq. It is believed that once the sultan started building Tughlaqabad, his religious teacher Nizam-ud-din Auliya wanted a stepwell to be built for the public as a symbol of his piety. The sultan, who was determined to complete his fort first, refused the saint, who went against the wishes of Ghiyas-ud-din and built a well. Infuriated, the sultan ordered Nizam-ud-din Auliya to leave the fort, but legend holds that before he left he cursed the new city of Tughlaqabad proclaiming that it would soon be inhabited only by jackals, as indeed it was, owing to a lack of water.

Ghiyas-ud-din ruled for a short five years and his fort was built in less than three. His successor, the despotic Muhammed is best known for shifting his capital from Delhi to Daulatabad, and thereafter Feroz Shah Tughlaq built his own capital Kotla Feroz Shah, and so life in this fort was short-lived.

Tughlaqabad was conceived on a massive scale. Its perimeter wall was no less than 7.75 miles. Some 3 miles wide and roughly square in shape, the massive irregular red stonewalls, punctured for defence and supported with 61 huge bastions, taper upwards and are accessed by 13 entry gates. The sloping ramparts are built upon vaulted rooms that would have housed the garrison. It had clear demarcation for the palace citadel, which occupied a small portion of a fortified city.

The citadel itself could be reached through three gates and had a large audience hall known as Hazaar Ustan or Hall of a Thousand Pillars. The lofty gateway and triple-storeyed tower within the remaining rampart walls are still impressive. A description of the sultan's court by the chronicler Ibn Batuta provides an insight into court life at that time: *"On all the thirteen gates were ushers of different status. At the gate which led to the main audience hall stood the chief usher who introduced the visitor to the chief minister who took care of the visitor. It was only after crossing the third gate that one could enter the vast grandeur of the hall of a thousand pillars and have an audience with the Sultan."*

Tughlaqabad is full of underground chambers, or *tehkhana*s and it is believed to be connected to Old Delhi by an underground passageway. There is also a water tank measuring around 80 feet in depth that was possibly the quarry that provided stone to build the palace citadel. On the vast, fortified plain there is the Jami Masjid and there would have been many small settlements within its walls, with the services tucked around the walls but outside. Muhammad-bin-Tughlaq built his own citadel, Adilabad outside the fort to the southeast, and connected it with a causeway. Outside and connected by another causeway is Ghiyas-ud-din's mausoleum, which would have stood in the middle of a water tank. It is elegantly embellished with sloping walls and provides the best evidence of the architecture of that period.

In the 19th century, General Cunningham noted: *"The fort stands on a rocky height, and is built of massive blocks of stones so large and heavy that they must have been quarried on the spot. The largest stone that I observed measured fourteen feet in length by two feet two inches and one foot ten inches in breadth and thickness, and must have weighed rather more than six tons …the walls are built of large plain dressed stones, and there is no ornament of any kind: but the vast size, the great strength and the visible solidity on the whole, give to Tughlakabad an air of stern and massive grandeur that is both striking and impressive."*

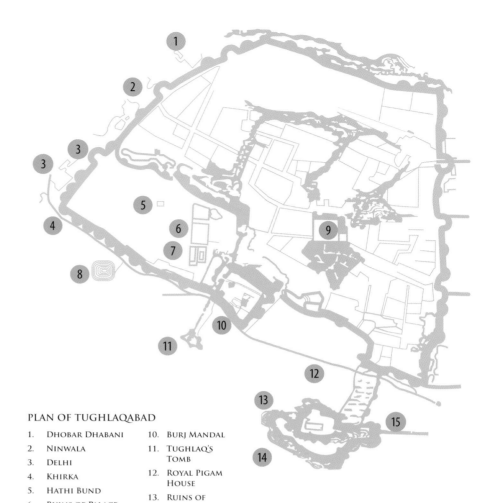

PLAN OF TUGHLAQABAD

1. DHOBAR DHABANI
2. NINWALA
3. DELHI
4. KHIRKA
5. HATHI BUND
6. RUINS OF PALACE
7. SHEIKH INAYAT ALI'S VILLAGE
8. DAK BUNGALOW
9. JAMI MASJID
10. BURJ MANDAL
11. TUGHLAQ'S TOMB
12. ROYAL PIGAM HOUSE
13. RUINS OF TUGHLAQ PALACES
14. TEHKHANAS OR UNDERGROUND CHAMBERS
15. FORT

Below: *Ruins inside the fort. The circular pit in the foreground was the mechanism used for crushing lime for mortar used in stone masonry*

Kotla Feroz Shah

Right: *The Ashokan pillar above a three-storeyed pyramidical structure inside the fort*

Delhi was well known during the Tughlaq period as a prosperous and vibrant city. Even so, the fortunes of the Tughlaq dynasty were short-lived. After Muhammed-bin-Tughlaq's costly misadventure of shifting his capital to Daulatabad, his kingdom was significantly weakened. His nephew Feroz Shah Tughlaq succeeded him to the throne at Delhi. A reluctant king, he assumed power in AD 1351 and started the construction of his new city Ferozabad almost immediately. A dedicated patron of the arts, Feroz Shah committed most of his career to building civic and secular structures, with the general philosophy of making his people more content and prosperous. He was responsible for a number of urban settlements, canals, tanks, and wells; gardens and orchards and inevitably hunting lodges, pavilions, and palaces. His first palace was built in Khirki, a village in south Delhi, where there are still the remains of a mosque. However the scarcity of water, which spelt the end of Tughlaqabad, was a constant concern and he was

forced to consider building his fort near the River Yamuna, where his court could be sustained. He thus began the construction of Ferozabad and Kotla Feroz Shah.

Development was divided into distinct areas, with the fortified seat of power, palaces, *zenanas*, and homes of noblemen housed within the citadel, Kotla Feroz Shah. A second level of fortification encompassed the homes of workmen, artisans, and farmers in the villages around. The city of Ferozabad comprised 18 villages.

To enter Kusk-i-Feroz or Kotla Feroz Shah, there was a large entry gateway with a barbican and bastions on either side. The citadel had high fortifications, with a double row of slits for arrows and circular bastions. Beyond were the public buildings, the hall of public audience, baths, stepwells, tanks, and garrison quarters. The stepwell, built in 1354, is an elegant union of function with artistic rendering. This was a recreational area with open *chattri*-style pavilions and two storeys of underground rooms with piers

opening onto the well. There was also a large network of tunnels connecting Feroz Shah Kotla's settlements, the evidence of which can still seen at Bara Hindu Rao.

The three palaces had the best location at the top with views across the river and steps leading down. There were many pillared halls and a pigeon tower. Jami Masjid, a congregational mosque which could house over a thousand people, was built in AD 1354 and is said to be the largest of seven mosques built in Delhi in that period. The mosque is an impressive domed building raised on a block of cells. The main entrance to the mosque is from the north, accessed by a flight of stairs leading to the next level to a domed chamber going into the *sehan*, or courtyard. The mosque is rubble masonry covered in plaster which would have been a reflective white colour. Contemporary historians have stated that the doorways of the mosque were covered with carved stone, and that an account of Feroz Shah's reign was inscribed in the centre of the courtyard beyond.

Feroz Shah Kotla has at its centre, the remains of a three-storeyed pyramid-like structure with an Ashokan pillar at the top. Inspired by the Qutb Mosque's iron pillar, Feroz Shah, in 1367, transported this at enormous effort, on a specially fabricated, 42-wheeled carriage and crossed the River Yamuna on a pontoon of boats joined together. The pillar was then installed on a pyramid, with three levels of small, vaulted chambers with corresponding terraces, tapering upwards. A staircase winds through the structure to the summit, where the pillar stands. Muslim clergy called these two pillars the work of djinns and Hindu *pandits*, calling them the walking sticks of Bhima, a hero in the epic Mahabharata.

The total expanse of the city was vast – as described by two travellers of that time, Afif and Barni. Because the Tughlaq dynasty's fortunes lasted a mere three generations, there was no renewal and layering of buildings seen in later forts. But the settlements, which he had developed with civic amenities including the Satpula Bridge at Jahanpanah, have served the city of Delhi well over the centuries.

Above: Entrance to Jami Masjid

Below: Ruins inside the fort

Mandu

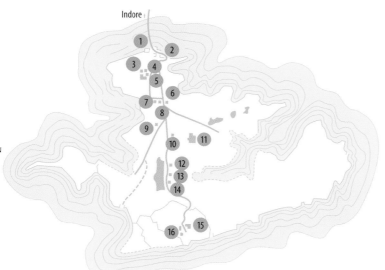

Below: *Jahaz Mahal as seen from across the lake*

Mandu, or Mandavgarh, a lost city at the edge of the Malwa Plateau above the Nimar Plains, is one of India's architectural gems. It is an enormous complex of pleasure palaces and pavilions enclosed by huge fortifications. Rebuilt in the 11th century, Mandu Fort stands at an elevation of 2,000 feet, extending over 13 miles along a crest of the Vindhya ranges, overlooking the River Narmada on one side and the Malwa Plateau on the other. Mandu, with its natural defences, was originally the fort-capital of the Rajput Parmara rulers of Malwa, around the 6th century. Towards the end of the 11th century, it came under the sway of the Taranga kingdom. The city reached its zenith in the early 15th century.

Originally, it is believed to have been the Mandapa Durg or attributed to the Goddess Durga as a hall of worship, or the Fort (*durg*) of Pavilions. Four hundred years after it was founded here, the Parmara kings moved their capital to Dhar some 20 miles away, and Mandu became a retreat, secluded within the jungles. Gradually, the Malwa Plateau grew in importance with the consolidation of the Slave kings in Delhi, and with their

growing ambitions to expand their territories, Malwa fell to them in AD 1305. A century later, with the Sultanate power in Delhi being eroded by the invasions of Timur, the Afghan Governor of Malwa, Dilawar Khan Ghuri, grew brave enough to encash on the weaknesses in Delhi and declare himself Sultan of Malwa. His rule was brief , lasting a mere four years but he established his capital at Mandu. His ambitious son Hoshang Shah was responsible for consolidating their position in Malwa and restoring its importance. It transformed from being the pleasure palace of Dhar to the capital of Malwa and it was during his reign that Mandu achieved its architectural excellence.

Dilawar Khan was responsible for building the great wall fortifying Mandu. Over 20 miles in length and with parapets extending more than 30 miles, it has two great entrance gateways securing the capital city from invaders. Delhi Darwaza, the main gateway is part of a series of gateways, each a fortified unit with bastions. Alamgir and Bhangi Darwaza lie beyond, while Tarapura Gate is articulated by three sharp right-angle turns, the most successful system of defence in a fort. Another gate Ram Pol, which lies towards the northeast, predates this construction and is said to belong to the original construction during the Parmara era. Raja Bhoj, one of the greatest kings of that period built the original palaces around Munja Talav where Sanskrit inscriptions and remains of temples still exist.

Dilawar Khan's son, Hoshang Shah took on his mantle and built what are arguably some of Asia's finest Islamic monuments. Hoshang Shah's successor was Mahmud Khan, a Khilji who, as minister to Hoshang Shah's son, poisoned him, rose to power, and established the Khilji dynasty at Mandu.

Mandu was then renamed Shadiabad, or City of Happiness and Peace, a city where he ushered in an era of prosperity. But he was an ambitious king and constantly at war with his neighbours in Gujarat and Mewar. His war with Rana Kumbha of Mewar was a victory of some irony as Rana Kumbha built his Vijay Stambh at Chittorgarh to mark his success while Khilji built a seven-storey tower at Mandu to mark his victory.

Baz Bahadur, the last Sultan of Malwa, was famed for his love of Rani Roopmati and in whose praise balladeers of Malwa still sing. Rani Roopmati's Pavilion gazes down at Baz Bahadur's Palace. The Rewa Kund palaces exemplified a life of pleasure and indulgence which eventually cost him the loyalty of his people and attracted the attention of Akbar. His army, led by Adam Khan, sacked Mandu and Baz Bahadur fled, leaving Rani Roopmati to consume poison

Above: Water body and pillared corridor inside Baz Bahadur's Palace

Above: *Hindola Mahal*

Facing page:
Delhi Darwaza
with fortifications

rather than surrender to the Mughals. Thereafter Mandu became a halfway house for the Mughals, especially Akbar and Jehangir, on their forays into the Deccan and they attempted to restore some of Mandu's splendour. Thomas Roe, Ambassador of the King of England to Jehangir's court, visited Mandu to participate in the emperor's birthday celebrations. Here he witnessed Jehangir laden with gems of every description, weighed in silver, precious stones, and brocades on gold scales, distributing silver nuggets to his courtiers. In the face of these unsustainable excesses, Mandu was bound to flounder; it fell to the growing power of the Marathas as Malhar Rao Holkar defeated the Mughal Governor of Malwa. Later, the British took over and Mandu, the quintessential pleasure palace became history.

Mandu has a magical quality, its landscape gently undulating, its lake reflecting its glory. Most of the buildings here, from the palace to his own tomb, were built by Hoshang Shah. His tomb is the first white marble construction in India with a large, well-proportioned dome, charming lattice work in marble, and corner towers which define its square form. It is believed that Shah Jahan sent his architects to study this tomb for inspiration when designing the Taj Mahal.

Hoshang Shah also built Jami Masjid, one of the finest buildings still standing in Mandu. Inspired by the great mosque of Damascus, as the Shahs traced their lineage to Damascus, this mosque was constructed on an enormous scale. Although simple in style, it is at a great height, with a huge, domed porch over the entrance pavilion, and is balanced by five colonnaded aisles with 17 domed bays. Although many of Mandu's mosques are built with material looted from temples, this was an original construction, in a Classical style, with a large congregational courtyard and arcades flanking it.

On the other side of the great mosque is Ashrafi Mahal, built by Mahmud Shah Khilji. This palace of gold coins or *ashrafi*s was designed as a *madrasa*, or school of Islamic studies. Here, the Persian art of glazing, brought from Multan, was used to embellish the façade of the *mahal*, a wonderful palette of turquoise blue and bright yellow. This 15th-century structure is the jewel of Mandu. Nearby is his famous seven-storeyed victory tower, of which only one storey survives.

Quite the most famous building in Mandu and certainly its most romantic is Jahaz Mahal or Ship Palace, located between two artificial lakes – Munj Talav (of much older provenance) and the Kapur Talav. Stretching 400 feet along the edge of the *talav*, this was essentially a pleasure palace for Ghiyas-ud-din's queens. It is a series of open-plan halls with large terraces, little *chattri*s and open pavilions, with fountains, bathing courtyards, kiosks, and cupolas. Jahaz Mahal and the adjoining Taveli Mahal reflected in the water, have an ethereal quality when silhouetted against an evening sky.

According to architectural historians, the use of a very large courtyard surrounded by residential apartments set a precedent for secular architecture and was used extensively in India thereafter. Built by Baz Bahadur in the 16th century, the palace, set in a spacious walled courtyard had spectacular views across the River Narmada. The rather massive Hindola Mahal was possibly a hall of audience. It almost seems to sway because of its sloping walls. It is an enormous hall with arcades along the sides, overlooked by a gallery possibly for the *zenana*, and is decorated with sandstone trellis work.

By the 16th century, Rajput power in Mewar was at its peak, and Mahmud II's minister Medini Rao allied with the Ranas of Mewar, necessitating the Sultan of Malwa to seek the help of the Sultan of Gujarat to quell the dissidents. Mahmud fell, and in the ensuing realignment and treachery, he lost Malwa to the Sultan of Gujarat. Both were extinguished in the bloody years of war ahead, first against Humayun and then Sher Shah who established his own Governor at Mandu.

Daulatabad

Daulatabad, or the Abode of Wealth is the culmination of the compounded avarice of many, an ugly history of merciless killings and destruction. Ironically, in its first manifestation, it is believed to have been a Buddhist monastery. Its known history is from the time of the Yadavas of Devagiri who founded their capital here in the 12th century. Perched upon a rock, it fuses with the rough basalt landscape, virtually inaccessible to all.

The Yadavas were a major dynasty following the Chalukyas, and exercised enormous power, with their kingdom stretching from the River Narmada to the River Krishna. It was also a kingdom known for its arts, literature, and wealth – a cultured and progressive dynasty. Inevitably it attracted the rapacious appetites of the Slave kings making inroads in North India. In AD 1296 Ala-ud-din Khilji captured the fort, after marching his armies across Central India with a few thousand horsemen to plunder Devagiri's celebrated wealth. Raja Ramachandra Deva was besieged and retreated into the citadel while Ala-ud-din looted Devagiri. On his way back to Delhi, he was

ambushed by the raja's son, which proved even more successful as his booty was reputed to include 6 tonnes of gold, 12 tonnes of silver, 50 pounds of diamonds, other gems, and at least 50 elephants and 1,000 horses. Ala-ud-din was a cruel and depraved ruler, his reign scarred by murder and pillage. In time, Devagiri was annexed, and as Raja Harpal Deva rebelled, he was flayed alive in 1318. Ala-ud-din was murdered by his most trusted advisor Khusro Khan. In turn, Khan was beheaded by the Turkish Ghazi Malik, later Tughlaq Shah, Sultan of Delhi and the Tughlaq dynasty was born.

Shah was murdered by his elder son Muhammed-bin-Tughlaq, and his reign was the fiercest of all the Tughlaqs. Known for even higher degrees of cruelty than Ala-ud-din, Muhammed made the foolhardy decision to not just shift his capital to Daulatabad, but to shift the entire population of Delhi. And so the well-documented tragedy of immense proportions commenced. Across 700 miles of rough road, his army, nobles, and the paraphernalia necessary to support this move set out on a monumental journey of no return.

Below: *View of Daulatabad Fort*

Facing page: *Entrance gateways*

Right: Detail of a cannon in the fort

Most died on the way south, many perished while returning, and it is said that while the animals were fed on *gur* (molasses) and rice, the people were left to die or eat each other. But Muhammed persevered and on reaching Devagiri, established himself at the fort with a manic determination, a failure which resulted in some extraordinary fort construction but doomed the king.

Muhammed-bin-Tughlaq named Devagiri Daulatabad, and although his attempt to shift his capital failed, it remained with his Governor until 1347, when the establishment rose against the Tughlaqs and resettled as the Bahmani Kingdom in Gulbarga. It remained with them until the Mughal strategists began to decimate the powerful confederation of Bahmani Sultans. It was strategically most important and coveted, given its location and the rise of Maratha powers in the 17th century. Its conquest was crucial for Shah Jahan who was aspiring to merit his succession to the throne. Prince Khurram's military strategies were honed here as he was appointed Viceroy to the Deccan. The Deccan Sultans were nefarious friends and foes and shifting allegiances resulted

Facing page: Stepwell inside Daulatabad Fort

Below: A panoramic view of the fort

in many re-groupings. Even though Shah Jahan made Daulatabad his focus, it took him almost 15 years to finally conquer this fort, and after he became emperor in June 1633, Daulatabad passed into the hands of the Mughals.

The fort's construction reflects its turbulent history. It has huge ramparts built in three distinct layers, and was one of 39 forts running north to south along the western edge of the Deccan Plateau. Towering 650 feet over the plains, its sheer walls were excavated to ensure it could not be scaled. Ambarkot is the outermost fortification at the base, and completely enclosed the hill where the community, which sustained the fort, would have lived.

The main citadel, Mahakot, is truly formidable, surrounded by a moat with a stone bridge. It was controlled by dams which could render the bridges impassable during a siege. There is then a defence tower and access to the fort is through a series of underground chambers and passages hewn out of the rock; and a stone barrier drawn by iron rings reinforced the security. The monumental doorway to the tunnel resembles the entrance doorway to the Kailasa Temple at Ellora not far away, reflecting the cross-cultural influences of the time. At the other end is a ribbed iron door 20 feet across and an inch thick; it could be heated red-hot from a small chamber alongside. A sophisticated air-ducting system could smoke out the tunnel and formed a lethal defence apparatus.

Beyond lies a shrine and a Yadava pavilion with a balcony overlooking a 100-foot chasm, believed to have been the residence of the Yadava rani but later occupied by Shah Jahan.

On a nearby bastion is the Kila Shikan or fort-breaker, one of Daulatabad's mightiest guns. Inside the Mahakot there are the ruins of a Shah Jahani palace, the Daulat Khana, a Jami Masjid and the baths. The Jami Masjid was built in the time of Khilji's invasions in 1318 and comprises a large, enclosed square with a pillared prayer hall on the west side, whose 106 pillars form 25 aisles, with a flat roof. Four external columns, recycled from old temples, support a corbelled dome over the *mihrab*. Nearby is the four-storeyed Chand Minar or Moon Tower built in 1435, which dominates the entire complex.

Kalakot is the innermost enclosure built on the northeastern side; one of its bastions houses the massive cannon, known as Creator of Storms, inscribed in Gujarati and installed by the Mughals. There is evidence of the royal palaces including Chini Mahal which may have been the reception hall, named after the blue and white tiles which used to adorn the interior. In 1687, Aurangzeb imprisoned the last of the kings of Golconda here for 13 years. An arched gateway leads through a long double-height hall with transverse arches, leading to further chambers at a higher level, which would have been the private chambers. These open onto a courtyard and across, there are remains of more apartments which would have been in heavily carved wood, the building type used in this region but which did not survive the ravages of time.

Daulatabad's hoary past is reflected in the massive entrance fortifications. While they may have destroyed all that lay before them, they were equally determined to fortify themselves against retaliations. It is therefore a powerful structure, visible across the countryside – a symbol of power and destruction.

Bidar

The Deccan Plateau of India provided an extraordinary canvas for building fortified cities. Invasions from the north meant crossing mountain ranges, rivers, and a hostile landscape. It was in the 13th and 14th centuries that the Khiljis and Tughlaqs successfully forayed this far, and initiated a period of vigorous construction of mosques, and palatial buildings, and the development of urban lifestyles.

In 1424, when Shihab-ud-din Ahmad shifted from Gulbarga to the more salubrious climate of Bidar, it became the capital of the Bahmani Sultans. There is no empirical information as to when Bidar was first built, but local lore ascribes it to the Mahabharata period. When the Chalukyas established their kingdom in the south in the 10th century with Kalyani as their capital, Bidar Fort, some 40 miles away, was part of their possessions. When the fort finally came under the Bahmani kingdom, it was almost completely reconstructed. The decision was necessitated by a wariness of the growing power of the Vijayanagara Empire, as well as the desire to create a mammoth fort-city.

The Bahmani kingdom survived several generations, but its kings did not distinguish themselves either in war or governance. However, Mahmud Gawan, Prime Minister of Bidar and a Persian scholar, founded a *madrasa* outside the gates of the citadel, three storeys high, with a monumental minaret heavily decorated with colourful glazed tiles in a chevron pattern. Its dome was among the earliest bulbous-shaped domes built in India. Within the fort, two large mosques, Jami Masjid and Solah Khamba Masjid, the latter with 16 pillars supporting a lofty dome, are also attributed to him.

The Bahmanis were destined to disintegrate in the face of inordinate excesses, which were compounded by the disaffection

Right: Tarkash Mahal, Solah Khamba Masjid and Lal Bagh garden, Bidar Fort

of the local people who were forcibly converted to Islam. Qasim Barid, who was the Turkish minister to the last Bahmani king, ensured that his son Amir Barid Shah became king, a line that continued until Bidar fell to Bijapur. Bidar remained with this dynasty until Aurangzeb annexed it in 1656. Almost a century later, it became part of the Nizam's domicile under the Asaf Jahs.

The fort dominates the landscape for miles around. It is bound by enormous battlement ramparts, which are surrounded by a moat. Situated at one end of a large plateau, it slopes towards the town on the other side, where the fortifications are higher and in three layers. The 6-mile long fort wall, built with huge blocks of reddish laterite stone, is strengthened with 37 bastions and has several gates with barbicans. According to the historian Ferishta, engineers and architects from Turkey and West Asia were employed to create this huge fortified city.

The massive entry gate built by Ahmad Shah in 1429 is actually a series of gates of great simplicity and elegance, erected one behind the other. The first is Sharza Darwaza or Lion Gate, with two lions sculpted on its façade; the second is the Gumbaz Darwaza, with sloping walls, pointed arches, and a dome. The southern Fateh Darwaza has squat octagonal towers, a drawbridge, barbican, and a winding road leading to spiked-iron covered doors. Fateh Darwaza is reinforced from behind by

Above: Fortifications and dome of Gumbaz Darwaza

Talghat Darwaza, accessible by a ramp. Munda Burj is the largest bastion, with heavy guns, cannons, and embrasures at two levels. The significant architectural achievement in Bidar is the sophisticated system of gates and sluices, which could be used when required to flood segments of the moat and thus conserve water. To the east is a dam across the three moats and in the west, towards the town, a central water channel cuts through the moats, protected by a Naubat Khana from where an alarm would be sounded if an attempt was made to breach them.

Secluded within layers of fort walls and well concealed from the administrative buildings, the royal palaces flourished. The Chaubara, a 70-foot tower, is the dominant feature of the fort city. Lal Bagh, in front of the Solah Khamba Masjid, was irrigated by water which flowed down from the Turkish pavilions on the south and carried on to the *hamam*s beyond. Imposing black granite steps lead to Gagan Mahal, a residential complex with a vaulted gateway and a series of chambers. The most magnificent of the palaces is Rangeen Mahal. Built by Barid Shah in the 16th century, it is covered with delightful arabesque designs, glazed mosaic, and spectacular calligraphy. Brightly painted murals enrich the walls of the *zenana*, which also has exceptionally detailed carved woodwork. Some distance away, Takht Mahal or the Royal Throne Pavilion, which once boasted a magnificent turquoise throne, probably of Persian origin, lies behind the Diwan-e-Aam.

The beauty of Bidar lies in its simplicity and elegance. The Bahmanis were not a peaceful dynasty. Fraught with hatred and bigotry, they however, built one of the Deccan's most handsome forts.

Above Left: Interior of Tarkash Mahal

Left: Domes of Solah Khamba Masjid or the mosque with 16 pillars

Facing page: Interior of Rangeen Mahal

Following pages (104-105): Intricately carved wooden ceiling of Rangeen Mahal

Bijapur

The Adil Shahi dynasty was founded in 1490 by Yusuf Adil Khan, and their architectural achievements were matched by their political prowess in the region. The Adil Shahis were Shia Muslims and tolerant rulers who did not persecute other faiths, and in time, they became influential in the Deccan because of their inclusive policies.

Yusuf Adil was a Turk in exile who attached himself to the court at Bidar. He was appointed governor of Bijapur, but as Bahmani rule declined, he proclaimed himself Sultan. He married the sister of a defeated Maratha chieftain and her influence came to bear on the court, where proceedings were held in Marathi. Considered a 'wise prince', he was a patron of the arts, and in his reign, Bijapur flourished as scholars, ambassadors, and learned men flocked to his court. He lived mainly in Raichur, in the great concentric fort of the Yadavas, and his kingdom stretched down to Goa, which he frequented until it was lost to the Portuguese. The Vijayanagara kings, however, were a continuous threat and eventually, in 1565, Ali Adil Shah allied with Ahmadnagar, Bidar, and Golconda to destroy the hold of Vijayanagara, at the time ruled by the powerful king Rama Raya.

Bijapur lies within two concentric circles of fortifications. Construction of the outer city walls, extending more than 6 miles with extensive moats, was started by Yusuf. Reinforced with 100 bastions, the fort was built to accommodate heavy artillery. Burj-e-Sherza, or the Lion Bastion, has two sculpted lion heads and houses the Mallik-i- Maidan, or Lord of the Plains, a massive cannon believed to be one of the largest cannons ever cast. Behind the *burj* and in the town is Haider Burj, with a spiral staircase leading to the top. It was obviously a vantage point for miles around, with a cannon called Lamchari, or Distant Flier mounted atop. Inside the fortifications is the citadel, which houses the royal palaces. Its entrance gateways are accessed over heavily arched bridges, of which only two survive. The gates themselves were made of iron, with spikes and barbicans fixed at sharp angles.

To commemorate the successful decimation of the Vijayanagara Empire, Ali began his most ambitious construction, the Jami Masjid, funded by his Vijayanagara booty. One of the finest mosques in India, it is remarkable for its harmonious proportions and dignified simplicity. The mosque's courtyard was an enormous 9,000 square feet, and was later extended to 11,000 square feet, to accommodate 5,000 people. The central bay is believed to have originally been covered with rich velvet carpets, but after Aurangzeb looted Bijapur, this design was incorporated in stone. The single hemispherical dome is immense. The old Jami Masjid, built soon after Yusuf's death in 1513, was also imposing in scale. In fact, all of Bijapur's mosques are quite remarkable for their refinement despite the large scale on which they are built. Without doubt, Gol Gumbad is the culmination of this obsession with size. Famed as the second largest dome in the world, it is the tomb of Muhammad Adil Shah. Its square base supports a dome some 150-

Right: *Athar Mahal overlooks the pond and houses relics of the Prophet*

Facing page: *Painted chamber inside Athar Mahal*

Far left: *Jal Mandir*

Left: *Interior of Mehtar Mahal*

Facing page: *Interior of Jami Masjid*

feet high, with a diameter of more than 100 feet, covering a great hall of immense proportions.

The royal complex is no less noteworthy. Gagan Mahal or Sky Palace, was the hall of public audience built by Ali Adil Shah in 1561. The façade has a large central arch nearly 60-feet wide and 50-feet high, with smaller arches on either side. Fine plasterwork motifs, notably with fish, distinguish it. Fish was the emblem of the Adil Shahis, and a motif widely used during Muharram processions in this region. There used to be an upper floor for the *zenana*, but like many of the palaces that were built in exquisitely carved wood, they have since crumbled. Nearby, Anand Mahal, built much later, was the Palace of Pleasure.

An extremely large courtyard lies at the centre of the palace citadel. Towards the northwest is Sat Manzil or Seven-storeyed Palace, of which only five floors remain. In contrast to its unadorned façade, the interior is profusely painted with murals. To its north is Jal Mandir, a small pavilion with brackets and eaves overhanging the pool within which a temple stands. It is part of an elaborate system of water channels so necessary in the hot desert plateau. Chini Mahal nearby was so named because of the Chinese ceramics found in its vicinity. Built later across the moat is Dad Mahal, the Hall of Justice, later converted into a shrine, and Athar Mahal, which is said to hold the relics of Prophet Mohammed. With a grand entrance that has teak wood pillars double the height of the gate, this palace, with its elaborate archways and painted ceilings, remains intact and provides a glimpse of what the palaces looked like in their day.

Another work of consummate design in the complex is the mausoleum of Ibrahim Rauza and family members. The hanging ceiling and exquisite, filigreed screens must have created a vision of paradise against the backdrop of the surrounding garden, as is evident from an inscription found here: "*Heaven stood astonished at the elevation of this building, and it might be said, when its head rose from earth, that another heaven was erected.*"

Once the Mughal incursions into the Deccan gained strength, the days of the Adil Shahis were numbered. Though Bijapur held firm, contracting suitable alliances (such as giving their beloved Padshah Bibi in marriage to the imperial family), they were finally worn down. The besieged fort collapsed, and the last Sultan of Bijapur was exiled to Daulatabad.

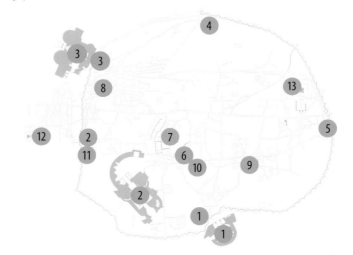

PLAN OF BIJAPUR

1. FATEH DARWAZA
2. MECCA DARWAZA
3. ZOHRAHAPUR DARWAZA
4. BAHMANI DARWAZA
5. ALIPUR DARWAZA
6. ARH QILA DARWAZA
7. ARH QILA WITH PALACE COMPOUND
8. HAIDAR BURJ
9. JAMI MASJID
10. MIHITARI MASJID
11. TAJ BAOLI
12. IBRAHIM RAUZA
13. GOL GUMBAD

Gulbarga

of the Deccan Sultanates – Bijapur, Bidar, Berar, Ahmadnagar, and Golconda. The Bahmani dynasty ruled over the Deccan for nearly 200 years, with Gulbarga as their capital.

Gulbarga Fort is a desolate structure, evocative of its barbaric history and its short-lived glory. It sprawls across the countryside, its ramparts and bastions soaring mightily into the sky. Constructed on the remains of a Warangal Fort built by Raja Gulchand, it was a *nara durg* with no natural defences, dependent on the might of its men. Completely overhauled and reconstructed by Ala-ud-din Bahmani, it was an engineering feat of its time, with a 50-foot thick double wall, the inner one higher than the outer. It had an almost impregnable defence system with a 90-foot wide moat with drawbridges completely surrounding its three miles of fortifications. The massive stone bastions that have outward projections provided enough space to house revolving cannons. The fortifications also had provision for dropping solids or liquids upon the approaching enemy, as well as merlons, and embrasures for musketry. 15 towers and 26 cannons ensured it was one of the mightiest of forts. The western entrance is colossal with four gates and four courtyards, each one so fortified that it would be impossible to pass through unscathed. The doors themselves were in metal ceated, with iron spikes to protect against an enemy mounted on elephants; iron chains to hold the doors and bars to close them present a formidable welcome to Gulbarga Fort. It is an excellent example of military architecture, and was probably inspired by the Syrians.

Inside are remains of large buildings, temples, and several beautiful courtyards. The large and foreboding Bala Hissar was used as the royal residence and certainly as a last refuge. The Jami Masjid built in 1367 is awe-inspiring as it covers 38,000 square feet and, being covered, is a unique congregational courtyard of a type not usually seen in India. The grandeur of the mosque is further enhanced with a repetition of ogee and cusped arches, with a trefoil at the centre for the *mihrab*, a style more visible in West Asia. The early tombs of the Bahmanis were simple stone and rubble masonry structures.

Ala-ud-din Bahmani died in 1358. By then, he had conquered considerable territories, including Goa on the west coast. His successor Muhammad I continued to wage war with neighbouring territories, particularly Warangal and Vijayanagara. Ferishta recorded that the Bahmanis used gunpowder against Vijayanagara long before the Mughals used it in North India. It is said that Muhammad's army was commanded by Venetians and Turks who were ferocious and brutal fighters. Muhammad's reign was undoubtedly the bloodiest, as he is also said to have

Above: *Ruins of Rana Mandal, a tall structure that has cannons mounted on it*

Facing page above: *Interior of Jami Masjid*

Facing page below: *Roof of Rana Mandal, overlooking Jami Masjid*

Gulbarga's history dates back to the 6th century, when the Rashtrakutas controlled the area. In the 9th century, it fell to the powerful Chalukyas, who reigned for almost 200 years. The Kalachuris succeeded them and remained in control until the 12th century. Then followed the rule of the Yadavas of Devagiri and of the Hoysalas of Halebid. The Kakatiyas of Warangal soon took over most of the area and then finally succumbed to the Sultanate in Delhi.

Rebellion sums up the history of the Bahmani kingdom, founded by Ala-ud-din Hasan Bahman in 1347. He established himself as Sultan with Gulbarga as his capital, thus marking the beginning slain more than 20,000 men in Gulbarga, often just on charges of petty theft.

The eighth Bahmani king, Feroz Shah was as depraved as his ancestors, even as he built much of Gulbarga's splendours, including public buildings and palaces. He was defeated in battle in 1420 and two years later, murdered by his brother Ahmed. He shifted the capital to Bidar in 1424, primarily to put some distance between him and the Vijayanagara rajas. The Bahmani wars were not only against Hindus; they were also wars between Deccan Sunnis and Shias. These continuous wars ultimately destroyed the dynasty. Gulbarga was razed completely by the Vijayanagara king Krishna Deva Raya in 1520. The Deccan Sultanate broke into individual entities and in due course, Aurangzeb overran all.

Centuries after its creation, Gulbarga is still famous for the *dargah* of Hazrat Gesu Daraz, the renowned Chisti saint, who migrated here in his old age and settled in a monastery close to Jami Masjid. But as he refused to bless the dissolute son of Sultan Feroz, he was banished to the outskirts of the fort city.

Murud Janjira

Right: A carving on the external wall near the entrance

Facing page: The main entrance as seen from one of the arches within the fortification

Below: A view of the fortifications from the highest point inside the fort

With a rich and colourful history, replete with pirates, mercenaries, and a unique location once commanding trade in the Konkan region of the west coast, Murud Janjira island lies a few miles off the Konkan coast in the Arabian Sea. Its name of both Arabic and Konkani origin was the principality of the Siddhi nawabs for centuries. *Murud*, the Konkan word for dry land, is used along with *janjira*, said to be a corruption of *jazira* the Arabic word for island. With a history dating back to 225 BC, it was once part of Kolaba, but when Kolaba merged with Gujarat, Murud's maritime importance was reduced . By the 8th century, Murud once again established itself as an important centre for trade with the Arabic world.

But it was in 1490 that Murud Janjira was fully settled by Malik Ahmed Sultan of Ahmednagar who extended his kingdom to include Janjira, leaving it to one of his Siddhi slaves, Yakut to command. Another more colourful account, perhaps apocryphal, credits the Siddhi slaves with acquisition by deception. A few Siddhi slaves of Ahmed Shah, dressed as merchants, brought a shipload of boxes from Surat said to contain wine and silk. They regaled the Kolis with wine, and once they were inebriated, the boxes, in which armed men were hidden, were opened and a full-fledged attack was launched, establishing the Siddhi dynasty.

Even though Ahmednagar and Janjira fell to the Mughals, the Siddhis remained in control of this island kingdom. The Siddhis, originally from Abyssinia, were renowned for their military skills and were much sought after. In time, they helped the Mughal armies establish themselves in the Deccan and so, not only retained their fort but also their lands, ruling over a prosperous state for more than 350 years. They remained impervious even to the Portuguese, who controlled most of the Konkan region at this time. They withstood as many as 16 sieges by Shivaji, who coveted the strategic location of Murud Janjira. The Siddhis consolidated their position when the Mughals sought their help to annihilate the British, who were well entrenched in Bombay. This fort has the distinction of being amongst the very few forts in India to remain unconquered.

It is an island which provides a natural landscape as a perfect foil to its architecture. In the 17th century, the Siddhis established their own kingdom and began the reconstruction of the fort. An Inscription above the entry gate marks the beginning of its current construction in AD 1696. The wooden fortifications were replaced with massive stone walls rising straight out of the sea, some 14-metres high and enclosing eight and a half acres. The

battlements, with strongly articulated bastions, are some 100 feet apart and almost 60 feet across. Each bastion had the capacity for at least ten cannons capable of sinking any approaching vessel. Its main entrance is carefully concealed considering its exposed location, and faces landward with steps to the sea; directly opposite there is a small postern gate opening onto a large pier.

To the right of the entrance lies the *dargah* of Pir Panchayatan, which predates this fort and remains a major pilgrimage destination. Additionally there were five mosques of which Jama Masjid was most important. To the left of Jama Masjid there are two freshwater tanks, an essential ingredient for a successful island fort. Three wells further augment the supply. The impressive ruins of Siddhi Surul Khan, with heavy, fort-like walls in stone masonry and charming ornamental windows of Saracenic style, is nearby, and beyond lay the nawab's and queen's quarters, flanking the main water tanks. At the centre of the fort, there are the remains of the Raj Durbar or King's Court. It was originally built with seven floors, but only four remain, and it would have been a symbol of power. It was built complete with an execution chamber at the third level, with a trapdoor dropping straight into the sea. At the highest level of the fort, there is the lighthouse, an ancient circular structure.

At its peak more than 1,500 persons lived in Murud Janjira besides the nawab and his immediate retinue. The interior was full of closely built houses packed around paved alleyways surrounding the inner citadel, which was built on higher ground and would have been a self-sufficient settlement.

The Siddhi nawabs moved their palace to the mainland early in the 20th century. It is located on a high spur just outside the town of Murud. It blends the superb craftsmanship of the west coast of India with European fashion so prevalent in palaces then. Its large halls were tastefully decorated, and there was a vast number of personal chambers with other European facilities such as swimming pools, tennis courts and other recreation. It has a museum today, which showcases Siddhi history.

Golconda

A diamond among the Deccan forts, Golconda Fort is a massive assemblage of granite and masonry, it towers from a hillock over vast plains that held some of the densest concentration of diamond and gemstones in the world. The fort is chiselled with such skill that the *baradari* pavilions and palaces seem to almost spring from the surrounding granite rocks.

Golconda had been at the centre of a bustling trade in gemstones, and caravan *serai*s for merchants, nobility, and fortune hunters, who streamed in from as far as Turkey and Persia, dot the landscape. The region was originally called Warangal, meaning 'solitary rock', and was ruled by the Hindu Kakatiya kings, who built a mud fort at the site around AD 1143, when an idol of the deity Mangalavaram was found by a shepherd boy here. Golconda later became part of the Bahmani Sultanate and the Bahmanis added considerable fortifications. In AD 1518, the fort's Turkish Governor proclaimed independence and, assuming the title of Sultan Quli Qutb Shah, ruled long and well until the age of 90.

One of the most visionary and liberal kings of medieval India, Quli Qutb Shah built most of the fort as it stands today, channelling the revenue gained from flourishing trade and prosperity into an impressive fort and palace. He replaced the old Warangal mud fort with a huge edifice of stone that is arranged in several layers. Later sultans added their own contributions to this unique fort.

The city of Golconda was enclosed by outer fortifications that lay well below the hillock. This city, however, was plagued by disease and lack of water and the later sultan, Ibrahim Qutb Shah built a bridge across the River Musi to allow expansion into healthier areas with a better supply of water. It was during Ibrahim Qutb Shah's reign that the famed diamonds of Golconda were discovered at Kollur near the River Krishna.

With the discovery of the diamond mines, Golconda quickly became an extraordinarily wealthy kingdom. The liberal attitude of the Qutb Shahi kings led to a vibrant cosmopolitan culture that was secure within the towering fortifications. Three granite walls of stupendous scale encircled the fort. The outermost wall was extended to encompass a smaller fort on a hillock and some settlements nearby, while the second wall girdled the hill at its foot. The third fortification guarded the hilltop and appears to be almost hewn out of the granite hillside, with huge boulders straddling its walls. This wall has at least 87 semi-circular bastions, is 60-feet high, and is fashioned out of massive granite blocks. Some of these still have beautifully engraved cannons in place.

The main entry to the fort is through the Fateh Darwaza, or Gate of Victory, reached through a long, narrow road lined with towering ramparts. Fateh Darwaza is heavily spiked to defend against battering by elephants, and attacking armies had to intoxicate their elephants to make them push against the gates. The gate is acoustically designed in such a way that any sound here could be heard at Bala Hissar pavilion at the top, almost a kilometre away, a curiosity that continues to amaze and attract visitors. The gate bears the figure of a Hindu deity and may have been built by the Kakatiya kings. The other gates Banjara, Bahmani, Patancheru, Mecca, and Jamali are all decorated with animal relief in fine plasterwork. Bala Hissar Gate has a monumental domed portico and marks the beginning of the palace precincts.

Stories of the fort are legion, with each bastion having its own tale. In the northwest comer lies Petla Burj, or the 'Big-bellied Bastion', jutting out from an angle in the wall and housing the famous Fateh Rahbar cannon. The 'Nine-lobed Bastion' lies to the northeast and is so called because it has a corrugated face with nine protrusions, a design that affords a great length of parapet for defence and an expanse from which to fire at all sides. Musa Burj to the south is named after Musa Khan, Abdullah Qutb Shah's general, and was built by the architect Dharmachar to protect the fort against the first Mughal invasion in 1656.

Right: *Bala Hissar Gate*

Facing page: *Interior of Rani Mahal*

Inside the fort are remains of mosques, palaces, and *zenana*s built by successive generations of Qutb Shahi kings. The road towards the citadel's west is lined with military barracks, while the road to the south runs past a large complex of palace buildings. The *shila*, or armoury, dominates the fort's outer section. Further inside lies Taramati Masjid, the royal mosque adorned with fine plasterwork. Cobbled pathways lead through Dad Mahal, a long arcade with massive vaulted ceilings, into the royal complex where pleasure palaces and fountains and chambers abound. The Rani Mahal overlooks the courtyard and opens onto a triple-vaulted hall that still contains remnants of refined plasterwork embellishments. Most of these buildings suffered severe damage during the Mughal sieges and few stand in their entirety. Steep flights of stairs and stone-flagged passages lead to the large Bala Hissar hall, which was probably used either as a *durbar* pavilion or as a safe house, since the road up the hill is lined with granaries, stores, and even the treasury. An elaborate water system was devised to raise water to the top with water channels and tanks all the way uphill. Immediately below lies Ibrahim's Mosque and the original Mahakali Temple.

The glory of Golconda was abruptly cut short when Muhammad Quli Qutb Shah moved his capital to Bhagnagar, in pursuit of his beloved Bhagmati in 1589. Bhagnagar grew into the city of Hyderabad and a mosque and a *baradari* built for Bhagmati still stand there. But the greatest architectural legacy Muhammad Quli

Qutb Shah left to Hyderabad is the Char Minar, a triumphal archway with four minarets that is in the heart of the city and represents the finest synthesis of Persian and Indian styles in Deccani architecture.

The Qutb Shahi kings were a peace-loving dynasty and the only major battle they were part of was that of Talikota, where they joined Bijapur and Bidar in forming a confederacy with Ahmadnagar against the Hindu Vijayanagara kingdom. But after years of keeping the Mughals at bay through appeasement and services, they failed to contain the ambitions of a young Aurangzeb, newly appointed Governor of the Deccan by his father Shah Jahan. Abdullah Qutb Shah was betrayed by his own chief minister Mir Jumla, who joined forces with Aurangzeb and captured Hyderabad for himself. Abdullah Qutb Shah fled Hyderabad for the safety of Golconda, but Aurangzeb kept at his heels and besieged the fort, pulling back only when Shah Jahan insisted, but not before he had irrevocably damaged Golconda's fortifications.

In 1724, Golconda eventually became the property of Nizam-ul-Mulk, the Nizam of Hyderabad. The Nizam's wealth was built on his control over the diamond mines in the region, and he collected so many diamonds that were hoarded in fort, which led to Golconda Fort being called the world's most remarkable diamond vault. The largest of the Nizam's diamonds, the Jacob diamond, was used as a paperweight in the last Nizam's office, as perhaps inverted snobbery of the wealthiest man in the world.

Below: A panoramic view of the fort

Left: *Interior of Rani Mahal*

Right: *The temple at the top of the fort*

Asaf Jahi Palaces

CHAUMAHALLA PALACE

Among the several states that emerged from the yoke of a declining Mughal Empire in the 18th century, only one managed to retain its independence and territory until the time of independence from British rule. This state was Hyderabad, the unrivalled and wealthiest power in the Deccan for over 200 years. Mir Qamar-ud-din Khan, initially an appointee of Emperor Aurangzeb with the title of Nizam-ul-Mulk, (Administrator of the Realm), declared independence amid the chaos that followed Aurangzeb's death, and assumed the title Asaf Jah. The Nizam soon took over Golconda and its diamond mines and, as the Deccan Sultanates collapsed around him, began building his capital of Hyderabad into the most magnificent city of its time. Each generation of Nizams grew wealthier and more ambitious than the one before, and built fabulous palaces, each larger and grander than the last.

The Nizams had enormous households and retinues. As palaces grew crowded, or as new *begum*s brought their influences to bear, a plethora of palaces were built. The most majestic of these is the Chaumahalla Palace, built in the 1750s by Nizam Salabat Jung. Among the first and finest examples of the fusion of Indian and European neo-Classical architecture, the palace was built to the southwest of the Char Minar, which marked the city centre. Salabat Jung was influenced by the presence of French traders and adventurers at his court, which explains the choice of European design in the Chaumahalla.

Later Nizams made several additions to this massive palace complex, which originally covered an area of 54.78 acres and consisted of a series of buildings arranged around two main courtyards. At the centre of Chaumahalla is Khilwat Mahal, a durbar hall twice as tall as the surrounding buildings. It is crowned with elaborate *chattri*s at every corner and its upper level is set well

Facing page:
Khilwat Mahal

Below: Rest rooms
for travellers in the
first courtyard

back to create a spacious terrace. Offices and residential suites are
built in a linear fashion around the vast gardens outside the *mahal*.
The offices of the Nizam's personal estate were located in the
eastern building, with the Aftab Mahal and Mehtab Mahal serving
as reception halls during state functions.

Behind Khilwat Mahal is an enormous water tank that defines
the landscape. The palaces beyond are secluded and were built
by different Nizams, accounting for their somewhat eclectic style.
At the other end of Khilwat lies Tahniat, where the Nizams held
state receptions and entertained British Viceroys and imperial
emissaries. The ministers and other state dignitaries of Hyderabad
State were received at the southern palace, Afzal Mahal, thus
establishing clear distinctions.

Khilwat Mahal played host to the British Viceroys Curzon and
Wavell. When the Prince of Wales visited Hyderabad, over 160
guests were treated to a lavish banquet in this grand reception
room. It also was the venue for the coronation of the Nizams.
Today, Chaumahalla has been reduced to a mere 12 acres, but is
being painstakingly restored and opened, for the first time in its
history, to the public.

FALAKNUMA PALACE

The Falaknuma Palace is, in many ways, the acme of the Nizams'
aspirations to modernise their lifestyle. Though it is undoubtedly
the more handsome of the two, the seat of real power remained
in the city, in Chaumahalla. Muhammad Quli Qutb Shah had earlier

built a palace called Tur Mahal on the site where Falaknuma stands.
Falaknuma was first built in 1872 for a Paigah nobleman, then the
most eminent of Hyderabad's nobility; and was later bought by
Nizam Mir Mahbub Ali Khan Bahadur, who ruled from 1869 to 1911,
to be his private residence.

Situated at an elevation of 2,000 feet, Falaknuma's enormous
Palladian façade dominates the skyline. An Italian architect
designed the palace and extensively used Italian marble. The
main entrance is reached by a majestic double flight of stairs,
the lower floors supported by Ionic pillars and the floor above, by
Corinthian pillars. The entrance hall has a huge marble fountain
surrounded by benches and Italian statuary. The frescoes on the
walls and ceiling, adorned with flying cherubs carrying flower
garlands, complete the European look. To the rear of the entrance
hall, a sweeping staircase leads to reception halls resplendent
with French tapestry and decorated with a mix of Kashmiri and
Victorian objects of art.

The Durbar Hall is classic French baroque, with heavy drapes,
mirrors, enormous chandeliers, and parquet flooring. A smoking
room, card room, and billiard room are connected to the dining hall
which could seat over a hundred people. The Nizam's armchair was
higher, compensating his diminutive height, while establishing his
position. The tableware was made of gold, and English musicians
entertained guests while dining.

The smooth functioning of the palace was made possible
by a staff of 500 while continuous visits by distinguished guests

*Facing page below
right:* Painting of the
Bismillah ceremony of
Prince Mukkaram Jah

*Facing page below
left and above:* The
recently restored interiors
of Falaknuma Palace

resulted in constant renovation of the palace. Showers of scented water in the bathtubs were installed for King George V, and a new electrical system introduced for the Prince of Wales in 1922.

Behind the palace and separated by a courtyard are the curved buildings of the *zenana*, shaped like a scorpion's tail. This wing grew to accommodate the expanding harem of the Nizams and is reputed to have once accommodated no less than 5,000 women. The *zenana* is also built in the neo-Classical style, but the pointed arches and onion domes reflect the Islamic building tradition of Hyderabad. This fusion reflects the dilemma of the ruling families in 19th-century India as they aspired to emulate the lifestyle of the British even while trying to preserve their own culture.

The extravagance of Falaknuma is best described by the Prince of Wales after his visit in 1922: *"The marble vestibule always seems delightfully cool on the hottest day. The walls and the ceiling of the vestibule are artistically painted and decorated. Beyond this is a waiting room, adjoining which is the library containing a most valuable collection of manuscripts and printed books. The staircase leading to the upper floor is of marble, with carved balustrades, supporting, at intervals, marble figures. On the walls of the landing are excellent oil paintings of the Asaf Jahi family, past ministers and notable personages, the whole forming a very interesting historical picture gallery, which adds greatly to the imposing effect of the staircase. The State Reception Room is decorated with costly draperies and furniture and the collection of jade in it is considered to be unique in the world."*

Southern Kingdoms

Hampi

PLAN OF HAMPI

1. IMPERIAL CEREMONIAL ENCLOSURE
2. EMPEROR'S PRIVATE QUARTERS
3. HAZARA RAMA TEMPLE
4. ENCLOSURE WITH LOTUS MAHAL
5. ELEPHANT STABLES
6. ACHYUTA DEVA RAYA'S TEMPLE
7. SULAI BAZAAR
8. HAMPI BAZAAR
9. VIRUPAKSHA TEMPLE
10. KRISHNA TEMPLE
11. VITTHALA TEMPLE

next six-and-a-half centuries, Pampa *tirtha* grew into a ceremonial centre of significance. In recent years, archaeologists have found evidence of Neolithic settlements.

Located at the edge of the River Tungabhadra, Hampi is spread over 9 square miles in the lee of a rocky outcrop, which together with the river provides a natural protection. The city expanded rapidly under the Vijayanagara Empire. Abdur Razzak, an ambassador from Persia, wrote of it in AD 1442: *"The city of Bijadnagar is such that the pupil of the eye has never seen a place like it and the ear of intelligence has never been informed that there existed such a place like it."*

The vast ruins at Hampi, once the famed capital of the medieval Vijayanagara Empire, are like pieces of a broken mirror that reflect fragments, but do not give the full picture, of the glory of a sophisticated and mighty empire, unique in the world. Through the 14th and 15th centuries, the city of Vijayanagara, the present-day Hampi in north Karnataka, stood as one of the wealthiest and most flourishing cities in the world. Travellers from Europe confessed that imperial Rome paled in comparison to this magnificent metropolis. But the Vijayanagara Empire, the last great Hindu empire in India, was to meet a tragic and cataclysmic end. In the space of six months, the Islamic Sultanates in the Deccan combined to utterly raze and pillage the capital of Vijayanagara. Half a million people were mercilessly killed and the majestic buildings brought down one by one. The ruins at Hampi now lie desolate, a brute reminder of the fate that befell the finest of civilisations.

Hampi is situated on an ancient site known traditionally as Pampakshetra and Kishkindyakshetra. The site is mentioned in the Ramayana as Kishkinda and has a sacred geography. Pampakshetra is believed to be where the marriage of Lord Shiva with Parvati was consecrated, and the city of Hampi grew around the ancient temple of Virupaksha, a manifestation of Shiva. The earliest record of settlement is a 7th-century copper plate that refers to the site as Pampa *tirtha*, after the river goddess Pampa who presided over the *tirtha* on the southern bank of the River Tungabhadra. Over the

Right: Octogonal tower and view of the complex

Left: *Lotus Mahal*

Before the rise of the Vijayanagara dynasty, Hampi was ruled in succession by the Kadambas, the Chalukyas of Badami, the Rashtrakutas, the Hoysalas, and the Yadavas. To the east of Hampi, Kampili was the seat of the Kalyani Chalukyas in the 11th century. The Delhi Sultan Ala-ud-din Khilji captured Kampili in 1326 taking with him two treasury officers, the brothers Harihara and Bukka, who converted to Islam and professed loyalty to the Sultan. They were soon sent back to the South to quell an insurgency, and there they grew in power, finally declaring independence and reconverting to Hinduism. Claiming lineage from Virupaksha, Harihara assumed the title of Hastinapati, or Hampi, and established, after his father's name, the Sangama dynasty. Bukka succeeded Harihara in 1354 and began work on a sophisticated palatial, civic, and religious complex that was to be his capital of Vijayanagara, the City of Victory.

Bukka's successor, Harihara II, was as powerful and waged war with the Bahmani Sultans. In 1565, at the battle of Talikota, the Deccan Sultanates defeated Vijayanagara and the Sultan of Ahmadnagar decapitated king Rama Raya, leaving the city of Vijayanagara to plunder and destruction. Vijayanagara remained part of the Bijapur Sultanate until Aurangzeb decimated it in the 17th century.

Hampi is one of the richest archaeological treasures in India. An outer fortification encloses the temples and the royal palaces. The fortifications are almost circular with gateways leading to the city within. Pavilions and watch towers still stand in the remains of palaces and royal reception areas. The most imposing structure is the Mahanavmi Dibba, a multi-level platform 40-feet high and tapering towards the top. It is elaborately carved with depictions of the court, wars, and hunting expeditions. The highest platform served as the throne of the Rayas from where they presided over religious ceremonies like Navaratri and Diwali.

On the southern side are two spectacular bathing tanks with steps leading down in complicated geometric patterns. The Queen's Bath is built in the Deccan Sultanate style with a vaulted and domed roof and balconies overlooking the tank. A sophisticated water system connected the tanks with the bathing pavilions.

Lotus Mahal is a two-storey pavilion with projections on all sides, and an upper floor with cusped arch openings. The beautifully plastered superstructure is supported by 24 square pillars. The ceiling is elaborately ornamented with stucco arches, friezes, and ledges, mostly with animal motifs but noteworthy for the *Yalis*, the guardian deities. The superstructure consists of nine towers that form a pyramid shape. These used to be fully decorated and covered with polished lime plaster. The Lotus Mahal is also known locally as Chitrangini Mahal, but the *Svaramelakalanidhi*, a contemporary text, refers to it as Ratnakuta, the centre of arts.

The elephant stables are a handsome ensemble consisting of 11 chambers. They are crowned with a sequence of plain or fluted domes, alternating with 12-sided vaults capped with ribbed finials arranged symmetrically on either side of a central

two-storey upper chamber. The linear arrangement of the domed chambers is similar to that in Bahmani architecture and so is the decorated stucco, which is also seen on the octagonal pavilion that faces a huge courtyard where parades were held for the kings.

The Virupaksha Temple dominates the skyline and continues to attract thousands of devotees. It is situated on the banks of the River Tungabhadra and is part of a larger complex of tanks, *mathas*, and related shrines. It was originally built in the 7th century and is among India's oldest temples where worship has continued unbroken to the present day. The temple has three *gopurams*. The eastern one is 160-feet high and was built by Krishna Deva Raya in the 16th century. The northern *gopuram* has five storeys and lies in front of the third *gopuram*, which has three storeys. All the three *gopurams* have wonderful stucco work depicting religious images. Krishna Deva Raya also constructed the central pillared hall known as the Ranga Mandapa. Two mythical lion-like creatures form the balustrade at the entrance to an open pavilion. This hall has five aisles and

Facing page above: Tank close to Vitthala Temple

Facing page below: Interior of Lotus Mahal

38 rows of pillars sculpted with mythical creatures like *Yalis* that are shown standing on crocodiles. The Krishna Temple complex nearby is in ruins. The 'Hazara-Rama' Temple, its name inspired by the thousand images of Rama carved on the walls, lies close to the royal enclosure and is richly carved in bas-relief depicting scenes from the Ramayana.

The centrepiece of Hampi is the Vitthala Temple complex. A vast number of structures, large and small, make up this damaged temple complex. A stone chariot, intricately carved with mythical battle scenes, is one of the jewels of Hampi and seems to be inspired by Harihara II's victories in Orissa, where the Konark Sun Temple is built in the form of the Sun God's chariot. Nearby is a many-pillared hall called the Maha Mandapa. The balustrade is dramatically carved with giant *Yalis* fighting elephants. The hall stands on an ornate platform carved with floral motifs. The reliefs on the lower level of the platform depict chains of horses, trainers, and traders. The Maha Mandapa is also known as the hall of musical pillars, as its elaborately carved giant monolithic pillars resonate with musical tones when skilfully tapped.

Vellore

One of India's finest military forts, Vellore is an almost perfect *jala durg*, a fort defended by water. Its formidable façade of huge granite fortifications is surrounded by a very broad moat. Located on the banks of the River Pallar, it conforms to the ancient principles of defence stipulated in the *Shastras*. The water of the moat was infested with crocodiles and its causeways could easily be flooded. The very name Vellore means a 'City of Spears', evoking its martial history of battles and bloodshed. Its chequered history is clearly reflected in the various layers of construction that each successive ruler added to the fort.

Built in the 14th century by Chinna Bommi Nayak, a chieftain of Vijayanagara, the fort was called 'Raya Vellore' to differentiate it from the 'Uppu Vellore' situated in the Godavari Basin. Constructed during the reign of Krishna Deva Raya, the fort grew in prosperity when Dutch, French, and Portuguese traders established bases along the Coromandel Coast in the 17th century. However, this period of peace was short-lived as the Sultan of Bijapur seized the fort in 1656 as part of the Deccan Sultanates' collaborative campaign to annihilate Vijayanagara.

In 1676, the Marathas led by Shivaji attacked the fort. Shivaji was intent on establishing a base in the Deccan and entered into an agreement with the Golconda Sultan to defeat the Adil Shahis of Bijapur, who had wrested the fort from Vijayanagara. The Bijapur army heroically defied the siege for 14 months, and the Marathas had to fortify the neighbouring hills from which they could bombard Vellore. The Maratha triumph proved to be as brief as Bijapur's and 30 years later, the fort fell to Daud Khan's Delhi army in 1707, the year of Aurangzeb's death. The Mughals established the Nawabi of Arcot and gave it the charge of Vellore Fort. Dost Ali Khan, who became nawab in 1732, gifted the fort to one of his sons-in-law, which led to a bloody succession struggle. Meanwhile the French and British trading companies, having risen in strength over the years, became involved in the struggle for the control of the fort. Finally, the British East India Company took over

Right: Interior of the Jalakanteshwara Temple complex

the fort after a series of what are known as Carnatic Wars and used it as an important garrison right up to the time of Independence. Haider Ali of Mysore attacked the fort in 1780 but the British defied the siege for two years. Haider Ali's son, Tipu Sultan, was kept prisoner, along with his family at Vellore Fort after the British victory at Srirangapatnam in 1799.

Vellore Fort was also the site of the first Indian sepoy mutiny against the British, half a century before the first Indian war of Independence in 1857. Early in the morning on July 10, 1806, some 1,500 Indian soldiers of the Madras Regiment attacked the European barracks and killed 100 soldiers and 15 officers. The immediate provocation for the revolt was an order forbidding the wearing of caste marks and beards. The rebels urged Tipu Sultan's sons to lead the attack. Reinforcements were rushed to the fort and the rebellion was quashed by noon, after almost 800 Indian sepoys had been killed. Tipu's family was moved to Kolkata, though they were later buried in Vellore just outside the fort.

Vellore Fort hugs the contours of the land, its gray-blue granite wrapping itself along the River Pallar. The massive ramparts are interspersed with bastions and square towers at regular intervals. There are two distinct fort walls, the outer one slightly lower than the inner, so that both walls could be used in tandem for the firing of guns and cannons as well as spears and arrows. The crenellated parapets are made of brick, in which embrasures are cut. The embrasures are possibly a later European addition. To the south is a raised bastion with a flagstaff. It was entered through massive gates and was protected by a drawbridge, a system that was altered in the 18th century to adapt it for artillery defence. The broad moat surrounding the fort receives water from the Suryagunta tank, a large reservoir nearby. The moat is said to have contained more than 10,000 crocodiles at one time. It extends to 8,000 feet outside the fort and in some places is as deep as 190 feet.

The most significant structure within the fort is the Jalakantheshwara Temple dedicated to Lord Shiva. It was left untouched even during the Sultanate and Arcot occupations. In its entrance courtyard is a magnificent Nandi bull statue in

blue granite and an impressive gateway with a seven-storeyed *gopuram*, also of granite. The gateway is flanked on either side by magnificent statues of a dancing Parvati while the temple itself is heavily carved in the Vijayanagara style with *gopurams*, *mandapas*, and cloisters of sculpted stone.

Within the fort, the parade ground is flanked by the old royal palaces, which are two-storey buildings with large internal courtyards. The Tipu and Haider Ali Mahals were built by the British to imprison the survivors of the family. The charm of Vellore Fort is that despite its turbulent history, a temple, a mosque, a church and a variety of British military buildings blend into harmony with the forbidding granite ramparts. Today, the Pallar flows gently by; there are no crocodiles, and the fort is easily accessed by a bridge that hundreds of devotees cross every day to worship at the Jalakantheshwara Temple.

Above left: Fortifications surrounded by the moat

Above right:
Entrance gopuram *to Jalakanteshwara Temple*

PLAN OF VELLORE FORT
1. JALAKANTESHWARA TEMPLE
2. MAIN GATE
3. MOSQUE
4. ASI OFFICE
5. ARCHAEOLOGICAL MUSEUM
6. ST JOHN'S CHURCH
7. HAIDER MAHAL
8. TIPU MAHAL
9. UPPER RAMPARTS

Gingee

The great fort at Gingee straddles the three hills of Krishnagiri, Chandragiri, and Rajagiri. It is the quintessential *giri durg*, or hill fort. The building is a stupendous array of fortified walls and bastions scattered in ruins over a large area in the Eastern Ghats. Situated in an idyllic rural landscape, its remains are now one with nature. The fortifications rise and descend with the contours of the hills, forming a rough triangle. Rajagiri is the highest hill and houses the main fort and palace of Raigarh.

Gingee was a Chola fort; the Cholas were the most powerful rulers of Southern India from the 9th to the 13th centuries. They built strong defences against their traditional enemies, the Pandyas of Madura, but by the mid-15th century Vijay Ranga Nayaka, the Pandya Governor of Thanjavur, had taken control of the fort and extended the fortifications to the Chandragiri and Krishnagiri hills, retaining the citadel at Rajagiri.

The Pandya Nayakas reigned supreme during the 16th and 17th centuries and built remarkable temples and palaces in the fort. After the collapse of Vijayanagara, Gingee fell to the Sultan of Bijapur. When Maratha king Shivaji entered into an alliance with his arch rival Golconda, the Marathas stormed Gingee making it their stronghold till 1698, when the Nayakas briefly regained power under Raja Sarup Singh. This was a short-lived rule, as the fort was besieged by the Mughal general Zulfikar Ali Khan during the reign of Emperor Aurangzeb, a siege that lasted seven years. Throughout this period, the Marathas laid siege to the Mughal forces looting their supply lines and completely demoralising them. However,

infighting among the Marathas gave the Mughal armies the edge, who finally conquered this invincible fort and made Gingee their southern capital until 1730, when the capital was shifted to Arcot. Gingee played a crucial role in the battles between the French and British as they struggled for supremacy in a beleaguered India. The French commander Bussy finally took Gingee in 1750 and a mere 10 years later, it became the last French fort to fall to the British, culminating their seven-year war with the French in South India.

The great fort at Gingee, now deserted, was one of the most impressive forts in India. The three hills on which the *giri durg* is built are high and difficult to ascend, with their rocky escarpments contributing to the fort's impregnability. A main outer wall stretches to the fortifications protecting Chandragiri and Krishnagiri. From the centre of the fort's triangular formation, three main lines of walls lead in succession to the citadel of Rajagiri at the summit. Supplementary walls running between the hillocks enclose the ravines and provide additional fortifications.

Entrance to the complex was gained through the gate at the centre of the wall forming the base of the triangle, about halfway between Chandragiri and Krishnagiri. The citadel's outer bailey, partially moated, contained the granaries and the later multi-storey, *prasada*-like Kalyana Mahal built by the Nayakas. This bailey was entered through a great triple gate, with a barbican and heavily guarded courts, with a complex passage that had 90-degree turns at six places. The next two gates, serving as entry and exit of a second bailey, stand diagonally across each other and at different heights. Over the lintel of the second gate is a small circular carving of Kirtimukha – 'Mouth of Glory' – with a demonic head. A deep and rocky chasm lies on the way to the summit. A drawbridge used to exist over this leading to a narrow and forbidding passage to the inner sanctum.

The route to the citadel is defended by seven gateways. Three of the gates in the second and fourth walls have large courtyards between them. The royal compound of the Nayakas consisted of a number of buildings, the best preserved being the Kalyana Mahal or the *zenana*. This complex has apartments on four sides of a square water tank, in a classical Hindu plan. These chambers were reserved for the Nayakas' entourage. At the centre of the courtyard is a large tower pavilion of seven storeys, each having pillared arcades with a single entry from the southern side. Above the first storey, the tower is laced on its four sides with arched openings from which the women of the court could look out without being observed. This multi-storey tower would have provided ample space on the upper floors for the privacy and security of the Nayaka. A highly sophisticated water system with three tanks, fed

Right:
Kalyana Mahal

Facing page: The vast fortifications of Gingee

Above: Palace complex on top of the hill

Right: Ceiling detail in the palace complex

Below: Ceremonial seat with a granite bolster in the parade ground

by two springs could lift water as high as six storeys, ensuring that this *mahal* was always well served.

To the north of the Kalyana Mahal stands a six-storeyed tower with arcades on its four sides, and a small chamber with a steeply pyramidal roof at the top. To its west lies a double row of small chambers with shallow vaults, each with an arcaded verandah, which are likely to have been stables for horses. These form the northern boundary of the Kalyana Mahal complex, creating a spacious parade ground. To the west of this ground, foundations of what would have been the royal residence are visible, with a square, central room, evidence of a colonnaded verandah, and subsidiary chambers.

Immediately below, and reached by a spiral staircase, is a large square stone slab with a bolster that formed part of a ceremonial seat. The slab is hewn from gray-green granite and raised on a stone structure. It is speculated that the Nayaka rulers used this as a seat for presiding over the vast parade ground. A vaulted granary, a watch tower, and an oil press also form part of this complex.

To the south of the Kalyana Mahal is a large bathing tank carved out of rock and surrounded by a covered colonnade. Access was limited and achieved through several steps around the tank. It was used possibly for ritual purposes. The tank would have provided vital water storage during the seven-year siege of the fort.

Granaries with pointed arched vaults are prominent in the royal complex at Gingee. Each one is varied: one has four interconnecting chambers but an unadorned façade, while another is single-chambered but with decorative features, including a frieze of foliage motifs and *Yali* heads at the arched ends. The open pavilions nearby, with fanciful arches and fluted domes, would have been pleasure pavilions.

A huge gun crowns the Rajagiri citadel. The Prisoner's Well is a gigantic boulder, pierced by a large opening and balanced on a rock with a low, circular brick wall. It is believed that prisoners were thrown in and left to die of starvation.

Below: *The palace and temple complex atop the hill*

Srirangapatnam

Above: Gateway to the fort complex

For a brief period in its otherwise peaceful history, the Srirangapatnam Fort was the bloodiest and most war-ravaged citadel in India. In the mid-18th century, Haider Ali, having risen from the fighting ranks of the Mysore army to become de facto king, jolted the small kingdom of Mysore out of its bucolic existence and pitchforked it into the heat of the battles for power raging across India. Feared for his cruelty against enemies, Haider Ali worsted the Marathas, conquered Calicut, and attacked the British East India Company. He modernised the army, employed European officers and artillery, and, in 1781, plundered Tanjore so mercilessly that folklore in the region still remembers the attack as *Haiderakalabam*, or the apocalypse wrought by Haider. His son Tipu Sultan was as ferocious and was known as the 'Tiger of Mysore'. A friend of Italian nationalist rebels and an admirer of European technology, Tipu fought to the bitter end, defending Srirangapatnam from the Company.

Poised on an island in the sacred River Kaveri, Srirangapatnam is a perfect *jala durg*. Its name is derived from the ancient temple of Sri Ranganatha Swami on the island. In 1610, the Wodeyar king of Mysore shifted his capital from Mysore to Srirangapatnam, extending his territories and consolidating his holdings across peninsular India. Following the defeat of the Vijayanagara Empire in the 16th century, the Sultans of Bijapur and Golconda held sway across most of South India. The Mughals decimated the Sultanates and established governors, but soon the Mughal Empire was in decline, renewing the struggle for power in the Deccan, this time between the Nizam of Hyderabad and the Marathas.

Haider Ali swept across the region, destroying all that lay in his path. The Marathas and the Nizam were so alarmed that they joined forces, but they still could not muster the strength to face the marauder and so, allied with the British, who themselves were looking to increase their power in the region. Even the combined armies of the British, the Marathas, and the Nizam were routed by Haider Ali, who also seized Mangalore and had reached the gates of Madras when the Company negotiated a peace treaty in 1769. In 1771, the Marathas attacked Srirangapatnam but were betrayed by the British, who, instead of facilitating them, used the opportunity to capture Mahe, a French protectorate of Mysore. Haider Ali bought off the Marathas but remained on the offensive against the Company, capturing Arcot. On his death in 1782, Tipu Sultan became the ruler of Mysore.

Tipu's soldiers defeated British armies in the east, repelled a joint Maratha-Hyderabad invasion from the north, and captured territories in the south. At one point, Tipu even captured Hyderabad but returned it after the Nizam promised peace. The British, however opposed this agreement with Mysore and provoked Tipu into attacking Travancore and setting off a three-year war between the British and Mysore. In 1791, Lord Cornwallis captured Bangalore and attacked Srirangapatnam, but had to retreat after his plan failed. In 1792, he returned with a larger force, and captured Srirangapatnam. Tipu had to surrender half his lands to the Marathas and the Nizam. The 'final struggle' took place in 1799, when Lord Wellesley sent in his army, finally destroying the power of Tipu Sultan, and restored the Hindu Wodeyars to the throne. The assault against the island fortress, a joint military operation by 40,000 troops, culminated in the capture of the city on May 4, 1799, and the death of Tipu Sultan. As a result, the British were able to secure control of all of Southern India, establishing the transition from trade to military power.

Srirangapatnam Fort is accessed through its main southern gate, the Mysore Gate. During the assault by Cornwallis, some 10,000 prisoners kept in the fort escaped through this gate. Nearby is the flagstaff erected by Lord Wellesley, the first Duke of Wellington, who, prior to defeating Napoleon, had earned fame for the defeat of Tipu Sultan.

The Elephant Gate, built in 1793, is large enough to accommodate caparisoned elephants and was once secured by a drawbridge. The Delhi Gate was accessed by the Delhi Bridge,

which Tipu dismantled for defence purposes, but the stone bases still remain. The northern rampart leads to the Sultan Battery, below which are the dungeons where prisoners were confined in appalling conditions, often for years. Standing up to their necks in water, they were chained with their arms crossed, and compelled to eat like animals, with the food being placed on stone ledges above. Further east along the ramparts is the 'Gateway of the Fallen Fortress', or the Bidda Kote Bagalu, with underground vaults also used as dungeons.

The Temple of Sri Ranganatha Swami stands at one end of the parade ground. Nearby is the 18th-century Narasimha Swami Temple built by the Wodeyars. The Lal Mahal, the palace of Haider Ali and Tipu Sultan, once described as India's finest building, no longer exists. The Jami Masjid built by Tipu is a graceful structure with onion domes and a mound nearby marks the grave of Mir Muhammad Sadak, executor of Tipu's heinous tortures, and also his most trusted lieutenant.

The *gumbaz* built by Tipu is an extravagant mausoleum complex with great gardens and a *naubat khana* straddling the gateway to the main hall containing the graves of Haider and Tipu. These are elegant square buildings, each with an onion dome and four small minarets. They are raised on an arcaded verandah with elegant polished stone pillars and an ebony door inlaid with ivory. This door was restored by the British when they occupied the fort. Just outside the fort is Daria Daulat Bagh, Tipu's summer palace. Built on the remains of the Mahanavmi Mandapa of the Mysore Rajas, it was briefly used by Haidar Ali as barracks. Tipu transformed it into an elaborately painted and gilded hall, with the murals depicting his successful wars against the British. The garden itself is a classical *char bagh* and exotic plants brought from Kabul, Lahore, and beyond were grown here.

Rebuilt many times, the Srirangapatnam Fort stands as a reminder not only of the tragic fall of Tipu Sultan, but also the rise of the British Empire in India.

Above: Wall painting, Daria Daulat Bagh

Below: Colonel Bailey's dungeon

Right & below:
Wall painting, Daria
Daulat Bagh

Facing page: Interior
of Daria Daulat Bagh

Mysore

The extravagant opulence of the Mysore Palace gives no hint that the fortunes of the state of Mysore were fraught with peril for most of its history. Wedged between the aspirations of the British Empire and the ambitions of Tipu Sultan, the tiny Mysore state survived four Anglo-Mysore wars that also saw the Marathas and the Nizam of Golconda fighting for a share of this kingdom deep in the hills of Karnataka. The Wodeyar kings, who were once vassals of the Vijayanagara kingdom and had been ousted by Haider Ali, returned to the throne when the British established the princely state of Mysore and gave it to the Wodeyars in return for a heavy tribute. Towards the end of the 19th century, the enlightened, progressive, and extraordinarily wealthy Krishna Raja IV (ruled 1894–1940), whom Mahatma Gandhi called a 'saintly king', ascended the throne and began to develop Mysore as a modern city, with the fortified palace at its centre.

The original palace building was destroyed in a fire during a marriage ceremony in 1897. Work on a new palace commenced immediately and was completed in 1912. British architect Henry Irwin was commissioned to design the palace and it was built in an Indo-Saracenic style unique to Mysore. The palace epitomises the eclectic fusion of European and Indian art and architecture, and is the iconic image of the city.

A three-storey building 245 feet in length and 136 feet in breadth, the palace is approached through an imposing Jaya

Facing page:
Amba Vilas Palace

Below:
The palace illuminated

Martand Gate that has a cusped archway and is over 65-feet tall. As mandated in the sacred texts, the gate is situated to the east. The massive façade of the building is counterbalanced with delicate detailing that lends its curious architecture great charm. Vast onion domes, turrets, and minarets combine to make an excessively busy exterior. A huge portico has polished granite columns supporting cusped arches, covered by a *bangla*-style roof with domed *chattri*s. Behind the portico is an enormous 12-sided tower with a gilded dome and surrounded by clusters of smaller domes. During Dussehra, a major festival in Mysore, more than 50,000 light bulbs illuminate the building exterior.

The palace's interior are as opulent as the façade. A huge ceremonial staircase, flanked by marble statues of guards and with a teak ceiling carved with Hindu mythological figures, leads to the huge public halls. The Durbar Hall is the most majestic – 165 feet in length – and is dominated by short southern-style pillars that are heavily ornamented and gilded. Wide cusped arches support a richly decorated ceiling, painted in an eclectic style with blue skies, stars, and lotuses. The walls are painted with images of Hindu gods and goddesses, the most important being Chamundeshwari,

the patron deity of the Mysore rajas. The most impressive focus of the Durbar Hall used to be a massive gold throne, which stood in the centre under a gold umbrella topped by a gold bird holding a string of emeralds in its beak.

The Amba Vilas, or the hall of private audience, lies to the south and has heavily decorated short columns with a carved and inlaid teakwood ceiling. But the exceptional feature of the hall is undoubtedly the cast ironwork. Richly decorated cast iron pillars, fashioned in Glasgow and brought to Mysore, support a stained-glass roof of great luminescence, especially when lit by the huge chandeliers. The floor is of marble and inlaid with semiprecious stones. A richly carved rosewood door leads to the temple of Lord Ganesha, exclusively used by the royal family.

At the centre of the Mysore Palace is a colonnaded courtyard that separates the private royal chambers from the public halls. The royal chambers consist of the *zenana* and the king's chambers. These have now been converted to museums displaying the royal collection of armoury, trophies, and paintings. One remarkable exhibit is a wooden elephant decorated with 84 kg of gold.

Perhaps the most impressive building in the palace is the Kalyana Mandapa, or wedding hall. It is a cast iron structure with an octagonal dome of stained glass that is supported by clusters of cast iron pillars with ornate capitals. The floor is of Victorian tiles while the walls depict Mysore's famed Dussehra procession.

Adding to the palace's exoticness are ballrooms and libraries made of Burmese teak, and a dining room upholstered in red velvet. Writing on the intricately executed multiple moldings, Hayavadana Rao noted:"*They break the surface into many projections, recesses, niches, and panels*" and are "*relieved with a superabundance of deep, sharp, and fine carvings of scrolls, foliage, birds, animals and statuettes of very chaste and elegant design*". Philip Davies was less complimentary and regarded Irwin's design as "*ostentatious, ill-mannered, and vulgar*","but conceded that it was "*enormous fun*".

Facing page: Pillared hallway leading to Amba Vilas

Above: Stained-glass ceiling of the Kalyana Mandapa

Far left: The Kalyana Mandapa

Left: Corridor around the Kalyana Mandapa

Padmanabhapuram

Right: The Mantrashala, or the council meeting room

Facing page: Looking down on to the temple courtyard from the Upparika Malika

Following pages (144-145): Interior of the temple located on the topmost floor of the Upparika Malika, used by the king for his prayers

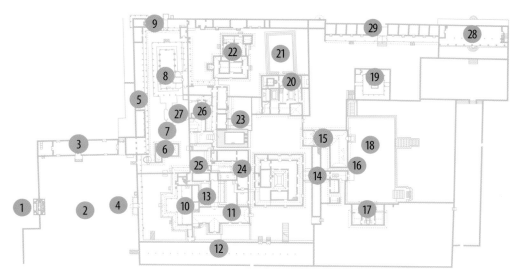

Distanced from the pressures of invasions, conquests, loot and pillage that marked much of India's medieval history, the royal seat of Travancore situated in the seaward side of the Western Ghats was among the earliest powers to have established trade relations with the Arabs, Portuguese, and Dutch. The original seat of the kingdom was Kanyakumari, where the Cheraman dynasty reigned until 1790. Raja Martanda Varma in the mid-18th century rebuilt the *garh-mahal* in Kanyakumari and expanded the palace, naming it Padmanabhapuram, city of the Lotus Padamnabha, an *avatar* of Vishnu. In 1790, Raja Rama Varma II shifted the capital to Thiruvananthapuram and Padmanabhapuram became the royal summer residence.

There are no records of the origin of Padmanabhapuram, but its earliest structures are dated to the 16th century. Of the *garh-mahal*s of India, the major structures of Padmanabhapuram are singular in that they are primarily constructed of wood rather than the more permanent stone or masonry. Although this form of construction was prevalent along Western India, very few such buildings remain. Padmanabhapuram's excellent state of preservation is due to the fact that it has had an uninterrupted custodianship and its sanctum sanctorum still holds the lineage deity of the kings.

Located inside the granite Padmanabhapuram Fort, which is spread over 186.25 acres at the foot of a hill, the palace is defined by a high wall on the western side and is divided into four distinct courtyards. The first courtyard is entered through an imposing gateway with a pitched roof portico that leads to an open area used for public ceremonies. Across this is a *padipura*, a traditional Kerala doorway with a high gabled roof and richly carved woodwork, which opens into the smallest of the four courtyards with the *pumukham*, or hall of public audience, facing it. The hall itself is on the second storey and is built on large circular wooden pillars. Intricately carved screens decorate the entrance gable and extensive slatted screens are angled to filter the sunlight. To the north is the Navrathri Mandapa, where festivals were celebrated. This has a high roof, profusely carved granite pillars, and a burnished black lime plaster floor. On one side is a small structure with wooden screens; this secluded the royal women when they came to watch the performances.

Small and unpretentious doors connect the adjoining courtyard complexes, each of which served a different purpose. The next courtyard leads into the interior, incrementally increasing in privacy as it moves from the official to the private realm, into the core of the palace known as Thai Kottaram, the Queen Mother's Palace. It is one of the oldest structures and is built around a small courtyard with a shallow pool in the middle. It forms the centre of the palace layout, which is designed according to the *Vastu Purusha Mandala*, the ancient Indian diagram representing the cosmos. The Brahma Sthana, or the crossing point of the two main axis, falls immediately outside, in alignment with the main entrance gateways. Considering the palace was continuously added to over generations, it nonetheless conforms to the prevailing science of building known locally as *Thachu Shastram*.

The third courtyard is the royal apartment complex, with its most notable building being the Upparika Malika, a four-storey masonry tower that soars over the palace. Each floor of this building has a chamber, a treasury, a resting room for the king, and a fasting room for ritual purposes. The uppermost storey contains the personal prayer room of the Varma kings and is reached by a ladder, unlike the lower floors that are accessed by narrow stairs. This shrine room is heavily decorated with frescoes depicting mythological scenes and pictures of gods, and a bed is provided for Lord Padmanabha. To this day, the royal family conducts its rituals in this room. The lower rooms have slatted angled shutters, a sophisticated system to divert sunlight while allowing those inside to survey the court below. Beyond lie the queens' quarters, the Lakshmi Vilasam and Pilamuttu Kottaram, and the Homapura, a building with its own stepped tank and temple that was used

Right: Curved brackets
in the Mantrashala

Right: The verandah
of Thekke Kottaram
or the South Palace

Far right: Carved
gable on the entrance
to the Mantrashala

by queens to perform sacred rituals. The Uttupura, a two-storey dining hall, is an extremely long pillared hall and is entered from the upper storey.

The fourth courtyard is to the east and has additional dining areas as well as residences built around the Kalkulam tank, that has a flight of stairs descending to the water. The courtyard also houses the Indra Vilasam, a suite of public and private rooms meant exclusively for foreigners.

Padmanabhapuram has an interesting layout as it incorporates royal and civic use in a system of two-storey buildings. The lower floors house the administrative offices and through the day would have bustled with the comings and goings of a busy court life, while the upper floors were kept for the royal family and their personal retinue, a feature common to all Kerala's grand *manas*. The official meetings of the king took place in the Mantrashala on the first floor, which has balconies from where the king gave

public audience. Around the palace is a cluster of many buildings – the mint, an armoury, *langars*, and offices – that gives the complex an almost urban setting.

Padmanabhapuram is possibly the best-preserved wooden palace in India. Built on a stone base, the superstructure makes extensive use of intricately carved wood in doors, windows and roofs. Wood and stone pillars support elaborate wooden ribbed rafters while the walls are made with plastered masonry or wooden screens. The wooden screens filter the light, provide privacy and ventilation, and are used in the roofs as well. The walls are rendered in the finest shell lime plaster that glistens in light, and together with the black lime plaster flooring, makes for a unique ensemble. This perfect play of light and shade is still visible, for even though Padmanabhapuram is now in custody of the state government, the descendents of Raja Martanda Varma still perform the royal rituals here and keep alive the glory of this magnificent palace.

Above: *Curved timber trellises embellished with coloured mica for the window shutters*

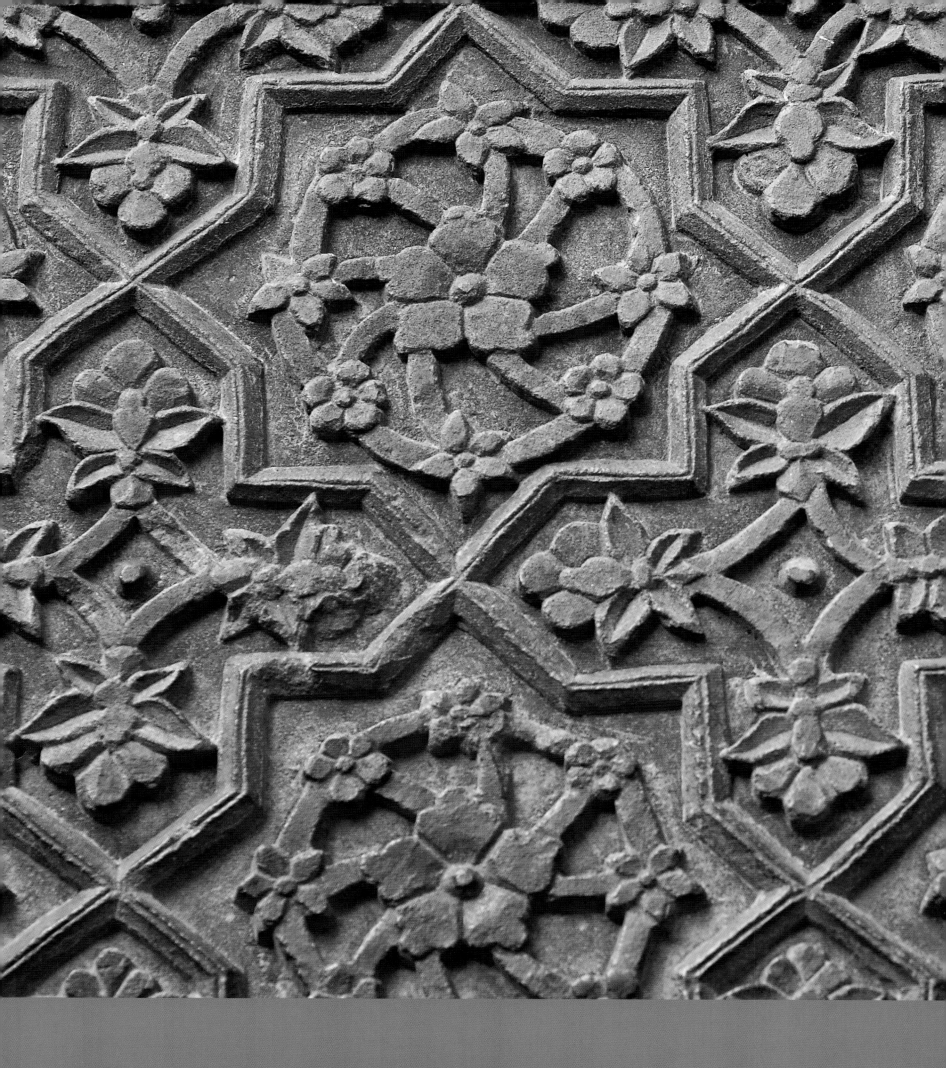

Mughal Forts

Purana Qila

Purana Qila established the sixth of the fabled seven cities of Delhi. Its founder was the Mughal emperor Humayun, who called it Dinpanah, or 'Refuge of Faith', but the major part of the fort was built by the Sur emperor Sher Shah, whose dramatic growth in power began in Eastern India, demolishing early Mughal ambitions. Humayun had to find refuge in Persia and it was not until ten years after Sher Shah's death that he managed to recapture Delhi in 1555.

Sher Shah was a prodigious builder. He began work on what must have been the most ambitious civic project of the time, a road from Peshawar in the subcontinent's northwest mountains to Murshidabad near the east coast of Bengal. This road is now called the Grand Trunk Road and is India's busiest highway. Sher Shah ruled from Purana Qila and called it Shergarh. The fort stood on a site believed to have been the Pandava capital of Indraprastha mentioned in the Mahabharata. The Archaeological Survey of India's excavations, however, have dated the site to no further back than 2nd century BC, and the area has been continuously occupied ever since.

After Humayun recaptured it, the fort was renamed but it was a hundred years later, after Shah Jahan built the Lal Qila in his new, walled city of Shahjahanabad, that it came to be known as Purana Qila, or Old Fort. The settlement inside the fort, however, continued to be called Dinpanah until well into the 20th century. And a refuge it certainly remained: thousands of refugees from West Pakistan, after India's partition in 1947, stayed here in camps for several years; even the last Mughal emperor Bahadur Shah Zafar took refuge here during the 1857 rebellion against the British. One of the fort's gates, Kabuli Darwaza, acquired the epithet Khooni Darwaza or 'Bloody Gate' after Bahadur Shah's sons were killed here.

Purana Qila was the citadel of a much larger fortified city. It was located at the edge of the River Yamuna and water was plentiful. Bada Darwaza is the main gate and was built in 1533–34. It is a three-storey structure with two massive, curving bastions made of rubble masonry. A *chattri* on one of the bastions indicates that the gate would have once been much grander. The gate itself is dressed in deep red sandstone, inlaid with coloured stones and black marble. On the second floor are three openings, two of which have *jharokhas*, and all are embellished with green and blue glazed tiles.

The northern gate is known as Talaaqi Darwaza or the 'Forbidden Gate'. It is not clear why this gate was so named but popular legend holds that a princess closed the gate on her husband when he returned defeated from war, and would only reopen it if he came back victorious. The prince never returned as he was killed in

battle and the gate has remained closed ever since. This gateway has huge bastions with *jharokha*s similar to Bada Darwaza. The inside of the roof is exquisite, with finely incised plaster work amid medallions, mirrors, and panels of blue tiles. To the south of the fort lies the Humayun Gate, with a view to his tomb.

It was during Sher Shah's reign that much of the fort's interior was built. Sher Shah's mosque, Qila-e-Kuhna Masjid, dominates Purana Qila. Built in 1542, it is located near a well and stands at the centre in alignment with the Bada Darwaza. The central arch is large and extensively decorated with white marble. The outer arches, which include the *sawal* and *jawab* – architectural elements often used to provide balance and symmetry – are of red sandstone and Delhi's famous gray quartzite. The ceiling of the *liwan* (the vaulted portal) is decorated with glazed tiles in blue, green, yellow, and white, combining Persian-inspired encaustic tile work and marble mosaic. The *mihrab* here is particularly ornate, carved and inlaid with sandstone and black and white marble. All five bays of the mosque are decorated with carvings and show traces of paintings on the ceilings.

Sher Shah also built Sher Mandal in 1541, south of Qila-e-Kuhna Masjid. This is a squat octagonal tower of red sandstone that is topped with a diminutive dome. Each side of the octagon has a recessed arch decorated with carving and inlay in white marble, while the second storey has a chamber with decorative tilework and stucco. It is reached by a steep flight of stairs. It was probably designed to function as a pleasure retreat, but when Humayun regained the fort, he converted this double-storey building into his library. A year later, in 1556, Humayun tripped and fell down the stairs of Sher Mandal and died of his injuries. His son, Akbar,

lived briefly in the fort before shifting his capital to Agra. Purana Qila fell into disrepair but it left a distinguished legacy as the first Mughal fort.

Above: Bada Darwaza

Left: Façade detail of Qila-e-Kuhna Masjid

Facing page: Interior of Qila-e-Kuhna Masjid

Lal Qila

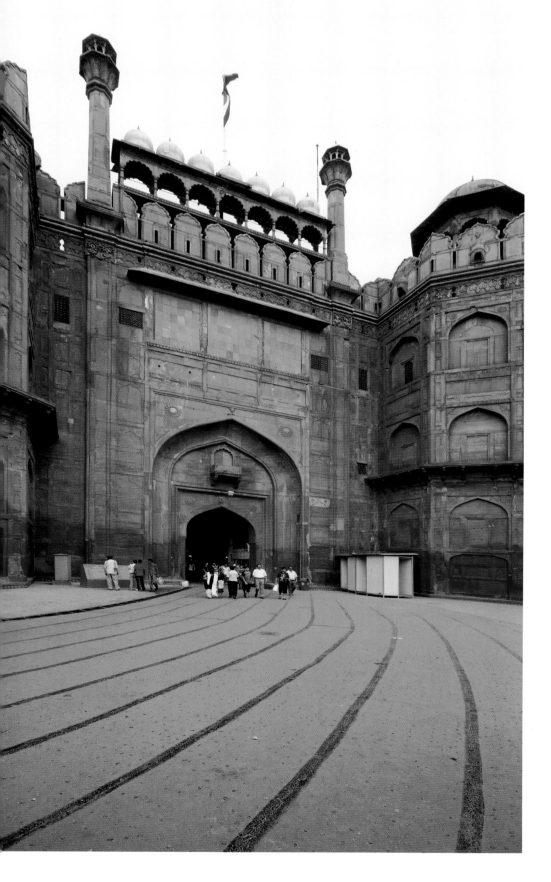

If there be paradise on earth, it is this, it is this, it is this. Inscribed on the roof of the Diwan-e-Aam in Delhi's Lal Qila or Red Fort, these words celebrate the Red Fort as the culmination of the great imperial ambitions of the Mughal Empire. Though Shah Jahan built the even more wondrous Taj Mahal a few years later, the Red Fort remains the most important legacy of India's greatest builder. The fort has always represented the heart of India's power, passing from Mughal to British to finally independent India's hands, and the nation's Prime Minister continues to deliver the Independence Day address from the Red Fort's ramparts. The fort also stands at the heart of Shahjahanabad, the 'seventh' city of Delhi that Shah Jahan built, which is now known as 'Old Delhi' and is one of the most densely inhabited areas today.

Shah Jahan shifted his capital to Delhi when Agra could no longer handle the scale of the emperor's movements, his army of elephants and horses severely restricted by its narrow streets. Delhi offered virgin lands on which to build a fortified city befitting the Shahenshah of Hindustan. This walled city would be Shahjahanabad, city of the ruler of the world, the most magnificent the world had seen. On his astrologer's advice, Shah Jahan selected a site just south of Salimgarh, (built by Salim Shah in 1546), started on an auspicious date in 1638, and in nine years, the structure was ready. The fort was first called Qila Mubarak, 'Fort of Good Fortune', and Shah Jahan moved into it in 1648, the 20th year of his reign. Through 'the great gate facing the river', he held his first *durbar* amid lavish celebrations lasting several days. Known by many names, including Qila Shahjahanabad, and during the reign of the last emperor of Delhi, Bahadur Shah II, as Qila-I-Mu'alla or the 'Exalted Fort', it became the Red Fort under British occupation.

During a 17th-century earthquake that lasted a month and two days according to the court chronicle *Tarikk-i- Muzaffari*, the fort was significantly damaged. Later, in the invasion by the Afghan Ahmad Shah Durrani and then during the Mughal-Maratha conflict, European-made guns bombarded the Mussaman Burj with cannon balls, causing major damage to the Diwan-e-Khas. The Mussaman Burj is a semi-octagonal tower on the riverside where the emperor appeared each day before his subjects, a custom of public appearance called *darshan*. The Mughal emperor Akbar II added a projecting balcony in 1806, which reinforced the tradition

Left: *Entrance to Chhatta Chowk*

Facing page: *Royal apartments connected with the Nahar-i-Bihist*

of *darshan*. It was from this balcony that King George V and Queen Mary appeared before the public in 1911, after the great Delhi Durbar.

The Red Fort was conceived and designed on a massive scale. The chief vision was Shah Jahan's, but the architects were two Persians, Ahmad and Hamid-ul-Sar. The huge crenellated ramparts, in perfectly dressed red sandstone, ran along the River Yamuna on one side and faced the city of Shahjahanabad on the other. The fort is a rough rectangle, some 3,000-feet long and 1,600-feet across. It rises over 60 feet above the river and is surrounded by a broad and deep moat on the side of the city. It presents a spectacular façade and was originally, according to the 17th-century European traveller Bernier, "*surrounded by large gardens full of flowers and shrubs which contrasted with the stupendous walls to produce a beautiful effect*". The vast expanse of land between the fort and the city was used to house the cavalry and the retinue of visiting rajas, who never actually lived inside the fort.

Two enormous gates punctuate the fort walls. Lahore Gate is the majestic main access to the new city's central concourse, Chandni Chowk. Aurangzeb later added a barbican for further security, or as Shah Jahan was to lament: "*a permanent veil for the bride*". Lahore Gate rises three floors, flanked by two octagonal towers with *chattris* and a panel of little white marble domes between them. This gate leads to the market that is now known as Chhatta Bazaar, but in Shah Jahan's time was called Meena Bazaar or the Bazaar-e-Musakkaf. In the 17th century, the shops along this covered, vaulted

arcade catered to the huge population living inside the fort as well as visitors; everything, from jewels and brocade to furniture, was available. Further south, Delhi Gate, guarded by two massive stone-sculpted elephants, opens towards the bazaar, and the roads from these two entrances lead to the great square court where the Naqqar Khana or Drum House would announce the opening of the Diwan-e-Aam.

Regarded as the Red Fort's finest building, the Diwan-e-Aam is some 50-feet long and 24-feet wide, an enormous open hall with deep, overhanging eaves. It is supported by 32 absolutely symmetrical shell-plastered and gilded sandstone pillars, and a heavily decorated ceiling inlaid with gold, silver, and gems. Set in a recess of the rear wall is a marble *bangladar* baldachino known as the Nashiman-i-Zill-i-Ilahi or the 'Seat of the Shadow of God', panelled with marble and inlaid with precious stones. The pietra dura work includes some Italian themes like Orpheus charming the beasts with his music. Here the emperor sat on his magnificently bejewelled Peacock Throne, which was looted by Nadir Shah in 1739. In front of the baldachino is a four-legged marble dais that was used by the Wazir when presenting petitions to the emperor seated above. The pillared hall created three aisles and nine compartments within which the hierarchy of nobility and advisors was maintained. The Gulal Bari outside was reserved for minor officials and the public stood in the large enclosure beyond.

Located discreetly away from the public eye, along the ramparts on the riverside are the palace buildings, exquisitely wrought in white marble that is etched, inlaid and adorned. Flowing through the centre of these buildings is a water channel known as Nahar-i-Bihisht, or the 'Stream of Paradise'. Rang Mahal lies at the centre of these palaces and is a large hall, originally painted on the interior, from which it derives its name, the 'Palace of Colour'. The marble basin at its centre once had an ivory fountain, which was the centre of the *nahar*.

In Khas Mahal, the water channel flowed beneath a marble latticework screen of remarkable delicacy, surmounted by a marble frieze depicting the scales of justice over a crescent and surrounded by the planets. Khas Mahal faces the Diwan-e-Khas and includes the Tasbih Khana where the emperor prayed. Behind it is the Khwabgah or the sleeping chamber of the king, and to the south is a long hall with painted ceilings and walls that was either the *tosh khana*, (robe chamber), or *baithak*, (sitting room). Beyond lay more palaces including the palace of Mumtaz Mahal and the royal *hamam*s. The Mussaman Burj was used primarily for the emperor's *darshan* but also for his own pleasure, such as viewing elephant fights on the river's edge.

Moti Masjid near the *hamam* was built by Aurangzeb for his private worship. It is a simple structure on the outside, with three bulbous domes rising above the fort's skyline; but has an elaborately carved white marble interior. To the north is Hayat Baksh Bagh, or the 'Life-Bestowing Garden', with marble pavilions at each end. A red sandstone pavilion in its central pool was added by Bahadur Shah Zafar, the last Mughal emperor, who was tried for treason in this fort after the 1857 rebellion. After that, the fort became a garrison of the British Indian Army and, until recently, also of the Indian Army.

Below: *Detail of a carved stone window in the Diwan-e-Aam*

Right: *Rang Mahal – the fountain in the middle is fed by the Nahar-i-Bihisht*

Agra Fort

Above: *The main
entrance to Agra Fort*

Arguably the most important fort of India, Agra Fort became the seat of the imperial Mughals when Akbar shifted his capital from Lahore to Agra, a city he described as the *"emporium of the traffic of the world".* In popular imagination, the fort is more closely associated with Emperor Shah Jahan, who was imprisoned here by his son Aurangzeb and left to die a melancholy death, his days and nights spent gazing at the Taj Mahal, the memorial to his beloved wife Mumtaz Mahal.

Agra Fort was originally a brick fort built by the Chauhan Rajputs. It was recorded for the first time in AD 1080 when Mahmud Ghazni's army attacked it. Sikandar Lodi of Delhi moved his capital here in the 15th century but his son Ibrahim Lodi was defeated by Babur in 1526 and the Mughals captured the fort which was said to hold a vast treasure, including the Kohinoor diamond. Babur lived here briefly, as did his son Humayun, who was crowned here. After Humayun's defeat by Sher Shah and his retreat to Persia, Sher Shah held the fort for five years before the Mughals returned with their Persian armies to oust him.

It was Akbar who built most of the present-day fort, demolishing the existing structure and building a massive fortification in dressed red sandstone, over 70-feet high and 1.5 miles in circumference. It was built in the shape of an expanded bow, its straight side separated from the River Yamuna by a moat. Inside, only a few remain of the *"five hundred buildings in the wonderful designs of Bengal and Gujarat"* recorded by Abu'l Fazl, Akbar's court historian. Of these, Delhi Gate, Akbar Gate and Bengali Mahal were built during the reign of Akbar.

The *mahal*s or palaces have been built along the fort wall on the riverside, capturing not only the best views but also the benefit of a cool breeze off the water. More importantly, Akbar could view his favourite sport – elephant fights – on a flat strip of land between the wall and the riverfront. Should an elephant become too enraged, it could be skewed into the river to cool down.

Jehangir and Shah Jahan added their own buildings to the fort, often by demolishing the earlier ones, creating a rare amalgamation of the aesthetic sensibilities of three different Mughal kings. Shah Jahan's architectural vision shifted from the red sandstone of Akbar's period to finely carved and inlaid marble. He redid several of the sandstone palaces into dainty, richly embellished marble structures. When Agra Fort fell to the British, many of its buildings were destroyed.

The fort appears invincible from outside. It has massive double ramparts interspersed with bastions. Towards the city, there is an additional moat after the first one. The main gate on this side is Delhi Darwaza, a heavily decorated gateway with a panel displaying the surrender of seven elephants to a mythical beast, symbolising the indestructible power of the empire. The magnificent Hathi Pol lies immediately beyond, providing a second layer of entrance. It had two huge sandstone elephants flanking it, which were destroyed by Aurangzeb in an attempt to erase as much as he could of its Hindu features. Akbar Darwaza, renamed Amar Singh Darwaza by Jehangir, was guarded by two barbicans. It is a massive structure with galleries built in tiers, which appear to amplify the size of the gate. Towards the riverfront is Khizri Darwaza, which once opened onto a pier and bathing ghats that have been lost due to the river slowly changing its course.

The fort is spatially organised as a city of grand scale. Military facilities bound the outer walls on the city side, securing the part of the fort that once bustled with public buildings, markets, and servant quarters. The royal residence lay on the other side, with Jehangiri Mahal being the main *zenana*. This palace has a most perfect synthesis of Hindu and Timurid architecture, its long halls, arched recesses, pavilions, and pillared courtyards all elaborately carved with Islamic as well as Hindu motifs. Constructed around 1570, it is entered through an impressive gateway and a courtyard that overlooks the river through a carved screen wall. Heavily carved brackets, piers, and cross beams still hold remnants of gilded decorations. Almost every surface is ornamented with birds and fruit and floral motifs. Carved elephants abound, and elaborately adorned doors, windows, and lintels create an exquisite space, delicate and immense. It is the most significant surviving building of Akbar's time.

Near the northern entrance is the Diwan-e-Aam or the Hall of Public Audience. The most ingenious aspect of this hall's design is that the throne is approached from the sides rather than from the front. The alignment of the pillars is so precise that visitors arriving through the gates on the right and left have an uninterrupted view of the seat of the emperor. The raised platform on which the legendary Peacock Throne or Takht-e-Taoos stood is beautifully inlaid with precious and semi-precious stones. Behind the throne is a pavilion with a delicately carved screen through which women could view court proceedings.

Opposite the Diwan-e-Aam and across a courtyard lies the Diwan-e-Khas, the Hall of Private Audience. This is a heavily decorated pavilion, with fine inlay work in precious stones and a screen wall at the back. Outside is a terrace with a huge marble throne platform. Between the Diwan-e-Aam and Diwan-e-Khas is the Macchli Bhawan, or the Fish Mansion, meant for the amusement of the harem. This paradisical garden with fountains and pools full of fish was looted by Raja Surajmal and transported to his palace at Deeg.

Khas Mahal was built by Shah Jahan in his favourite white marble. It was the emperor's personal chamber with three pavilions on the riverside and a fountain courtyard on the other. The central pavilion with cusped arches is flanked by two *bangla*-style pavilions that have gilded domes. There is a small room with little niches where, it is believed, women could put their jewels, the niches being so narrow that only a woman's slender hand could

Above: Interior of Khas Mahal. Khas Mahal overlooks Angoori Bagh — a typical Mughal garden

PLAN OF AGRA FORT

1. AMAR SINGH DARWAZA
2. DELHI DARWAZA
3. HATHI POL
4. JEHANGIRI MAHAL
5. DIWAN-E-AAM
6. MACCHLI BHAWAN
7. DIWAN-E-KHAS
8. MUSAMMAM BURJ
9. SHEESH MAHAL
10. KHAS MAHAL AND ANGOORI BAGH
11. NAGINA MASJID
12. MOTI MASJID

Left: *Angoori Bagh in the foreground. Khas Mahal is located at one end, facing the river*

Facing page: *The carved marble fountain at the entrance to Mussaman Burj — the octogonal tower that overlooks the Taj Mahal*

pass through. Khas Mahal overlooks Angoori Bagh, the 'Garden of Grapes,' so called because of the profusion of carvings of grapes. This is a classic *char bagh* garden and is said to have been inspired by the gardens of Kashmir. On the other side of the garden is the tiny Mina Masjid built by Aurangzeb to allow his imprisoned father to worship.

Sheesh Mahal is the 'Palace of Mirrors'. It consists of two large halls completely covered with mica mosaic, embedded in lime. The curvature of the mica is such that candlelight is reflected many times. When the hall was lit with candles, every surface came alive in myriad lights, casting a magical quality. Sheesh Mahal also had ponds and channels of water running through it, which were connected with the royal baths.

Musamman Burj is an octagonal tower with an open pavilion built by Shah Jahan for his wife Mumtaz Mahal. It is enclosed with beautifully carved marble lattice screens to ensure the queen's privacy while she looked out at the river. The *burj* is surrounded by a verandah that has a marble fountain at the centre and a courtyard with squares laid out for a game of *pachesi*, a form of backgammon. It was from here that the imprisoned Shah Jahan spent his last days gazing at the Taj Mahal.

Moti Masjid or the 'Pearl Mosque' is a perfect gem set in the centre of the fort beyond the Diwan-e-Aam, its dome dominating the skyline. Nagina Masjid or the 'Gem Mosque' is a private mosque built by Shah Jahan for the ladies of the court. The level below it used to host the Meena Bazaar, a market only women could enter. Both the mosques carry Shah Jahan's stamp of white marble.

Akbar's son Jehangir shifted his court to Lahore and often stayed in Kashmir, where he built exotic pleasure gardens. But

Shah Jahan returned to Agra and infused a new life into the fort, a life that was effectively snuffed out when the emperor became a prisoner in his own fort. Aurangzeb built an additional wall around the fortifications, but Mughal power had already grown too diseased to be revived by brick or stone. Aurangzeb, having proclaimed himself 'Alamgir', King of the Universe, in 1658, left Agra for his Deccan campaign in 1682 where he spent the remaining 27 years of his life, and never set foot in Agra again. Agra Fort is today a UNESCO World Heritage Site, a testimony to the grand architectural achievements of the Mughal Empire.

Following pages (160-161): *The balcony of Mussaman Burj and the fortifications on the riverside*

Below: *Exterior of Jehangiri Mahal built by Akbar for his son Jehangir*

Fatehpur Sikri

Above: *Anup Talav seen from within a pavilion at the southern end*

Facing page above: *Stone carving on a wall in the Turkish Sultana's house*

Facing page below: *The Diwan-e-Khas with its central pillar*

The most eloquent testament in stone to the great humanist vision of Mughal Emperor Akbar is the 'lost' city of Fatehpur Sikri, the new capital Akbar built for his empire. A mere fifteen years after it was built, the city was abandoned for lack of water. Akbar went back to Agra but the fort at Fatehpur Sikri still lives, sustained not so much by tourists (though it is a UNESCO World Heritage Site) as by pilgrims and worshippers visiting the shrine of Sufi saint Sheikh Salim Chisti. Salim Chisti had advised Akbar to move his capital here and he would be blessed with sons. And so it was no sooner than Fatehpur Sikri was built that Salim, later to be Emperor Jehangir, was born to Jodha Bai, believed to be the Rajput princess of Amber.

Following his victories in Gujarat in 1572, Akbar ordered a new imperial capital to be built near Agra with the name Fatehpur, 'City of Victory'. The fort was built on a grand scale, but the most remarkable feature were the buildings inside, built in an unprecedented architectural synthesis of diverse cultures. Akbar's love of red sandstone found unbridled expression. Exquisite palaces were built for his queens and his most prized courtiers called *navratna*s or nine jewels, and exotic chambers designed for meditation and spiritual and theological debates. Fatehpur Sikri was the crucible of Akbar's idea of a new faith, *Din-e-Ilahi*, an enlightened and rational synthesis of the universal values of Hinduism, Jainism, Buddhism, Islam, Christianity, and Zoroastrianism.

Fatehpur Sikri's spectacular architecture owes much to the Gujarati craftsmen Akbar brought with him from his campaign in Gujarat. These craftsmen were masters of carving and decoration, having inherited their skill from generations of temple builders. The craftsmen worked the rich red sandstone, quarried from the area around Sikri, into some of the most delicately carved buildings ever built in India.

The Diwan-e-Aam, Hall of Public Audience, in Fatehpur Sikri is a large courtyard facing a pavilion with innumerable *jharokha*s, each a combination of an enormous eave and a delicate balcony. The central and much larger *jharokha* housed the emperor's throne. Beyond this lies the Hall of Private Audience or the Diwan-e-Khas. This is arguably the most ingenious building in Fatehpur Sikri. From outside, it appears to be a huge, two-storey structure but is actually just a single hall with a double height ceiling. A massive central pillar, with brackets radiating outwards supports, the wide, circular platform from where the emperor presided. From this throne-platform, four 'bridges' of red sandstone connect to a balcony that runs along the upper level of the chamber and was used by the nobles of the court. Servants and others stood at the lowest level.

A courtyard paved with red sandstone flags, the *pachesi* court connects the Diwan-e-Khas with Anup Talav. The legendary musician Tansen is said to have performed on an island in the middle of Anup Talav. A section of the courtyard is marked with slabs of marble as in a board of *pachesi*, and it is said that slave girls were used as pawns. Akbar sat at a height directing the movement of his live pieces.

Fatehpur Sikri consists of two distinct sets of buildings, demarcating sacred spaces from secular ones. The sacred section is dominated by the Jama Masjid and is entered through a colossal gate, Buland Darwaza, the largest and highest gateway in all Indian forts. Once flanked by two massive stone elephants, the towering gateway rises 176 feet from the ground, its recessed central arch dominating not just the fort but the entire area. Inscribed on the arch in Islamic calligraphy are the words: *"The world is but a bridge; pass over but build no houses on it."*

To the left of the Jama Masjid is the tomb of Sheikh Salim Chisti, its white marble glistening like a pearl in the vast sandstone courtyard. Akbar had the shrine built in red sandstone in 1571, but Shah Jahan rebuilt it in white marble. Four carved pillars support a low dome and the walls are intricately carved screens. Next to it is the Jamaat Khana, made of red sandstone and also with carved screens and a low dome, containing the grave of Islam Khan, a disciple of Salim Chisti. In contrast to the delicacy of these two shrines, the Jama Masjid is sparingly but elegantly carved. The

Right: *One of the rooms surrounding the courtyard in Jodhabai's Palace*

Below: *Panch Mahal*

domed ceiling of the mosque still has traces of turquoise, mauve, and sea-green decoration.

The other part of the fort houses the imperial buildings. Built largely of red sandstone, they surround Anup Talav at the southern end of the courtyard. Akbar's famous library is known as Daftarkhana and beyond it are the royal chambers, laid out over a complex network of water channels designed to cool the interiors. The Miriam Palace is clearly the finest, embellished with gilding and frescoes that depicted scenes from Firdausi's Persian epic, *Shahnama*. Jodhabai's Palace is the largest palace and is also known as Jehangiri Mahal. As Jodhabai was a Rajput, her palace has several Rajput architectural elements that can be said to have been borrowed from the palaces at Mandu. The palace is built around a courtyard with pillared chambers on all sides. It has space for a temple where the queen could worship, and a *hawa mahal* or wind pavilion where she could enjoy the breeze while remaining secluded from the outside gaze. The two pavilions at either end have sloping roofs covered in blue tiles that are clearly visible from the rest of the fort.

Panch Mahal is a distinctive palace, its five stories tapering as they go up. It consists of 84 pillars, each differently carved and embellished in Hindu and Jain tradition. It was a pavilion for Akbar's vast harem.

At the foot of the hill on which the buildings stood, grew a township, originally a small hamlet called Sikri that was incorporated into the fort and thus the name Fatehpur Sikri. This was the commoners' space, containing markets, residences, mosques and temples. The Hiran Minar located here marks the grave of Akbar's favourite elephant. Beyond this lay the caravan *serai*, the polo grounds, and a lake. A mile of fortifications, strengthened by eight double-towered gates, protected this short-lived but remarkable city.

Maratha Forts

Shivneri

Right: *Gateway leading to the fort complex*

Facing page above: *Interior of Shivaji's house*

Facing page below: *The rock-cut Ganga–Jamuna Talav's waters percolate and collect in these tanks*

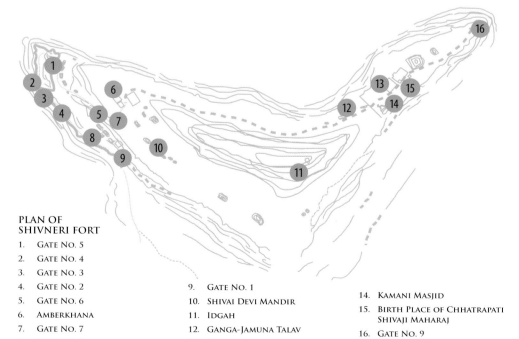

PLAN OF SHIVNERI FORT

1. Gate No. 5
2. Gate No. 4
3. Gate No. 3
4. Gate No. 2
5. Gate No. 6
6. Amberkhana
7. Gate No. 7
8. Gate No. 8
9. Gate No. 1
10. Shivai Devi Mandir
11. Idgah
12. Ganga-Jamuna Talav
13. Hamam
14. Kamani Masjid
15. Birth Place of Chhatrapati Shivaji Maharaj
16. Gate No. 9 Kadelot Tok

The meteoric rise to power of a group of chieftains bound by a common hatred of the Deccan Sultanates and the expanding Mughal influence in the peninsula is one of the centrepieces of medieval Indian history. This surge of rebellion against the Mughal empire began in a rugged territory of the Deccan that is now Maharashtra. The rebels banded together under the identity of the Marathi language, calling themselves Marathas. The Marathas declared the Muslim kings 'invaders' and raised their battle cry in the name of defending the motherland. Not since the early Rajput resistance against the Delhi Sultanate, three hundred years earlier, had there been such a formidable challenge to Muslim dominance. The Marathas grew exponentially in strength: they broke the backbone of Mughal power, seized huge parts of Western and Central India, and were the main contenders for the throne of Delhi in the chaotic power struggle that followed Aurangzeb's death, in which the British East India Company eventually emerged the victor.

All this was the work of a single, remarkable man, Shivaji Bhonsle. Born in Shivneri in 1627, where his father and grandfather had held *jagir*s, Shivaji was not of the nobility. He was an extraordinary warrior and military strategist, a quick brain, fleet-footed and an inspiring leader of men. The Fort of Shivneri, which his father Shahaji controlled, was captured by Shah Jahan when Shivaji was still a teenager.

At the age of 19, Shivaji embarked on his mission to avenge his father's defeat at Shivneri and to establish *swarajya*, self rule, over his homeland. He won it back after a long and protracted struggle, and it remained his greatest prize. Shivneri was one of the oldest forts in the region, and was given to Shivaji's grandfather Maloji Bhonsle in 1595 by the Bahmani king Bahadur Nizam Shah II. The fort was famed for its riches. The English traveller Frazer visited Shivneri in 1673 and wrote that he found it invincible, and so well stocked that the provisions could last a thousand families for seven years. A perfect hill fort, a *giri durg*, it is roughly triangular in form and the battlements and fortifications start halfway up the hill. It is reached after a steep climb through seven spiral gates. To the right of the entrance is a fortified enclosure with mud walls. In keeping with Shivaji's reputation of ruthlessness, there is an overhang here, where executions took place, with prisoners plummeting to the depths below. At the centre is a small pond known as Badami Talav, and nearby there is a statue of Jijabai holding an infant Shivaji. There are also remains of a mosque and prayer hall.

Raigadh

Above: *Ruins of watch towers in the fort*

Facing page: *One of the gateways*

PLAN OF RAIGADH FORT

1. Maha Darwaza
2. Chor Dindi
3. Wagh Darwaza
4. Ghubladha
5. Wadi
6. Nana Darwaza
7. Ganga Sagar
8. Citadel
9. Bazaar
10. Jagdishwara Temple
11. Shivaji's Samadhi

The first fort Shivaji captured was Torna. This provided him the resources to start the reconstruction of Raigadh Fort, which in time became his capital. The main palace at Raigadh was constructed using wood, and so only the bases of the pillars remain. The ruins of three watch towers can be seen directly in front of the palace grounds, overlooking an artificial lake created next to the fort. It also provides a view of the cliff from which the sentenced prisoners were thrown off, called Takmak Tok. The king's Hall of Public Audience has a replica of the original throne. The main entrance to the fort is the majestic Maha Darwaza, though the king and his entourage used the Palki Darwaza, or Palanquin Gate.

Shivaji built more than a hundred forts in the Deccan and by the time he died, his kingdom was defended by 240 forts. Some he conquered and some were built from scratch, and these were the bulwarks of his military campaigns. He was a wily strategist and many of his sieges were successful not because of his endurance but his deviousness. His forts reflect the tenets of *Adnyapatre*, a contemporary text on kingship, which states: *"Fort … the essence of an entire kingdom. A country without its forts is a country which turns to ruin, its people un-sheltered with just one invasion of an enemy. If the country is destroyed, what is left to be called as a kingdom? A fort is the root of a kingdom, a fort is the treasure, a fort is the strength behind an army, a fort is Raj Lakshmi, a fort is the perfect place to live and a fort is a place where you can sleep without fear. Indeed …the fort is the protector."*

Lohagadh

Within a formidable network of forts which exemplify Maratha supremacy in the 17th century. Lohagadh, the Iron Fort was one of Shivaji's most coveted. It towers 3,400 feet above the landscape around and is located at the summit of a long, serpentine mountain, with the rivers Pavana and Indrani protecting its base on either side. It predates Shivaji by many centuries and is believed to have been occupied by the Satvahanas, the Chalukyas, Rashtrakutas, Yadavs, Bahmanis, Nizamshahis, and the Mughals before it was captured by Shivaji in 1648. He lost it to the Mughals, but recaptured it some twenty years later and it remained with the Marathas until the British took control of the region in the 19th century. Its importance to Shivaji was its virtual invincibility and it served as his treasury. It was here that Shivaji stored his plunder, or spoils of war, which financed his wars against the Mughals and the British. Local legend has it that some of this treasure still lies secreted away in the fort, yet to be discovered.

Lohagadh's height gave it a significant advantage over the enemy. On an adjacent hill, Shivaji built Visapur Fort at a higher elevation. This later proved to be a strategic error as, once it was captured by the British in 1818, it gave them a base from which to bombard Lohagadh, forcing the Marathas out. The steep and treacherous staircase up to Lohagadh winds along the contours, which in the rainy season, becomes a waterfall, making it even more difficult to negotiate. It is punctuated by four monumental gateways: Ganesha Darwaza, Narayan Darwaza, Hanuman Darwaza, the oldest, and Maha Darwaza, which has some decorative sculptures. Between the second and third gate, there are stone cellars that were possibly used as granaries, and beyond Maha Darwaza, there are some tombs in a building. Within, there are several water tanks, one of them being spring-fed thus ensuring pure drinking water. At the summit, there is a Mahadev temple with steps leading down to a water tank.; and there is also the grave of a Pir. Near the edge of the fortification, there is a spacious rock-cut cave called the Lomesh Rishi cave. During the Peshwa period under Nana Phadnavis, extensive building was undertaken inside the fort, especially augmenting the water system and building a stepwell. There are remains of a large number of buildings which would have served his military.

Lohagadh is forbidding in its location. Its fortifications encompass the entire hilltop; its narrow, long, fortified western end is called Vichhu Kanta, the Marathi word for 'scorpion's tail'. derived from its curious shape. There is a watch tower from where it was possible to guard the entire fort and perhaps many miles around, and was also used to monitor octroi collections in the region as this was a major trade route in the western Sahyadris. It still stands virtually unassailable, shrouded in mystery.

Left: *Vichhu Kanta or scorpion's tail – the cliff that juts out over the surrounding valley*

Below: *Intermediate doorway leading up to the fort*

Facing page: *The approach fortifications, showing the strategically designed bends and curves that add to the defence*

Sea Forts

VIJAYDURG

Vijaydurg and Sindhudurg bear testimony to Maharashtra's martial and maritime supremacy during Shivaji's reign. Vijaydurg is an ancient site, originally called Gheria. It was once part of the Bijapur Sultanate before it was acquired in the 17th century by Shivaji who gave it the name, Vijaydurg or Victory Fort. Vijaydurg was extensively reconstructed by Shivaji who built huge fortifications, giving it its architectural grandeur. It is one of the strongest marine forts on the west coast of India, with a superb location.

Built on a hill at the mouth of River Vaghotan, the fort stands on a promontory into the sea, protected on three sides by the sea with a moat to the east, long since abandoned. The three-layered fortifications provide a massive stone façade, and, as in other Maratha forts, make it virtually impregnable. The multiple layers of fortifications have 27 bastions, some of them double-storeyed. Its main entrance faced east, away from the vagaries of nature but also with clear strategic intent. Within its massive walls, there is a second, almost concealed gateway. Within the citadel, there were many buildings, largely military and functional, though few remain. However, water supply, the most essential element was in abundance with several wells and large tanks. In recent years, a submerged wall 100 metres east of the fort has been discovered. Almost 9-feet high, 20-feet wide and nearly a quarter of a mile long, this too seems part of the grand architectural plan for security. Vijaydurg finally fell when the Peshwas allied with the British in 1756, but remained with the Peshwas until they too surrendered to the British.

Below: Bastions overlooking the sea

Above: View of the fort from the riverside

Left: Painting on the mud-plastered walls of Dhulap's house near Vijaydurg

Following page: Overlooking the entrance to Sindhudurg from one of the windows in its fortifications

SINDHUDURG

Sindhudurg stands on a rocky outcrop of 48 acres known as Kurte, just off the Konkan coast. It was built by Shivaji in 1664, after successive futile attempts to capture Murud Janjira and symbolised the Marathas supremacy of the west coast. Shivaji employed an architect to design this mammoth fort and sourced his building skills, including 100 Portuguese, from Goa, where construction was prolific. There are records stating that it took 3,000 workers three years to build, with Shivaji's pillaging of Surat paying for the extravagance. It is approachable only by boat through a narrow, barely navigable channel, which limited access to the fort, and was its defence. It also highlights the enormous challenges which would have been faced during the construction of the immense fortifications. It is surrounded by rocky outcrops and simply navigating the waters to Sindhudurg was not always possible.

The fort is well preserved and has walls 27-feet high, ramparts as wide as 9 feet and some 4 miles in length punctuated with 47 bastions. The unique feature is that the foundations of the fortifications were laid in molten lead, and a further 2,000 *khandi*s or 72,000 kg of iron reinforced the fort walls. It was an engineering feat of its time.

The main gate of Sindhudurg faces east towards the city. Flanked by two huge bastions, a nearby parapet with two small domes has what are believed to be Shivaji's footprints embedded in the lime concrete. Within the fort, there is a Shivaji Temple, built by his son Rajaram, unique in itself, with an image of the Maratha warrior. After Shivaji, Sindhudurg was ruled by the Angres, Peshwas, and then Kolhapur. It was briefly captured by the British in 1765 who called it 'Fort Augustus'. Later in 1818, the British dismantled the fort's defence structures, destroying its legacy.

Above: Fortifications jutting into the sea

Below: Approach to the fort and its surrounding rocky outcrops. These are only seen during low tide

Maheshwar

After Aurangzeb's death in 1707, the Maratha Empire founded by Shivaji expanded to fill the vacuum created by the Mughal retreat from South and Central India. The Marathas had become a hydra-headed force, with different commanders having created their own dominions and armies. Of these, five Maratha clans rose to prominence: the Peshwas of Pune, the Gaekwads of Baroda, the Scindias of Gwalior, the Bhonsles of Nagpur, and the Holkars of Indore. Maheshwar Fort was the main citadel of the Holkars, from where they ruled Central India's Malwa plateau. The Holkars are among a handful of dynasties who accepted a woman on the throne. Queen Ahilya Bai ruled for 30 years as one of the most visionary and accomplished sovereigns of the time.

Situated on an isolated hillock on the banks of the sacred River Narmada, the Maheshwar Fort is believed to stand on the site of Maheshwari, mentioned in the Mahabharata as the capital of King Kartavirya Arjuna. Maheshwar is also considered to be Mahisatti or Mahishamati, capital of the 7th-century BC *mahajanapada* of Avanti. During the reign of Mughal emperor Akbar in the 16th century, Maheshwar and Burhanpur became important military bases. The Marathas raided Malwa in 1730 and Malhar Rao Holkar, the Maratha commander who led the attack, declared his independence and made Indore his capital.

It is said that during one of his military campaigns in Central India, Malhar Rao stopped at a village called Chondi and saw the eight-year-old Ahilya Bai serving at a temple. He brought the girl with him as a bride for his son Khande Rao. Khande Rao was killed in battle in 1754 and when Malhar Rao died 12 years later, Ahilya Bai succeeded to the throne. She shifted the capital to Maheshwar and ruled from there until her death in 1795. The Holkars became feudatories of the British Raj after the third Anglo-Maratha War in 1818, and were granted the title of 'Prince of Indore'.

Ahilya Bai was an extraordinary woman. She led the army with four bows and quivers fitted to the corners of the *howdah* of her elephant. She was a prodigious builder, erecting temples and pilgrimage centres across the length and breadth of India, and extensively renovating the Maheshwar Fort. She had the fort extended and the fortifications strengthened with new merlons to install modern weaponry. The height of the outer wall was raised 6 feet and in many places, the wall's lower part was reinforced with stones found near the river and from local black igneous rock. This created a vast façade of dark stone that is broken only by the bastions. Kamani Darwaza on the northern wall is possibly a Mughal gate and overlooks the town. Another gate nearby is the exclusive royal entrance and leads to the palace.

The *rajwada* on the southwestern corner is the fort's highest point. Constructed in 1766 by Ahilya Bai, it is a simple and elegant structure built around rectangular interlinked courtyards. The *wada* or palace is a classical example of the Maratha architecture of the period, with its heavily carved wooden pillars, beams, and brackets set against masonry walls. The royal apartment is located on top of a huge *burj* with spectacular views of the Narmada. Within the palace complex is the royal throne with a life size statue of Ahilya Bai. On the western side of the *rajwada* are gardens and orchards.

Ahilya Bai was a great patron of the arts. The famous Marathi poets Moropant and Anantaphandi, and the Sanskrit scholar Khushali Ram stayed at Maheshwar on her invitation. Craftsmen, sculptors, and artists received generous patronage and the famed Maheshwari textiles, especially the silk sarees, were first woven on a large scale in her reign. Ahilya Bai's greatest architectural legacy, however, are the exquisite temples built along the Narmada, joined to the river by series of steps that almost seem to cascade. The perfectly dressed stone of the temples serves as a foil to the rough-hewn fort walls. The temple of Ahilya Bai dominates the landscape and is heavily carved and decorated. It is dedicated to Lord Shiva and has been open to people of all faiths since its inception.

Below: Ahilya Ghat at the base of the fort. Located on the ghat are the Ahileshwari Temple and Ahilya Bai's samadhi

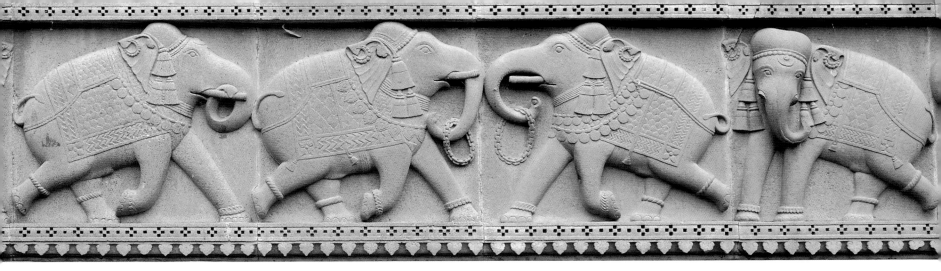

Far Above: *Carving on the walls of the Ahileshwari Temple complex*

Above: *Statue of Ahilya Bai in her Durbar Hall*

Left: *Entrance to the Ahileshwari Temple complex*

Below: *Timber brackets on the columns inside Ahilya Bai's Palace*

Indore

Above: *The Durbar Hall overlooking the entrance courtyard of the old Rajwada*

LAL BAGH

Like most princely states in India at the time, the Holkars of Indore, too, sought to build for themselves a 'modern' palace at the turn of the 19th century. Shivaji Rao Holkar began work for a new royal residence in Indore but it was under Tukoji Rao III (1903–1925) that the Lal Bagh Palace was completed. Also known as the Red Palace, Lal Bagh is one of India's finest neo-Classical buildings. It stands amid a vast, open scrub, with its pink façade now faded but still evoking its once legendary beauty. The formal garden is reached through the vast entrance gates bearing the Holkar coat of arms, eerily similar to the British monarch's. The exterior is relatively austere, broken only by Corinthian, Doric and Ionic columns, but to the north is an impressive, large, circular entrance or *porte-cochére* leading into a circular hallway and then to the reception rooms. These rooms are built in European style with huge marble arcades, stucco, and gilded walls and ceilings. A large banquet hall has a first floor balcony, perhaps as a concession to the ladies who were still in the *zenana*. Adjoining this hall are smaller, more intimate dining rooms, and there is a clear distinction between the Indian and western dining rooms.

The Durbar Hall projects outward on the east side and is one of the most lavishly decorated buildings. A huge purple silk throne, flanked by enormous crystal candelabras, replaces the old *rajgaddi*. Gilded lamps, mirrors, European marble sculptures, and imported marble fireplaces, Aubusson carpets, and crystal chandeliers create a palatial space not very different from any of Europe's grand palaces. The hall's crowning glory is, without doubt, the painted ceiling in rococo style, the central theme showing the Greek sun god Helios riding his chariot through the clouds.

The Dance Room is a charming building that attests to the Holkars' love for music and dance. It is built in the classic Indian tradition of a *nrityashala* (dance school) – a central open space surrounded by colonnades and devoid of furniture.

RAJWADA

The Indore Rajwada was built over two hundred years ago as the Maharaja of Indore felt the need to restore his capital to the city from where he could administer his properties. A towering seven storey complex in the centre of town, its very scale signified its importance. At the centre of Khajuri Bazaar this building is an elegant amalgam of French, Maratha, and Mughal architecture. The lower floors were constructed with stone and masonry while the upper structure is in the traditional Maratha style with wood and mud-brick plaster, employing fine wooden carved detailing on eaves, brackets and doors. However its interiors were rich with tapestries, chandeliers and other European fittings, making it an extremely usable building ideally suited to the climate. An enormous entrance gateway rises to almost the height of the building and is an intimidating entry. It has enormous wooden doors held with iron clasps Built around a huge courtyard, the front of the palace was the administrative section along with halls of public audience and other civic activities. To the rear of the courtyard were the private apartments. The royal apartments were located on the upper floors and provided both privacy as well as security. The Indore Rajwada has been burnt and rebuilt three times, the last time in 1984 when the entire superstructure was lost. The descendents of the Holkar maharaja have in recent years put a lot of work into rebuilding the Rajwada and restoring the building. Nonetheless it is still a mere shadow of its former glory.

Above: *The restored courtyard of the Rajwada that was destroyed in a fire during the 1984 riots*

Left: *Entrance façade of the Rajwada*

Gwalior

Left: *Gwalior Fort dominates the surrounding landscape*

Like many of the classic forts in Central India, the Gwalior Fort stands majestically atop an isolated hill. The region is believed to be the Gopakshetra mentioned in ancient Hindu texts, and Sanskrit inscriptions record that Mihirakula, the Hun, built a sun temple here in the 6th century AD. The region later became part of Kanauj under the Pratihara king Mihira Bhoja before falling to the Kacchawaha who reigned for over 200 years. The Kacchawaha chiefs believed that Suraj Sen founded the fort in the 4th century while out hunting on this hill, then known as Gopagiri. Here, a hermit, Gwalipa gave Suraj Sen water to drink, which miraculously cured his leprosy. The hermit told Suraj Sen that if he adopted the name Pal his family would rule at Gwalior. When the 84th Pal descendent, Tej Karan, broke this tradition, the Pratiharas captured Gwalior but soon lost it to Qutub-ud-din Aibak in 1196. In 1398, as Timur sacked Delhi, the Tomar chief Bir Singh Deo declared Gwalior independent and bought his peace by paying tribute to the Delhi Sultans. In the 16th century, Ibrahim Lodi invaded Gwalior with *"30,000 horses and 300*

elephants" but a year later, the fort fell to Babur, who described it as *"the pearl in the necklace of the forts of Hind".* The Mughals held Gwalior until 1754, when the Maratha advance into Central India led the Mughals to retreat to the safety of Delhi. However, the fort remained heavily contested until the Maratha warrior Mahdaji Rao Scindia established himself here in 1784 to take on the emerging British power. Gwalior also played a significant part in the 1857 rebellion, with some of Jayaji Rao's forces siding with the Rani of Jhansi.

Most of the fort was built by Raja Man Singh in the 15th century, on a hill that is virtually sheer, and where it was not, it was scarped. The massive ramparts are reinforced with bastions, often capped with delicately poised *chattris*. The most striking feature of the fort are the extensive bands of brightly coloured glazed tile, creating a delicacy in the otherwise formidable façade. The fort is reached by a steep road twisting its way through the hillside and is entered through seven gates, five of which are straddled by palaces. Raja Man Singh's Palace is above the Hathiyarpur Gate, which was built

between 1486 and 1517 and is a showcase of medieval Hindu architecture. Although most of the richly tiled façade of the palace has not survived, the interior still has wonderful tiles, bands of mosaic elephants, and peacocks in blues, greens, rose pink, and gold, including a whimsical frieze of Brahmani ducks in brilliant turquoise waters.

Man Singh's two-storey palace is laid out around a series of courtyards and is heavily carved with stone. The *zenana* is on the upper floor, above the king's chambers, and the terraces have exquisite pavilions. There are huge halls with fine stone screens, where royal ladies used to learn music. Below the palace are circular dungeons built in the Persian style; these once housed prisoners of the Mughal state. Aurangzeb had his brother Murad Baksh imprisoned, and later executed, here.

Mughal emperors Jehangir and Shah Jahan added the Jehangiri Mahal and the Shah Jahan Mahal to Man Singh's Palace. These include a beautiful *baradari* pavilion, delicately executed in a synthesis of Hindu and Islamic architecture. The fort is also renowned for its extensive network of tanks, stepwells and channels that managed a huge quantity of water. Suraj Kund to the west is the largest tank and it is believed that it was water from this *kund* that cured Suraj Pal of leprosy.

Close to Suraj Kund is the sacred centre of the fort, the 9th-century Teli-ka Mandir, a rectangular Shaivite shrine with a towering 80-feet high *shikhara*. The temple is unusual in that it has only a *garbagriha* and no *mandapa*. The Chaturbhuj Temple, built during the Pratihara dynasty, is a monolithic rock-cut

Above: Stone screens in the zenana *at Man Mandir Palace, inside Gwalior Fort*

Left: Vaulted chamber at Man Mandir Palace

temple of Vishnu, while the two Saas Bahu Temples were built in the 11th century and their extravagantly carved images of a dancing Vishnu have survived. The most outstanding sacred structures, however, are the five gigantic Jain *Teerthankara* images carved into the rock face below the fort. Just 70 years after they were made, Babur ordered *"these idols be destroyed"* and they were mutilated, though they have since been restored with stucco.

Gwalior was historically a centre of the arts, as literature, music, and poetry over the centuries found patronage from among its many ruling dynasties, founding one of India's most renowned schools of music. Outside the fort are the mausoleum of Tansen, the legendary singer at Akbar's court, and of the Sufi saint Ghous Mohammad. Ghous Mohammad's tomb is one of the earliest Mughal buildings in India and has huge hexagonal towers at the corners giving it the shape of an octagon with a high dome that was once tiled. A school was founded within the fort in 1897 and the buildings today resound with the chatter of children.

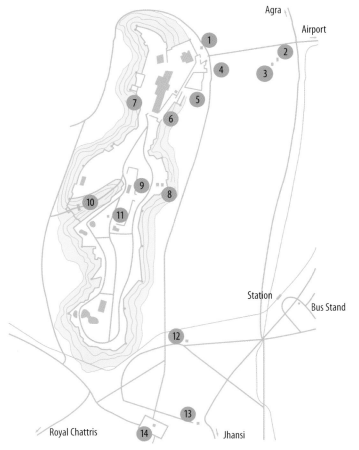

PLAN OF GWALIOR FORT
1. JAMI MASJID
2. TOMB OF GHOUS MOHAMMED
3. TOMB OF TANSEN
4. ALAMGIRI GATE
5. CHATURBHUJ TEMPLE
6. HATHI POL
7. MAN MANDIR
8. SAAS BAHU TEMPLES
9. SURAJ KUND
10. JAIN SCULPTURES
11. TELI-KA-MANDIR
12. TOMB OF RANI OF JHANSI
13. MOTI MAHAL PALACE
14. JAI VILAS PALACE

Facing page: Carved stone brackets and sun shades were once embellished with glazed ceramic tiles

Below: Carved stone screens filter light and provide spaces for women to watch the activities in the courtyard

Jai Vilas

Shortly after the British government restored Gwalior Fort to the Scindias, having taken it for a few years after the 1857 uprising, Jayaji Rao started the construction of Jai Vilas Palace, or Victory Palace, to mark the Prince of Wales' visit to India in 1876. It was one of the most ambitious palaces of its era, and was designed by Colonel Sir Michael Filose, whose family had lived in India for several generations and who reputedly had Italian blood, perhaps accounting for the palace being designed on the lines of a grand Italian Palazzo.

The building is laid out in a huge square, with four elongated wings around a central courtyard accessed through a heavily detailed cast iron gate. The public rooms, the Durbar Hall, and banqueting rooms are located at the centre of the south wing, while offices and royal apartments are housed in the remainder of the complex. The Italian façade is detailed with columns and pilasters painted white to simulate marble. The roof is a wonderful amalgam of turrets built in an eclectic fusion of Indian and Elizabethan features.

French, Italian, and Victorian elements merge to create an opulent architectural flourish. A grand staircase leading up to the Durbar Hall has cut crystal balustrades, while the Durbar Hall itself is lavishly embellished with gilded furniture and golden drapes. Its two crystal chandeliers are so huge that it is said two elephants were made to stand on the roof to ensure it was strong enough to take the 9,000 lbs weight of the chandeliers. The two chandeliers hold 248 candles each and were provided with glass chimneys so that when the *pankha*s, or fans were used, the candles didn't flicker. Crystal furniture stands on carpets that are said to be the largest in Asia and were especially woven for this hall.

The Dining Hall is equally munificent, with silver and crystal jostling for visibility. A silver model of a train chugged on silver rails around the dining table, serving port and wine after dinner. Not far from this is the royal guest house with suites adorned with coloured glass and painted with scenes from Hindu mythology. Another room is themed on erotica, with a life size statue of the Greek mythological figure of Leda at the centre. The Scindias were also legendary hunters of tiger, and tiger skins displayed on the palace walls attest to their prowess as well as to a life of absolute excess.

Facing page:
The Durbar Hall

Below: Main façade

Above: *A crystal train carrying port and wine ran on tracks on the dining table*

Left: *Indian-style dining room*

Right: *Detail of the Durbar Hall*

Facing page: *The grand double staircase leading to the Durbar Hall has a crystal balustrade*

Laxmi Vilas

Facing page above:
The Indo-Saracenic façade of the palace

Facing page below: *Courtyard within the palace*

Below: *The Durbar Hall*

Gaekwad rose to power as a general in the Peshwa's armies in the 18th century. The Peshwas were the powerful prime ministers of Shivaji's Maratha Empire, their hereditary position attainted by virtue of being high caste Brahmins. Pilaji Rao Gaekwad, the first ruler of Baroda, and eldest son of Jhingojirao Kerojirao Gaekwad, established himself at the fortress of Sonagad in AD 1726 after he was appointed by the Peshwa to collect revenues from the territories in Gujarat. He set about carving out a kingdom out of these territories and was granted the title of 'Sena Khas Khel' by the Peshwa.

Vadodara is believed to have a history of over 2,000 years but its recorded history starts in AD 812 as it became a node for traders in the region since it lay on the western route to the coast. The Gupta dynasty ruled here followed by the Chalukyas and then was annexed by the Solankis. In the 13th century, the Delhi Sultans swept across India and ruled until the Mughal Empire was established in the 16th century. Towards the end of Shah Jahan's rule the Marathas began their forays into Sultanate territories and beyond. Before the Gaekwads came to power, the Babi Nawabs of the Mughal Empire ruled Vadodara. Except for a brief interlude, the Gaekwads have ruled here since, even after the Marathas were defeated in the Third Battle of Panipat in 1761 and the Peshwa influence weakened; the Gaekwads accepted British sovereignty and ruled in relative peace.

Laxmi Vilas, one of several distinguished buildings heralding hybrid architecture, showcasing Indian, European and Moorish elements, provides an interesting transition from the traditional to the aspirations of a Raj lifestyle. Begun in 1878, it took twelve years to build the modern residence of Sayaji Rao III Gaekwad. Laxmi Vilas Palace is an extravagant creation by any standards and was reputedly the most expensive private construction of the era. It was designed by Major Charles Mant, the architect of Mayo College, in an exuberant Indo-Saracenic style. Mant died during the production of this extravaganza which was completed in 1890 by Robert Fellowes Chisholm. These two architects were the pioneers of the Orientalist style, combining western and eastern decorative elements especially in the arches and domes. Laxmi Vilas is a masterpiece which manages to achieve a harmony in both scale and proportion. The roof of Laxmi Vilas is a charming, if eclectic profusion, of *chattris*, cupolas and *bangladar* eaves. The central dome and a tower encompass every possible design and style. The entrance to the park is through an arched monumental gateway, framing the architectural triumphs within. Set in an enormous English-style garden with huge Italianate sculptures; the palace is faced in red sandstone from Agra, with dressings of blue stone from Pune and marble from Rajasthan.

Laxmi Vilas is designed in distinct sections with the public reception rooms, including a durbar hall and a European-style banquet hall to the north in front of the royal chambers of the maharaja and the *zenana* in the south. Each of these complexes are, as was the tradition, built around a courtyard, or a quadrangle, each with separate entrance porticos and interconnected within. The interiors of the palace are equally eclectic, with gilded mosaic on the walls of the vestibule, stained glass, marble sculptures, Venetian chandeliers and European period furniture.

The Durbar Hall is of immense scale with crystal chandeliers, imported stained glass windows depicting the marriage of Lord Ram and Sita, and a geometric wooden ceiling executed in a Moorish style. Projecting *jharokhas* rest on carved wooden brackets depicting flying musicians. The flooring is in Venetian mosaic, with Italian marble employed throughout, stained glass from England and Italianate sculptures along the grand staircase, all the acme of flamboyance. It is the pioneer, or even the culmination of fantastical architectural and interior style, implemented with remarkable aplomb.

The huge entrance lobby to the maharaja's royal apartments has a beautiful Grecian urn in the centre while an inner court has a marble pool with a fountain and statues and the surrounding arcades are in the Moorish style. The interior of the palace is equally opulent, designed and decorated with beautiful fittings including 18th-century furniture, in leather, brocade, gilded and wood panelled, with a significant collection of Indian and European art. Today this is housed to the south of the palace in the Maharaja Fateh Singh Museum, with a fine collection of European art, including works by Murillo, Titian and Raphael, as well as Chinese, Japanese and Indian exhibits; most notably a superb collection of court paintings by Raja Ravi Varma.

In 1984 his descendent Lt Col Fatehsingh Rao Gaekwad said that when he moved into the palace as a child: *"The size of this palace just hit us, it was enormous. Just within the palace itself there were over a thousand people doing various jobs, and there was always a servant or two lurking behind every door. It took us as children at least a year or two to find our way around and even today there are parts of the palace which I haven't visited in the last ten or fifteen years".*

Under Sayaji Rao III the Indo-Saracenic style of architecture flourished as he built some of Vadodara's most notable buildings. The Kirti Mandir of the early 20th century is the Gaekwad family cenotaph with the vault painted by one of India's most eminent artists Nandlal Bose. A large number of distinguished buildings are attributed to Sayaji Rao, including the hospital, high court and secretariat, all largely designed by Mant.

Sikh Forts

Bahadurgarh & Gobindgarh

BAHADURGARH FORT

On the outskirts of the city lies the great Sikh fort of Bahadurgarh. It is an exemplary *nara durg*, or one that is protected by a strong force of fighting men. The fort is circular, with a succession of entrances and a double layer of fortifications. Most of the buildings within were for military use, but there are *gurudwara*s, a mosque and some royal apartments. It is considered one of the best fortified forts built in Punjab.

The original fort is said to have been built by Nawab Saif Khan in 1658, in the ancient village of Saifabad. It is believed that Guru Tegh Bahadur visited the nawab at Saifabad and prophesied the rising of a great fort at the spot. In 1837, Maharaja Karan Singh of Patiala laid the foundations of this fort which considering its scale, was completed in a record eight years. He named it Bahadurgarh, after the guru, and built a *gurudwara* in memory of his visit. This fort has two circular ramparts and is surrounded by a moat. An inscription on the inner gate provides evidence of when it was built.

Bahadurgarh is stupendous in scale, with a circumference of more than a mile and the walls rising over 20 feet The beautiful *gurudwara*, a fine example of Sikh architecture is situated in the Panch Bati garden near a water tank. A mosque built by Saif Khan in 1668 stands nearby. It is said that Saif Khan, a relative of Emperor Aurangzeb, became a hermit and settled here in Saifabad. He is buried here, just behind the fort, and his grave is still cared for. The two inscriptions in the fort testify that the village and the mosque were founded in 1668 during the reign of Aurangzeb.

Below: Fortifications and the historic gurudwara inside the fort

cannon were mounted on its ramparts. The maharaja devoted his attention to securing the fort. He expanded the moat and added three lines of defence, further fortified the bastions to protect the *tosha khana* or treasury, which is situated deep within the fort, masked by an unpretentious doorway. It was also used as a palace until Rambagh Palace was built in Amritsar. The additions made by Ranjit Singh showcased the Sikh position of grandeur, wealth, and great political stature. At its peak, Gobindgarh housed 12,000 troops. A British diplomat of the time estimated the wealth inside the fort to be over a hundred million rupees.

Around 1850, the British Government established a base in Amritsar and set about demolishing fortifications around the region. They destroyed the two outer fortifications of Gobindgarh and built a large cantonment around the fort in a virtual cordon. They gradually took over Gobindgarh, and built living quarters inside; barracks overlaid palaces and gardens as they established their supremacy. Without the outer fortification, Gobindgarh shrank in size and stature as its innermost and private sections were clearly visible. Interestingly, the land that was reclaimed from the demolition of the outer fortifications came to be used as a moat, filled from Mati Jheel or mud pond and it has four star-shaped islands on each flank. During this period the British lived in the central building which is on a raised height, and the bastions were occupied by troops. There followed a period of bloody history as eventually General Dyer, of Jallianwala Bagh infamy came to live here. It is a modest establishment, its ghoulish past evident in the *phansi ghar* or hanging room, alongside the house.

The fort is entered through two gateways traversed in a sharply curved road. It is an exemplary form of a medieval fortress of the Misl period. Originally built in brick and mud mortar, it was consolidated and strengthened by Ranjit Singh after he annexed it. It is perhaps the only surviving fort of Ranjit Singh even though it has been so extensively demolished and overbuilt.

GOBINDGARH FORT

One of the most striking historic edifices in the holy town of Amritsar is Gobindgarh whose high fortifications and heavy batteries placed one on top each other gives it an imposing appearance. Ranjit Singh, chief of the Sukkarchakkia di Misl, declared himself Maharaja of Punjab in 1801, extended his territories to Amritsar in 1805 when he took over from his traditional rivals, the Bhangi chiefs. First built in 1760, it was known as Bhangiyan da Qila, or 'Fort of the Bhangis'; after Ranjit Singh took it over, it was restored and largely rebuilt under the control of the then Governor of Gobindgarh, Aziz-ud-din.

The importance of this fort is that it is located close to the sacred Golden Temple with its sacred tank, the centre of Sikh faith and belief. Maharaja Ranjit Singh, also known as the 'Lion of Punjab', was at the time attempting to consolidate forces against the colonial rulers and the construction of this fort was justified by the need to protect the Sikh's most holy shrine. It is also believed that Jaswant Rao Holkar, the Maratha king persuaded Ranjit Singh to build this fort in order to protect his treasure which, considering the Sikh and Maratha uprisings of the time, was no longer safe in conventional banks.

Gobindgarh is a formidable masonry structure with numerous bastions and iron gates. Twenty-five pieces of

Qila Mubarak

Above: *One of the courtyards in Qila Androon around which the various rooms are organised*

Patiala is a relatively young city, built only a few centuries ago, after the state was founded by Baba Ala Singh. Raja (Baba) Ala Singh, the first independent ruler of the state, founded Patiala in 1763. Ala Singh, Ram Singh's third son, was a brave soldier and an astute politician who laid the foundation of the Phulkian fortunes by creating the principality of Patiala. He carved out a state starting with a small *zamindari* of 30 villages and displayed great courage and shrewdness in dealing with the Mughals, Afghans, and Marathas. He managed to secure and establish his state and in 1763, laid the foundation of the Patiala Fort known as Qila Mubarak. This formed the nucleus of the present city of Patiala.

Early in his early career he waged war with the Bhattis and the Afghans. By 1732, he had conquered a vast territory around Barnala that served as his headquarters during the Durrani-Mughal clashes in Punjab. Ala Singh eventually established his hold over a huge swathe of lands, extending from Bhatinda to Sirhind and beyond. In 1753, he started building a fort about 100 km east of Barnala. The present city of Patiala, effectively the *patti* or land of Ala Singh, developed around it and became his capital. Ala Singh died in 1765 and was succeeded by his grandson Amar Singh, who was granted the title of Raja-i-Rajgan by the Durrani king Ahmed Shah Abdali, as a reward for helping Abdali against the Marathas and other Sikhs.

Amar Singh consolidated and expanded the kingdom while waging war for almost 40 years alternately with the Mughals, Afghans and Marathas. Theirs were almost continuous battles as they rose against British oppression; they adopted multiple military tactics, using swords, matchlocks, and daggers in a single assault. However the consolidation of their territories was eventually achieved through strategic alliances rather than military superiority. Under Amar Singh, Patiala became the most powerful state between the Yamuna and the Sutlej. His seven-year-old son, Sahib Singh, succeeded him and accepted British protection in 1809. This alliance signalled the beginning of an era of prosperity marked by increasing expansion and wealth.

Even though historians have tried to trace the origins of the name Patiala back to Vedic literature, the town as it stands today was built upon the nucleus founded by Ala Singh in 1763. It would appear to conform to the guidelines for fort construction laid down in the *Shastra*s. The king's palace is in the centre, along with it the sacred core where the *jyot* or lamp is lit and the administrative sections and residential quarters for the royal headquarters are built around it.

Originally a mud fort or *kachi garhi*, Qila Mubarak was consolidated by Baba Ala Singh after the conquest of Sirhind, as a victory fort. Qila Mubarak is constructed of a particularly large brick used in this region. The fort is an immense structure with 32 bastions, the largest with a circumference measuring 290 feet at the top. The walls of the citadel, which slope from base upwards, are of extraordinary scale and strength; they are as wide as 53 feet at the base and taper to around 35 feet at the top. The fort walls tower over the countryside at a height of 100 feet. The bastion tower or *burj* is 120 feet above the ground and is the remarkable feature of the fort. Overall there are four large bastions, one at each corner and 32 smaller ones, in absolute symmetry. It is one of the most impressive forts of Punjab. It was later raised to a sprawling double-storeyed structure with a massive gate and beautiful arches. Surrounded by high walls, it is an imposing structure and covers 10 acres in the heart of the city. The Qila Mubarak gate is in red sandstone decorated with lattice, covered by multiple arched openings. Between this first gateway and Qila Androon, or inner fort is a large forecourt flanked by the buildings of the secretariats and the Durbar Hall. The *androon* or internal gateway is a two-storeyed structure, square in design with *chattri*s at the top, and probably used by the king to preside over functions in the courtyard below.

Qila Androon consists of a series of interconnected courtyards with royal buildings leading off them. The entrance leads to a large, rectangular courtyard surrounded by high, wonderfully painted walls. To the west of the central courtyard are the private palaces; to the east the buildings were used for private audiences and events. Between these two is a passage leading to the highest bastion in the fort housing the '*jyot*' or sacred flame which Baba Ala Singh, the founder, brought from Jwalamukhi and which continues to be lit. Nearby there is a *gurudwara* and a temple.

The most important courtyard in the Qila houses the Rang Mahal which is an elaborately painted chamber with an alcove that housed the *takht* or throne of the king. The carvings, stuccowork, and elaborate painting are of exceptional quality and reflect the wide range of cultural influences during this period. It was an era when the fusion of Islamic art and traditional craftsmanship from the many regions of India were assimilated.

Below: Wall painting in the bed chamber

The Sheesh Mahal, located beyond the Rang Mahal, is a unique blend of the sacred and the secular. It has delicately painted rooms on the ground floor, a fountain in the central courtyard and numerous rooms with elaborate courtyards that open on to the Rang Mahal courtyard. The themes of the paintings on the ground floor of the Sheesh Mahal depict legends from the life of Krishna. Maharaja Narendra Singh, a great patron of the arts, commissioned Kangra and Rajput painters in 1847 to decorate the walls of the Sheesh Mahal and the Rang Mahal. Here, scenes from mythology, as well as floral motifs and mirror mosaics, express the cultural plurality of the region and the great wealth and style of the Patiala maharajas. A painted room on the second floor leads to the residential palaces. Other palaces such as Moti Mahal, or the Rajmata's Mahal, are also beautifully painted, palatial apartments. The Ran Baas was probably a guesthouse with courtyards, fountains, and small tanks. The first courtyard has a painted wall with a gilded throne. There is also a *char bagh* garden with marble paths and water channels with fountains – all elaborate but built at different times so they add their own eclectic style.

The Durbar Hall is symmetrical, with rooms on three sides. On the fourth side there are five grand arches through which one enters. The interior and exterior walls of the building are highly decorated with ornamental plasterwork. The false ceiling has elaborately painted *khatmbandi* or wooden tiles. The Durbar Hall itself has an amazing collection of Baccarat chandeliers installed by Maharaja Bhupinder Singh, a great patron of the arts.

In front of Qila Mubarak is the Qila Chowk which leads to the commercial areas including the Adalat Bazaar, which starts here and ends in another *chowk*. Undoubtedly the fort was the centre and nucleus of life in the principality of Patiala.

Left: *Thandi Burj, one of the corner towers of Qila Androon, always had a draft of cool air*

Above: *Phulkari-style wall decoration*

Facing page: *Alcove with rich wall adornment in the honeymoon chamber*

Kapurthala

The town of Kapurthala said to have been founded in the early part of the 11th century by Rana Kapur, a scion of the ruling house of Jaisalmer (Rajasthan) in the early part of the 11th century in the time of Sultan Mahmud of Ghazni. Although there are no records of this, the Kapurthala clan furthered this claim of lineage through marital alliances in the 19th century. Sardar Jassa Singh founded Kapurthala state in 1783 after successive battles with the Governors at Lahore. The fortunes of the Kapurthalas waned during the reign of Maharaja Ranjit Singh as he swept across the plains of Punjab, but as the Punjab treaty decreed, all of the Punjab princes came under the British yoke after successive Anglo-Sikh wars. The Maharajas of the Punjab became the British government's most loyal servants and Raja Randhir, the most loyal of them all was conferred the title of Raja-i-Rajgan in perpetuity after his assistance in quelling the First War of Independence.

Randhir Singh's grandson Maharaja Jagatjit Singh (1877–1949), the last ruler, was born in 1872, and was installed on the *gaddi* and

Above: *Façade of Jagatjit Palace*

Facing page: *The Durbar Hall, now the library of the Sainik School*

Right: *Wall and ceiling decoration in the formal drawing room, now converted into a museum*

Left: Chandelier inside
the Durbar Hall

Facing page: Balcony
that runs on the upper
level in the Durbar Hall

PLEASE DO NOT TOUCH ME

Far left: *The classical order in the column proportions of the main façade*

Left: *Formal dining room*

invested with the full powers of administration in November 1890. He left a lasting impact and was granted the title of 'Maharaja' during the Coronation Durbar held at Delhi in 1911. Educated in London and France, he was a Francophile and invested in the development of Kapurthala town. The extent of French influence in the architecture of the main palace, and some of the other buildings; its wide streets; the Indo-Saracenic influence in the civic buildings and the city layout was renowned in India. It was in its day, known as a city of palaces, mosques, temples, *gurudwara*s and gardens.

Most amazing of all was his palace, which he completed in 1908 for his most favoured wife, a European. He invited architects to submit designs and selected the French architect M Marcel whose design was not merely inspired, but emulated the great mansard roofs of Versailles and the Louvre. It was, in its day, known as Elysées Palace, a spectacular French chateau set in a grand park full of European mythological statuary, with figures riding seahorses grasping fish in front of the main entrance. The palace has a pink-and-white stucco façade with a huge copper clad mansard roof at the centre and smaller ones at either end. A *porte-cochère* gives way to sweeping staircases and a double-height Durbar Hall on the main floor. Today it is used as a library but there remain the elements of a grand palace.

The Durbar Hall was built by Maharaja Jagjit Singh. An inscription on its external façade states that construction was started in 1882 and completed in 1889. It consists of three structures joined together with rooms and doorways. The main structure, which was used as the Durbar Hall, has a rectangular plan, consisting of a central double-height hall with aisles on both sides and a double-height entrance hall. The entrance hall has recessed arches with statues. On the upper floors of the hall are projected, decorative *jharokha*s accessible from a narrow passage around the entrance hall at the first floor level. The central hall has a steel truss roof with a decorative wooden ceiling and cornices on all sides. It is separated from the side aisles through a row of cusped arches and circular columns. The upper floors are accessed by a staircase located in a narrow passage near the entrance hall.

The extensive parquet flooring has the state crest embedded in it. A screened upper gallery with a ceiling of stained glass would have been used by the *zenana* to observe the *durbar* proceedings. To the east, doors open into the dining room which is lavishly decorated in 17th-century French style with blue lapis lazuli marble pillars, gilded capitals, and fine Gobelin tapestry. To the west of the Durbar Hall is the formal drawing room in a Louis XVI style with heavily gilded and painted ceilings, fine European furniture, and ornaments. Kapurthala Palace was matched by a chateau built in the hills in the same style as an old country chateau in France with sloping roofs and multiple turrets.

The front façade of the building is dominated by an octagonal entrance porch and is made of fine exposed brickwork in lime mortar. The bricks are beautifully carved to make decorative columns and arches. The most important element of the front façade is an open-air pavilion at the top floor, covered with a framed dome and flanked by *chattri*s on both sides.

Maharaja Jagatjit Singh of Kapurthala secured for himself the acme of French lifestyle catering to every whim. It was an inordinately expensive venture and was unsustainable for later generations, who donated it so that it could be turned into a military school.

Facing page: *Formal living room, now converted into a museum*

Hill Forts

Kangra

The pride of place in Himalayan forts undoubtedly goes to the Kangra Fort, from which the town of Kangra or Nagarkot, the fort-city derives its name. It has endured a history of invasion and oppression but with it, rich tales of valour and resistance. Embedded in myth and legend, some claim that it is contemporaneous with the Mahabharata. Be that as it may, its possession by the Katoch dynasty of Jalandhara is recorded for at least 1,800 years or more.

Strategically situated above the River Banganga, and overlooking the verdant Kangra Valley, its value also lay in the prosperous valley irrigated by numerous streams, the forests, orchards and homesteads that it controlled. It was first assailed in the 11th century by Mahmud of Ghazni, who unexpectedly deflected his advance into India, swerving north to the Himalayan region of Kangra. The fort was noted for the immense wealth of its temples. It is well-established that vast quantities of treasure

Below: Ranjit Singh Darwaza, main entrance to the fort

were plundered from this temple. The treasure included a model of a house in silver, some 30-yards long and 15-yards wide; and jewels encrusted with rubies, diamonds, and pearls. The Muslim garrison held the fort for 35 years after which the Katoch dynasty resumed control and restored many sections that had fallen into decay. The descendants of the Katochs remained in undisturbed possession and control of Kangra Fort until 1360, with the arrival of the Tughlaqs.

Feroz Tughlaq like his imperialist predecessors, wanted to acquire as much territory as possible. More than wealth, he wanted control of the hugely productive lands and the strategic fort. He stormed Kangra but because of its sophisticated design, self-sufficiency in terms of water and supplies, Kangra Fort was able to hold out against the Tughlaqs for almost six months. Firoz Tughlaq unaccustomed to such resistance, sent several emissaries to the

Kangra Raja, assuring him pardon if he conceded. Diminishing supplies and sheer exhaustion resulted in his surrender but in an unusual concession, perhaps as an acknowledgement of his heroic stand, Tughlaq restored the fort to the raja, together with his conquered lands, and contented himself with the acceptance of a nominal suzerainty.

Two hundred years later, the fort was taken and permanently occupied by Emperor Akbar. But the Rajputs proved continuously troublesome to the Mughal governors of the Punjab and repeated expeditions were made to Kangra to control the intractable raja. Emperor Jehangir visited the fort and the Jehangiri Darwaza was built in recognition. The dynamic rule of Emperor Shah Jahan reduced the rajas of the hills to mere vassals, enjoying some power: the privilege of building forts, and even warring with one another. It is presumed that one or other branch of the Katoch family remained in occupation of the fort through its tumultuous fortunes.

When Guru Gobind Singh took up cudgels on behalf of the oppressed in his fight against the Mughals, he allied with the Rajput rajas of the Himalayas and encouraged them to retrieve control of their fortunes. The Kangra rajas recovered their properties and ushered in a period of relative peace.

The last of the Katoch family, the ambitious Raja Sansar Chand who succeeded to the throne in 1784, sought to extend his fiefdom; but he had to contend with Ranjit Singh, who was a growing power in Punjab. Defeated by Ranjit Singh in the plains, Sansar Chand turned his armies towards the Raja of Kahlur who in turn sought Gurkha support. With the help of Ranjit Singh, the Gurkhas were defeated; but he extracted his price and Kangra Fort was lost to the Katoch family.

After the defeat of the Sikhs and at the annexation of Punjab, the Kangra Fort too came under British administration. The devastating earthquake of 1905 caused immense damage of which the battered wall and fissured battlements bear ample evidence.

The fort gates or *darwaza*s are eloquent with history as each bears testimony to successive conquerors. Access to the fort is from the Ranjit Singh Darwaza leading to the Jehangiri Darwaza and through the Ahni and Amiri Darwazas. From the Jehangiri Darwaza, a path leads to the next gate known as Andheri Darwaza.

Further up is Darshani Darwaza, considered to be one of the oldest structures which opens into a spacious courtyard with chambers around it.

At the core of the fort lie the Lakshmi Narayan Temple and the Sitlamata Temple. Although seriously damaged in the earthquake of 1905, both these temples still have exquisite carvings. To the north of these two temples is the largely rebuilt Ambika Devi Temple which is still in worship. A Jain temple nearby has an inscription dated 1523.

Between the Sitlamata Temple and the Ambika Devi Temple, a staircase leads up to the Sheesh Mahal. This is clearly a misnomer for the *mahal* is a block of stone with a large terrace, on the edge of which stands a watch tower with spectacular views of the surrounding areas. Near Andheri Darwaza there are the remnants of a Jehangiri Mosque but more valuable is another structure, a stone stepwell by the name of Kapoorsagar which would have been the lifeline of the fort during its many sieges.

Above: Panoramic view of the fort above the river

Below:

Jehangiri Darwaza

Nurpur

Nurpur Fort was orginally known as Dhameri, not far from what is known today as Dharamsala. Emperor Jehangir made several forays into the Himalayas. When he fell in love with the beautiful wife of Sher Afghan, Mehrun-Nissa, the luckless husband was sent to war and certain death, while Jehangir spent years winning the love of the lovely widow who finally relented. Jehangir gave her the name, Nur Mahal, 'Light of the Palace' and later elevated it to Nur Jehan, 'Light of the World'. The town of Nurpur was named after her, following his conquest of the area. Nurpur has an old fort built by Raja Basu a thousand years ago. Today, it is largely in ruins but the fortifications still stand. There is a ruined but finely carved Krishna Temple within the fort.

Gurkha castles are an indispensable part of the heritage of Himachal. The erstwhile princely states of Hindoor, Kehloor,

Bhagat, Arkti, Mahlog, Kuthar, Sirmur, Jubbal, and Kyonthal which fell into complete disarray following petty battles were eventually brought under Gurkha control until 1815 when the British completely decimated the Gurkhas and pulverised them by incorporating them into the British army. While most of the structures built by the Gurkhas have crumbled, there are still some which speak of the rich history of the area. The castles of Malaon, Banasar, Subathu, and Dhar in Solan are evidence of their heritage. The Gurkhas did not uphold great traditions of kingship. Instead, it is said that most of their castles were built by force and with largely unpaid labour. Cruel and aggressive, they held control over most of the western Himalayan region until the British gained control in the 19th century.

Left: *Fort ruins*

Below left: *Wall painting at the Bris Raj Bihari Temple inside the fort*

Below right: *Main entrance to the fort*

Basgo

An arid desert at an altitude of around 4,000 metres, Ladakh was on the historic silk route, a crucial link between Central Asia and China. Caravans laden with riches, trading in gems, silk, tea, musk, and other products would cross here en route from China to Kashmir, Afghanistan, and beyond. It was not only trade which deeply influenced the culture of the region, but also the travels of monks, pilgrims, and craftsmen, a cross-fertilisation of cultures in an environment that dictated their lifestyle. It has remained, despite its volatile fortunes, a bastion of Buddhism in India.

The early history of Ladakh is largely in the oral tradition, but certainly many successive migrations took place, from the Dard of Iranian extraction, to Tibetans; and it was during the Kushan period, part of Bharat. While Buddhism went to Tibet from Kashmir in the 4th century, it was Ladakh where Tibetans returned to study the religion and religious practices linked to the university at Nalanda in the 7th century. Buddhism here too went through a period of turmoil following the assassination of King Lang Dar Ma who adopted the Bon faith. In time, there rose a king who sought stability, merging once again the spiritual and temporal. His descendents gradually re-established order and set up kingdoms in Guge, Tibet, Ladakh, Zanskar and Spiti in AD 930. They first established themselves at Shey.

The Buddhist renaissance, under the monk king Yeshe O, saw a continuous movement of monks and scholars, most notable of whom was Rinchen Zangpo. A scholar and patron of the arts, he brought artisans and craftsmen from Kashmir. It was under his influence that some of the most outstanding art and architecture in the region came to be built including Alchi and Wanla. The capital moved to Basgo in the 15th-century and although a large, fortified settlement was built, the region remained one of continuous conflict and invasions.

From Kashmir, Central Asia, Kashgar, and Baltistan, many attempts to capture Ladakh were made with inroads into the stability of Ladakh's kings. The 15th century fortress of Basgo withstood a three-year siege by Mongol and Tibetan invaders. The king finally abandoned Basgo in 1680 and moved into Leh constructing Leh Palace. He was further weakened by the Dogra's invasion in the 19th century, when they stormed Leh Palace and the king resettled at Stok.

Located an hour from Leh, Basgo today stands a shadow of its former glory, the mud-brick fortifications eroded beyond recognition and yet still, sentinels of past glory. Towering over the village of Basgo, the temples remain, still worshipped and still cared for. Built and rebuilt over the centuries lies the complex of temples dedicated to the Maitreya Buddha. The Chamba Lakhang

***Right:** Basgo Fort and monastery complex perched on a mud hillock*

Above: *Wall painting inside the complex*

Right: *Seated Buddha inside one of the temples within the fort complex*

Below: *The main temple and palace complex*

Facing page: *Richly painted interior of the main temple*

towers over the Serzang and Chamchung which have some of Ladakh's most significant wall paintings. Here in the wall paintings is revealed evidence of royal lifestyle as it depicts court scenes, royal retinues, and traditional robes. All of these provide crucial clues to understanding the court life at Basgo Fort.

Most of the original buildings have been lost with the passage of time, though there are efforts to recreate some of the ministers' chambers. However, watch towers, and remnants of the fortification still dominate the skyline. The region was one of continuous conflict and invasions. Below the Chamchung there is evidence of small rooms connected by long underground passages leading to the granary; and a derelict building that has local provenance as the Kalon's residence. Judging by the remains in the precinct around the temples, the major royal structures would have been nearby, reinforcing the strategic balance between king and priest.

Eastern India

Ramnagar

The sacred core of Varanasi, the ancient city of Kashi, occupies only one side of the River Ganga, while the other side is dramatically barren and fallow. On this bare side of the river, connected to Kashi by a narrow bridge, is the Ramnagar Fort, its ramparts visible from miles around. The fort was built in 1750 by Mansa Ram, a *zamindar* who had received a portion of Benaras from the Nawab of Awadh in AD 1737. Mansa Ram subsequently received Jaunpur and the rest of Benaras from the Mughal emperor, and thereafter, Mirzapur and Nandeshwar. Mansa Ram's son Balwant Singh rebelled against the Nawab of Awadh, and was defeated. In time he joined the British East India Company in

Centre: Carved ivory armrest on a howdah in the museum at Ramnagar

Below: The verandah of the palace overlooks a temple and the Ganga

invading Bengal at the Battle of Buxar in 1764, but the next year, Mughal emperor Shah Alam signed the Treaty of Benaras with the Company and returned the Zamindari of Benaras to the Awadh nawab.

Balwant Singh's son Chait Singh was given the title of 'Raja of Benaras' in 1770 but he soon rebelled against the demands made of him by the British. Chait Singh was quickly defeated and his territories, including Chunar Fort confiscated. The British placed various members of Chait Singh's family on the throne but kept eroding their authority, to the extent that even the rajas' personal lands were confiscated. Finally, in 1835, Ishwari Prasad

Narayan Singh was given the title of Maharaja in return for his staunch loyalty, which remained unwavering during the 1857 War of Independence. Ishwari Prasad's title was increased to 'Maharaja Bahadur'; he was given a personal 13-gun salute and was later knighted. The maharaja came to be known as Kashi Naresh, 'Lord of Kashi', and the family claimed descent from Lord Shiva, the supreme deity of Kashi.

Ramnagar Fort is built in Chunar sandstone and dominates the landscape with its massive fortifications. Inside its Durbar Hall is a subtle blend of Hindu and Islamic architecture, with decorative elements in marble adding lustre to an otherwise sombre interior. The hall has long terraces along the waterfront with spectacular views of the Ganga and Kashi on the other side.

The fort has a temple dedicated to Ved Vyasa, the legendary sage who wrote the Mahabharata, and it is believed that Vyasa's

ashram existed at this site. There are several other temples, of which the temples of Durga and Dakshin Mukhi Hanuman are important. The fort also houses a museum established by the current maharaja's father. It has an interesting collection of carriages and palanquins, and a quaint, 19th-century astronomical clock.

Ramnagar Fort's famed living tradition is the annual Rama Lila, the dramatic re-enactment of the Ramayana, which is performed inside the fort for several days leading up to the festival of Dussehra. The maharaja rides out on a caparisoned elephant to inaugurate the Rama Lila, and on the final day, anoints the child actor playing Lord Rama with *tilak* to celebrate the victory of good over evil. The Rama Lila at Ramnagar was first held over a century ago, and the enthralling power of the spectacle and the number of spectators still remain undiminished.

Above: *A panoramic view of the fort as seen from the river*

Below: *Coloured glass doors in the Durbar Hall*

Gaur

Above: *Tantipara Masjid*

Gaur is the last surviving mud fort in Bengal and is one of the few surviving mud forts in India, the *mahi durg* described in the *Arthashastra*. Built on the eastern bank of the River Bhagirathi and Mahanadi, its location is significant in terms of control over river trade of silk and cotton. Much of this was invested in buildings of great magnificence. At its peak, Gaur stretched across many miles. The land was fertile and prosperous; its very name is said to be derived from *gur* or molasses, a major produce of the area.

The area was known as Gauda under the rule of the famous Bengali king Sasanka, who emerged as a potentate from the collapsing Gupta Empire in the 7th century AD. After his rule, Gaur broke up and the kingdom was divided. The Pala dynasty, the last Buddhist dynasty, captured Gaur in the 8th century. It was also a prosperous city during the Sena dynasty. Originally Brahmans from the Deccan, they became Kshatriyas when they became soldiers. The Sena scholar King Vallal was a great reformer and introduced the concept of caste mobility. The last Sena king Lakshman founded the town of Lakshmanvati.

However, the well-documented history of Gaur begins with its conquest in AD 1198 by the Khiljis, who then ruled Delhi. The Gaur kings fought to retain their kingdom during a long period of hostility but were finally defeated by the Sultanate and it only reverted to them after the fall of the Tughlaqs.

At that time, one of the Afghani chieftains of the Tughlaqs, Fakhr-ud-din, broke away to found his own kingdom in Bengal. A period of war, attrition, and intrigue followed as they struggled to gain control of one of the wealthiest areas in the east. To build

his new capital in Pandua, Fakhr-ud-din plundered Gaur and took everything possible to transport. Eventually, Gaur was wrested back by King Ganesha from the Ilyasi Shah dynasty even as his son was forced to become a Muslim to avoid invasion from the Jaunpur Sharqis. Gaur faced a period fraught with conversions and religious hatred and the Ilyasis moved in swiftly to retrieve their kingdom.

Hussain Shah became the popularly elected king of Gaur, but it was under his son Nasrat Shah that most of Gaur was built. After its long history of turbulence, they ushered in an era of peace, prosperity and extensive construction. Nasrat Shah was a great patron of the arts and not only was the fort repaired but it was developed in a great confluence of indigenous Bengali and Afghani Islamic architecture. With the Mughals establishing themselves in India, Gaur was also desirable. Although Nasrat Shah made peace with Babur, Gaur was later occupied by Humayun. At that point, it was known as Jannatabad or 'Terrestrial Paradise'. It was later sacked by Sher Shah and was finally occupied by Akbar's army in 1576. This occupation followed an outbreak of plague that had occurred a year earlier and decimated the population inside the fort; and to that extent, it was worthless.

The main citadel stretched over a mile from north to south, the ramparts of such immense scale along the river and swamp that at places, the earthworks were as much as 6 miles wide. Designed against flooding, with two and three protective ditches; the ramparts, at some places 180-feet wide at the base and 30-feet high, were a formidable construction. Gaur, along with its settlements, covered a vast area in the 16th century. The Portuguese historian Faria e Sousa described it as having a million inhabitants.

The main citadel dates back to the 14th century. The ramparts of Gaur still exist; they were works of vast labour and even though they are now overgrown and have lost their masonry façade, it is still possible to visualise the scale of this fortified city. Barbak Shah remodelled the old city after his return from Pandua. He laid out a grand thoroughfare and built the great Dakhil Darwaza across, on axis with the entrance to the citadel. Dakhil Darwaza has a pointed arch, an Islamic contribution, but the beautifully coursed brickwork with terracotta ornamentation was wholly Bengali, thus a perfect blend of Hindu and Islamic architecture. To the west is the Golden or Baradwari Masjid built by Nasrat Shah, with 44 gilded domes of which only one remains. Its columns, faced with black marble and intricately carved, still stand, evocative of its early splendour.

Beyond the Eastern Gateway there is the great Feroza Minar which dominates the citadel and marks the triumph of

the Ilyasi Shahis. There is also the twelve-sided Chirag Minar illuminated with turquoise glaze. Lattan Masjid, built in the 15th century, has bands of yellow, green, blue, and white enamelled brick; and the Tantipara Masjid is decorated in Bengali style, with terracotta embossed brick. Here, the cusped arches and elaborate terracotta embellishments indicate a complete fusion of culture. The Piasbari tank, or 'Tank for the Thirsty', was designed only for prisoners who did not merit potable drinking water. To the south lies the Kotwali Gate and the intricately carved Lesser Golden Mosque built in the 16th century. Although the palace is no longer standing, there are tombs of Fateh Shah and Kadam Rasul, as well as a small mosque built by Nasrat Shah, with a slab reputed to bear a footprint of the Prophet. In nearby Pandua, the remains of the palace are hidden in the jungle.

Gaur was devastated by the plague in the 17th century and abandoned, gradually returning to nature, totally conquered by the jungle – inhabited by the Bengal tiger, python, and even crocodiles in its waters. In the last hundred years, it has begun to be recovered, an unique legacy of a fusion of artistic and architectural style developed by successive dynasties over a thousand years. Its sacred structures are still revered and are painted in the contemporary genre which is colourful, and indicative of the divergent interests of the classicists who salvage the bare bones of what was once a flourishing and brilliantly embellished complex of buildings.

Above: Vaulted interiors of Baradwari Masjid

Left: Feroza Minar

Hazarduari

During a time of increasing unease with the European influence pervading the courts of Indian princes in the 19th century, Humayun Jah, Nawab of Murshidabad completed an enormous neo-Classical palace known as the Hazarduari, its style reflecting the Palladian influence prevalent in the West and imported into Calcutta. The nawab invested in this enormous 'Palace of a Thousand Doors', even as he himself was dependent on the East India Company for stipends for his survival. For the British expansionist strategy, establishing control over the eastern ports at the delta of the River Ganga was essential. Murshidabad lies at the head of the delta dominating all trade from the hinterland of India and even China, and was thus extremely powerful. Further downstream, the Danes, Dutch, Portuguese, and French settlements lay between the Murshidabad nawabs and the East India Company headquartered in Calcutta. For the British, control of Murshidabad meant control of all trade on the Ganga, and they quickly established their supremacy.

The palace was designed by a British engineer, Duncan McLeod, who had served as chief engineer to the nawabs of Awadh for over a decade, even though he was also a Company servant. The Murshidabad Palace, unlike anything McLeod had designed in Lucknow, was modelled on the Government House in Calcutta, which had been based on Robert Adam's Kedleston Hall in Derbyshire. An imposing three-storey building set in sprawling lawns of 41 acres, the palace has an elegant, colonnaded façade, domed tower, high windows, and beautifully ornate pillars.

The layout, too, is unique, for it was the only palace built in India with all the rooms within a single building, in the European fashion, and not around series of courtyards, which defined the social mores in other contemporary palaces being constructed in India. Even so, the palace has a large and imposing Durbar Hall with an elaborate throne and his coat of arms.

It has been suggested that while Nawab Humayun Jah had no role in approving either the plans or the appearance of the palace, he laid the foundation stone himself. Inscriptions in English and Persian just behind the sculpted lions at the base of the massive staircase leading to the entrance, record the commencement

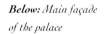

Below: *Main façade of the palace*

Left: *One of the structures opposite the main façade*

of the palace under the administration of Lord Bentinck in the presence of the Governor General's agent, the Commandant of the British troops; and also that "*all the European inhabitants of the station*" also attended. The nawab and his family never lived in the Hazarduari Palace. The building was intended for administrative purposes and was used to entertain the British.

The nawab's family resided in a smaller complex, known as Mubarak Manzil, located about five kilometres away. Built originally for the East India Company, the extensive, pillared verandahs of this palace are in the neo-Classical style and in direct contrast to the traditional palace architecture where secluded verandahs flanked the inner courtyards. However, inside this residential complex, Humayun Jah added a pavilion, which clearly was intended to serve as a throne room or audience hall. The building is a flat-roofed, rectangular structure with five arched entrances; and opens onto a marble terrace in the style of the Mughals.

The link between the Murshidabad nawabs and the Mughals is evident in the large, circular throne made from a single slab of black stone in the style of a Mughal *takht*; it is inscribed as the throne of Shah Shuja, Governor of Bengal, and dated 1643. It was a time when Indian and particularly Mughal culture was under threat as nawabs and rajas across India sought to emulate European lifestyles, and the nawabs of Murshidabad created their own hybrid architecture while doing so.

Tripura

Above: An old photograph of Ujjayanta Palace reflected in the pond

Right: Hunting trophies in the corridor of Andar Mahal

UJJAYANTA PALACE

To the far east of India lies the state of Tripura, where the indigenous Tripuri people have been ruled for more than two thousand years by the Debbarman family. The Manika Dynasty of Tripura claim their descent from the Mahabharata. The first ruler was Yajati, followed by Druha and Tripur. Following the meticulously maintained erstwhile royal chronicles, the present descendent, Pradyut Kishore is the 180th direct descendent.

Ujjayanta presides over Agartala town. Initially the palace was located some ten miles outside Agartala, the capital city, but after a devastating earthquake in 1897, the original palace or castle as it is known here, was destroyed. Rebuilt in the centre of the city at the turn of the last century, Ujjayanta occupies almost one square mile of land. The capital city itself had been founded in Agartala a mere 50 years earlier by Maharaj Krishno Kishore Manikya, away from its earlier location on the banks of the River Saidra. The palace is surrounded by a complex of temples in the unique architecture of the east and together, they form the hub of the city.

The palace built by Maharaj Radhkishorelan Manikya in 1901, at a cost of ten lakh rupees, was designed by Sir Alexander Martin and built by Martin Burn and Co., in a fusion of European architectural styles. It is set in enormous gardens of fantastical scale and designed with pools, fountains and pathways, laid out in the Mughal style.

left: Entrance lobby of Ujjayanta Palace

Above: Neer Mahal

Right: Formal living room of Andar Mahal, the privately owned portion where the royal family still lives

The two-storeyed building has three domes. The central one, which is almost 86-feet high is set on a block that is four storeys high. Two enormous water tanks on either side provide a perfect foil, balancing the building. Built in just over two years, the main building covers 80 acres, and the sumptuous interiors reflect the expansive tastes of the then maharaja. The Throne Room, Reception Hall and Durbar Hall were built on an immense scale with rich European-style embellishments. The curved wooden ceilings and exquisitely crafted doors made of Burmese teak are matched by superbly tiled floors. The interiors were furnished with crystal and chinoiserie reflecting the opulent tastes of the time. The Chinese Room was a creation of Chinese artisans especially summoned to the court to create this extravagance. The library is particularly noteworthy, with a rare collection of manuscripts, and a large collection of musical instruments. The maharaja was a great patron of the arts and literature, and was known for his close link with Nobel laureate Rabindranath Tagore. The Swet Mahal, Banquet Hall and Lal Mahal blocks were added later, as the needs of the palace grew. In 1947, when India gained independence, Tripura seceded to the Indian State, and half the palace became the new assembly building, to house the democratically elected government. Inevitably, much of this area was misused, and much has been lost. In a very recent initiative the state has built new assembly buildings, and after 60 years the palace in its entirety will return to the Debbarman family, perhaps for a new role in the 21st century.

NEER MAHAL

Neer Mahal, the great lake palace of Tripura was built as a summer palace in 1930 by Maharaja Birbikram Kishore Manikya Bahadur, in the centre of a lake known as Rudrasagar, some distance from Agartala. Built by Martin Burn and Co., its most challenging feature is that it is only accessible by water and therefore, it must have been a particularly successful venture to achieve this charming palace with elegant detailing. The palace is a domed building in two distinct wings, its architecture a fusion of Hindu and Mughal elements. To the western side is Andar Mahal or the inner palace which was exclusively for the use of the royal family while the eastern wing was essentially for staff and administration. Andar Mahal is a small, intimate palace with a mere 15 rooms overlooking extensive Mughal-style gardens. There is also a small stage where theatrical performances were held, in keeping with their status as

patrons of the arts. Andar Mahal was truly a private venue where the royal family could retreat into complete seclusion.

A jetty was provided from where motor boats plied to the palace, with two sets of steps; one for the maharani and her retinue and the other for the maharaja. Rudrasagar has been beautifully preserved and is today home to many migratory birds making this a unique destination. Neer Mahal has regrettably not fared so well.

Below: *A portrait of Maharaja Bir Chandra Manikya*

Burdwan Summer Palace

The maharajas of Burdwan, unlike most Indian rajas, were originally a trading family from western Punjab, who moved to Bengal in the 17th century when trade in that region was at its peak. The founder of this family, Sangam Rai Kapoor was enticed by trade opportunities in the east, and decided to move permanently to Burdwan.

During Shah Jahan's reign, Sangam Rai's grandson, Abu Rai, supplied essential commodities to the Mughal armies. He was appointed revenue officer for the region, and also had to ensure law and order. Subsequently, his descendants flourished in Burdwan. In time, they acquired large tracts of land and during Aurangzeb's reign, in 1689, Krishna Ram Rai was recognised as *zamindar* or landlord. In due course the Bengal community fell into disarray and Shova Singh, the *zamindar* of the neighbouring Chetua Barda, seized Burdwan's estates. Rai fled to Dhaka from where, with the help of the Mughal Nawab Nazim, he was able to reclaim his territories.

The decline of the Mughal Empire under Aurangzeb was defined by chaos and lawlessness throughout India, and Rai was murdered in 1702. His sons fought to preserve the estate and extended the Burdwan properties so significantly that Mughal Emperor Muhammed Shah conferred the title of 'Raja' on the family. The title was later raised to 'Maharajadhiraj Bahadur.'

During the East India Company's history of rapacious acquisitions Burdwan faced its greatest threat. Many *zamindar*s of Bengal supported Nawab Nazim Sirajuddaulah in his struggle against the British. Maharaja Tilak Chand of Burdwan was finally defeated in 1760 by the Company sepoys. Eventually the British prevailed over the *zamindar*s and in what is known as the Permanent Settlement of Bengal bought their peace.

The *zamindar*s of Bengal had to pay enormous tributes to the East India Company and were faced with possible bankruptcy. The grandson of Tilak Chand, Mahtab Chand had to accept British suzerainty. This policy held him in good stead and paid rich dividends especially after the First War of Independence of 1857. He was given the title of 'His Highness' and presented with a coat of arms by Queen Victoria in return for his unwavering loyalty.

In time, as their position stabilised, they felt the need to expand beyond the palaces in Burdwan and built palaces in Kolkata and a summer palace in Darjeeling to maintain closer links with the Government. Burdwan Palace in Darjeeling is one of the best examples of the adaptation of English country life to an Indian ethos. Its Art Deco design combined English-style interiors with collections of the royal family and makes an eclectic home which is a prominent landmark in the hill town of Darjeeling.

Above: *The study*

Left: *Grand double staircase to the first floor which has the bedrooms*

Facing page: *The double height central lobby of the Burdwan summer palace*

Colonial Settlers

French Settlements

Once the Portuguese discovered the Cape route to India, other European nations quickly followed suit. The French, the Dutch, the Danes, and the British set the sails of their ships in the direction of India's famed fortunes. The French *Compagnie des Indes Orientales* was the major trader with India, importing fine muslin, pepper, and saltpetre from India in exchange for wines, gold thread, and iron products. By 1721, trade had expanded so much that the French established a base at Mahé, a tiny settlement on the Malabar coast. After this, they acquired Yanam in 1731 and Karaikal in 1738. But the major French settlement grew in Puducherry, or the 'new hamlet', which the French called Pondicherry (now renamed Puducherry). Apart from this, a settlement at Chandernagore on the banks of the River Hooghly in Bengal served as their second bastion.

The French allied with the Marathas in India and their military skills contributed to Maratha successes, with many fortune-seeking French soldiers joining their armies. With the death of Hyderabad's Nizam-ul-mulk Asif Jah I in 1748, Joseph François Dupleix, who was then Governor General of Pondicherry, unleashed an all out attack in the region over the next 12 years, resulting in the French controlling most of the Deccan and Karnataka and installed Muzaffar Jung as Nizam in 1750. Jung secured the French possessions within his territories, which at the time extended as far as Cape Comorin. It was a brief period of glory, however, as the French remained ensnared in the region's politics, fighting with the Marathas against the powerful Tipu Sultan, and eventually losing to the superior might of the British.

Pondicherry was where the Portuguese established their first factory, which they lost soon to the Danes. A Dutch base was attempted here as well. But it was with the arrival of François Martin from France that building work began in right earnest. He made strategic alliances with the regional powers to obtain permission for erecting structures that would secure his people. This was the beginning of the Pondicherry Fort within which the French settlement developed. Later, a Maratha *farman* dated July 15, 1677, permitted the French to build godowns. In 1689, Sambaji, son of Shivaji, permitted Martin to make use of the defences that he had

erected to build a regular fort. Because of the war that broke out between the French and the Dutch, the latter attacked Pondicherry and were briefly successful in building an earthen rampart around the city. Once the French regained control they completed the fortification, strengthening and extending it and then adding a star-shaped outer fortification around the old one. South of the fort, the Capuchin monks built a church and laid the foundation of the development of the city. A moat was constructed around the fort and the earth from here was used to develop low-lying land. Later, in its more sophisticated phase, it was known as the Grand Canal, and beyond it were the Indian settlements. Pondicherry was the administrative head of the French settlements of Mahé, Yanam, and Karaikal.

It was under Dupleix from 1741 to 1754 that Pondicherry achieved its zenith. The outbreak of war between France and England in 1740, as a result of the War of the Austrian Succession, set off hostilities between the two European powers in India too. Bourdonnais captured Madras in 1746, and an English naval squadron attacked Pondicherry in 1748. In the month-long fighting, the English suffered considerably greater losses. The English withdrew, but before they could launch a second attack, peace was signed in Europe in 1748 and Madras (now Chennai) was restored to the English.

Above: *Interior of Eglise de Notre Dame des Anges*

Right: *Exterior of Eglise de Notre Dame des Anges on Rue Dumas*

Facing page: *Stairwell in an old French residence which is now occupied by the Ecole Française d'Extrême-Orient*

Right: *A street in the old part of Pondicherry*

Below: *Interior of Eglise de Notre Dame des Anges, Rue Dumas*

The new Governor General, M. Godheu, reached Pondicherry in 1754, and signed a provisional treaty of peace with the English. With this, the English in India succeeded in obtaining all that they had been fighting for, and the French in India renounced all they had sought. Three years later, the French renewed hostilities against the English. Comte de Lally, the Commander-in-Chief and Commissary of King Louis XV, was determined to retrieve the French losses. The Seven Year War in Europe spilled over to India. But Lally's attempts to oust the English from India failed, and he had to retreat to Pondicherry. The English captured all the outposts of Pondicherry and blockaded the town for four-and-a-half months. Lally surrendered, and on his return to France, was executed. The English razed the Pondicherry Fort to a two-feet ruin, which lay buried under the debris of the destroyed buildings.

At the end of the Seven Year War, the Treaty of Paris, signed on February 10, 1763, restored Pondicherry and its dependencies to the French. Dupleix had the city rebuilt, with the basic structure of the town being retained and lying within a circular road. The French town had pride of place along the waterfront with a number of elegant European buildings, gardens and, tree-lined avenues.

Dupleix's other major achievement was Chandernagore, built along the Hooghly upstream from Calcutta (now Kolkata). Late in the 17th century, a French factory was established here in the face of opposition from the Dutch, who already had a presence here. But Aurangzeb permitted the French to build not only a factory, but also a fort to protect it. Thus was the foundation laid of Fort d'Orleans, but it was only under Dupleix that it flourished. By Indian standards it was a small fort, some 600 square feet, built in brick with a bastion at each corner. West of the fort was a tank known as Lal Dighi, and public buildings like hospitals as well as private residences were concentrated near this reservoir. The fort has at its front, a classic French promenade called Quay Dupleix. The administrator's house, with a huge verandah, dominates the waterfront and has large, European-style rooms.

In 1756, Robert Clive, empire builder for the East India Company, destroyed Chandernagore. He returned the fort to the French on the condition that no new fortifications would be built. The Administrator Chevalier responded by building a ditch around the city. From then till 1816, the English continuously attacked Chandernagore. But the Dupleix Palace survived, its spectacular view of the Hooghly secure.

Karaikal was a large settlement south of Pondicherry, located at the mouth of the River Kaveri which the French acquired from the Thanjavur state in 1739. Fort Dauphin at Karaikal was constructed on the same lines as a French fort, projecting outward along the delta and controlling all the trade. The city was developed on the gridiron pattern, an urban planning design unique to Indo-French settlements in India. French motifs were introduced into Indian domestic architecture through Ionic and Corinthian pillars and pilasters.

Yanam was the smallest French settlement in India. Covering an area of only 913 hectares, it was founded by the French on the banks of the River Coringa in 1723 and became a colony under Pondicherry in 1814–15. The town conforms to the grid pattern of street layout, optimising the Coringa riverfront as a quay.

Mahé was seized by the French in 1725 from the *Vazhunnavar* or ruler of Badagara, and was named Mahe after its conqueror Mahé de Bourdonnais. The fort is squarish, with four pointed bastions thrusting outward to optimise the line of vision. Once a town of considerable importance, Mahé's recurrent losses to the English in the late 18th century damaged its trade and it declined into a picturesque backwater.

Above: Library of the Ecole Française d'Extrême-Orient

FRENCH ARCHITECTURE

French houses were built on a similar ground plan, though with strong variations in size, orientation, and detail – a local version of *hotel particulier*, the typical 'private house' of the 18th-century French urban upper class. The major feature is the symmetrical plan and main façade, which usually opens onto a garden and not the street. Only finely decorated gates are visible from the street. Lateral façades (usually plain and rather severe) enhanced the effect of the straight and perpendicular streets. In front of the main facade, columned porticos were built to provide protection from the sun and rain, and provide a pleasant transition from the garden. The plan consists of large, interconnected rooms without corridors. High ceilings and appropriate alignments of doors and windows were incorporated to improve natural ventilation. In fact, they proved to be better adapted to the South Indian climate than to France, where large rooms with high ceilings were difficult to heat in winter.

A major diversion from the French model was the use of flat, terraced roofs, which were uncommon in France. Contemporary references mention strong winds and cyclones as the main reason for this, but we can also assume the influence of Mediterranean architecture, particularly Greek, which represented for the French the typical response to a hot climate. Terraces could be used in the evenings, although they were not very useful during the rainy season and were difficult to maintain.

Since stone was not easily available in Pondicherry, it was scarcely used. Brick was the main building material and was used with lime mortar for all masonry work. Usually Burmese teak was used for timber.

The architectural decoration, using classical orders and motifs, was directly adapted from Europe, with the difference that while the original was carved in stone, the adaptation used local materials.

Government and public buildings followed a style and pattern similar to private houses, but were larger and more profusely decorated. They were usually two-storeyed, with flat roofs and wide porticos along the main façade.

Indian houses in Pondicherry display, to some extent, European influence on the traditional Tamil style. The entrance is from the street, through a finely carved wooden door, behind which lies the traditional verandah with timber columns. Inside, the major feature is the *murram* (central courtyard) with the *kudam* (main room) opening on one side. The courtyard, utilities and garden are at the back. Because of French influence, the ceilings are higher, and decorative elements such as classical columns and balustrades are frequently used. In several cases, the local style is more evident in the ground floor structures, which have more of wood carving, while the French influence is stronger in the upper storey.

Portuguese Forts

The turn of the 15th century witnessed two major historic events in India: the advent of the Portuguese by sea, and the arrival of the Mughals by land. While the Mughal dynasty and its impact in India were established, the expansion of the Portuguese at the same time is also significant. The Portuguese were amongst the first of the European nations to establish trading settlements in India, given that they pioneered the European sea route to India.

"Within fifty years of da Gama's arrival the Portuguese had occupied some 60 miles of coast around Goa, with territories stretching up to 30 miles inland. Northwards from Bombay to Daman, the key, with Diu across the Gulf, to the approaches to rich Gujarat, they occupied a still narrower tract with four important ports and several hundred towns and villages, port fortresses and trading ports – Onor, Barcelor, Mangalore, Cannanor, Cranganore, Cochin and Quilon. Even on the east coast at Negapatnam and San Thome, further military posts and

settlements were created, while as the 16th century drew to a close, a wealthy settlement grew up at Hughli in Bengal."

The first Portuguese settlements were factories or trading stations defended by fortresses. The Portuguese were primarily interested in trade and, therefore in ports, to control trade. A string of coastal forts were established to defend their businesses and ensure uninterrupted trade. These were situated in strategic locations along the coast, controlling trade with the interiors. Fortuitously, the west coast of India provides a natural landscape with capes, islands, or enclaves defined by rivers or canals to build these defences. The forts at Dahanu, Chinchani and Tarapur, Mahim, Colaba, Matunga, Mazagaon and Bandra were all Portuguese fortifications of which no evidence remains. Thane Fort is now used as a jail, while Bombay Fort has few remnants. The island of Gharapuri was a strategic outpost in Bombay Harbour where the historic rock-cut temples were used to store ammunition. Ironically these caves were named Elephanta by the Portuguese who destroyed the elephant sculptures located at the entrance of the ancient temples.

South of Bombay Chaul and Bankot; Janjira, Sindhudurg, Ananvel, Ratnagiri, Vijaydurg, and Suvarnadurg provided them control of most of the west coast. Fort Victoria in Bankot was built by Abyssinian pirates as a shelter and taken over by the Adil Shahis.

Above: Interior of St. Paul's Church

Right: Entrance to Diu Fort from the jetty

Facing page above: Cannons mounted on a fortification in Diu Fort

Facing page below: A view from the jetty

Following pages (238-239): The fort at the edge of the sea has basalt rock formations on one side

It was later used as a naval depot by the Portuguese, controlling the passages of vessels at the mouth of the River Savitri. Few of these forts survive today – a lone bastion at Tarapur and traces of the fortifications at Asava are a few remains, while the fort at Revdanda at the mouth of the River Kundalika, is one of the most imposing forts, not far from the ancient port of Chaul. Built in AD 1558 by the Portuguese as an advance position, this coastal fort is attached to the mainland by a narrow isthmus. The underground tunnels are an architectural wonder, originally accessible by six entrances, each well-concealed and extensive.

Bassein emerged as the most important fortified settlement and served as the capital of the Northern Province. It was captured in 1533 and a factory house was built two years later in the extreme east, next to the quay. Bassein was developed as a urban city with the Church of Nossa Senhora da Vida at the centre. With the advent of the missionaries, ecclesiastical buildings came up in frenzied haste with Franciscans, Jesuits, Dominicans, and Augustinians all vying with each other. A protective fort wall was built to safeguard the settlement in local basalt stone. A number of gates controlled access into Bassein but the most important was Porta do Mar, which secured the sea front.

The port town of Diu was the other important Portuguese settlement in India. The island was strategic and economically important as it controlled opium trade from the Malwa Plateau. Captured by the Portuguese in 1534, it had a fort with high walls and circular turrets. This was substantially renovated in the 1570s with the addition of bastions. The settlement at Diu was the backbone of Portuguese trade in Asia and remained with them

Right: One of the
gates to Vasai Fort

Facing page: Interior of
the Fransciscan Church
inside Vasai Fort

Right: Prayer ceremony at one of the churches inside Vasai Fort

Left: *A sketch of Reis Magos Fort*

Right: *View of Reis Magos Fort from the hill opposite*

till they left India in 1961. Port structures such as the jetty, shipyard, market, and quay were aligned along the canal, reinforcing their supremacy over the waterfront.

Daman too, in the early 16th century, was a major node for trade more because of its very great natural harbour for large ships. It comprised Damao Grande, large Daman and Damao Pequena, the small city. It was conquered in 1559 by the Portuguese who settled on the southern bank of the Damanganga.

The Fort of St Jerome was important as it also served the northern capital of Bassein. The gateway of the fort constructed in AD 1614 is an impressive structure flanked by two giant figures on either side, similar to the Indian *dwarapala*s. The fort area of Moti Daman contains the public buildings including the Governor's Palace and other administrative offices while Nani Daman has the residential quarters. Daman is the only city where the city and its fortifications were built at the same time.

The earliest Portuguese settlements, however, were established on the Malabar Coast, attracted by its rich spice trade, which had, for centuries, already attracted traders from east and west. The Portuguese had a brief and tempestuous encounter in Cochin, building what is erroneously called the Dutch Palace, which they gave to the Raja of Cochin, seeking his favour after a period of plunder. They built the fort, which was severely damaged in an attack by the Zamorin of Calicut but enlarged and rebuilt it in 1505, adding inner and outer fortifications to provide adequate protection. In 1663, the Dutch defeated the Portuguese, capturing the fort and renovating the palace for the raja in return for their 'colony'. It eventually fell to the British, who signed an alliance with the Raja of Cochin. The outer walls of Cochin Fort still provide protection against the force of the sea. Forts were also built in Mangalore, Cannanore, and Cranganore, of which there is no evidence today.

For the Portuguese, Goa was their 'capture'. It became one of the most powerful of their colonies, redefining Indian and Portuguese culture. Although Goa is best known for its fusion of Southern European culture, its history long predates its colonisation. It is believed to have been mentioned by Bhishmaparva in the Mahabharata as Gopakpattan or Gomanta and in Ptolemy's *Geography, Goa* is referred to as 'Gouba'. Its recorded history is from the Mauryan Empire in India in the 3rd century BC and later the Chalukyas of Badami in the 6th century, followed by the Rashtrakutas and the Kalyani Chalukyas. The Kadambas ruled Goa from AD 1020 for 300 years, as Goa became an important centre for maritime trade. It fell to the Sultans of

Delhi in the 14th century, then the Vijaynagara Empire and the Bahmanis in the 15th century.

Goa was with the Adil Shahis of Bijapur when the Portuguese landed. When Alfonso de Albuquerque captured Goa in November 1510, it was already a well-established settlement and was according to chroniclers, "*very large, with godly edifices and handsome streets and squares surrounded by walls and towers There is a very good fortress in it, and in the environs, many gardens and orchards of fine trees and fruits and many pools of good water*". The Portuguese moved quickly to ensure absolute control and within a decade, new buildings were built on the remnants of the older structures and construction mushroomed. Built in the Manueline style and later in Baroque, these European structures were translated by Indian artisans, as laterite became the preferred building material and craftsmen learnt a new architectural vocabulary. By the end of the 17th century, Velha Goa had around

Entrance to the fort is across a bridge that spans the moat

31 churches, 38 convents and monasteries and a large number of chapels and oratories protected by a fortified wall. The city reached its zenith around 1580 as 'Rome of the East', but not for long. There was no water supply and inhabitants were compelled to use the contaminated water from ponds and wells. By the turn of the 16th century, epidemic and plague devastated Velha Goa. Old Goa, as the colonial headquarters ceased to exist and the administrative headquarters and the Archbishop's Palace shifted to Panjim, securing the spiritual and temporal power at the summit of its lone hill, Altinho. Even today, the Archbishop's Palace towers over its surroundings; its elegant façade lies at the end of a long driveway. Within, elegant rooms furnished with period furniture give it an imposing aura. The official residence of the Governor General of Goa was Palacio do Cabo and it remains the residence of the Governors of independent India. Located on a promontory at some distance from the newly developing city of Panjim, Cabo as it is colloquially known, is a later Portuguese building with a panoramic view across the seas. Fort Aguada is across the bay to the north and Marmugao port is to the south. Because of its commanding position, it was originally developed as a fort for controlling entry to two of Goa's main maritime waterways – the Zuari and the Mandovi.

In 1541, a chapel was built by the Franciscans. It grew in importance and Antonio Bocarro in 1633 gave a detailed description of the fortress. It is located about 20 bracas (44 metres) from the base of the hill, with the church and the friary at the top of the hill almost 70 bracas (154 metres) above sea level. The fortress

Right: Main façade of the palace

Below: Interior of the Hall of the Patriarchs

was about 82-metres long, 20-metres wide and 1.32-metres high with a provision for artillery at intervals. Cabo Fort was constructed with laterite available at the site, and was built precariously along the slope of the hill.

A seven-storey house accommodated the captain and below there were about twelve incomplete small houses for the *bombardeiros*, or artillerymen. There were four bronze guns with gun carriages on the platform of the fortress. The Franciscan friars, who kept sufficient ammunition in the convent for these four guns, doubled up to act as informers from this outpost. The British briefly occupied it during the Napoleonic Wars but in 1813, the Portuguese reclaimed it and made it the Governor General's residence.

Cabo has a romantic legend attached to it as it is said Dona Paula de Menezes, the daughter of a Portuguese Viceroy threw herself off the cliff, when refused permission to marry a local fisherman, Gaspar Dias. The area nearby is now known as Dona Paula. In 1594, a small chapel dedicated to Nossa Senhora do Cabo, 'Our Lady of the Cape' along with a monastery was built at the end of the residence serving as a landmark for seafarers.

Palacio Do Cabo is a double-storeyed building with elegant public rooms and a vast verandah on the sea-facing side at the upper level. The rooms are decorated with fine Portuguese and Chinese artefacts including five tall Cantonese vases, believed to be over 300 years old, as well as two large-sized Cantonese bowls with a coat of arms and wooden ormolu-mounted chests with veneer wood inlay, and Carara marble tops. The chapel is still in worship but the monastery is now the guest wing of the residence.

Above: Portraits of previous patriarchs line the walls of the Hall of Patriarchs

Right: Interior of the chapel within Archbishop's Palace

Fort Dansborg

Below: Fort Dansborg *overlooking the sea*

Facing page above: *View of Fort Dansborg from the jetty*

Facing page below: *Main façade*

Nearly four hundred years ago, Danish sailors arrived at the picturesque Tamil coastal village of Tarangambadi. Its strategic location instantly made it attractive to the Danes as a trading post for their ambitions in the East. This windy beach town is a hollow remnant of Danish presence on the East Coast. Today, along the grandly named King's Road is a small memorial where the Danes landed. The massive Fort Dansborg is the centrepiece of the settlement, its forbidding walls built in a stolid style, reflecting a short but volatile history as the Danish tried to establish an eastern outpost. Today its walls are a sad reminder that this tiny town was once a much coveted port.

The founding of the first Danish East India Company was based on the hopes and ambitions inspired by expansionist ventures of the Portuguese, British, and Dutch companies. The Danes, too, sought a role in the promise of wealth from India and their merchants set sail to establish trading posts.

In October 1620, they arrived at the court of the Nayak of Tanjore and within a month, they concluded a treaty between the

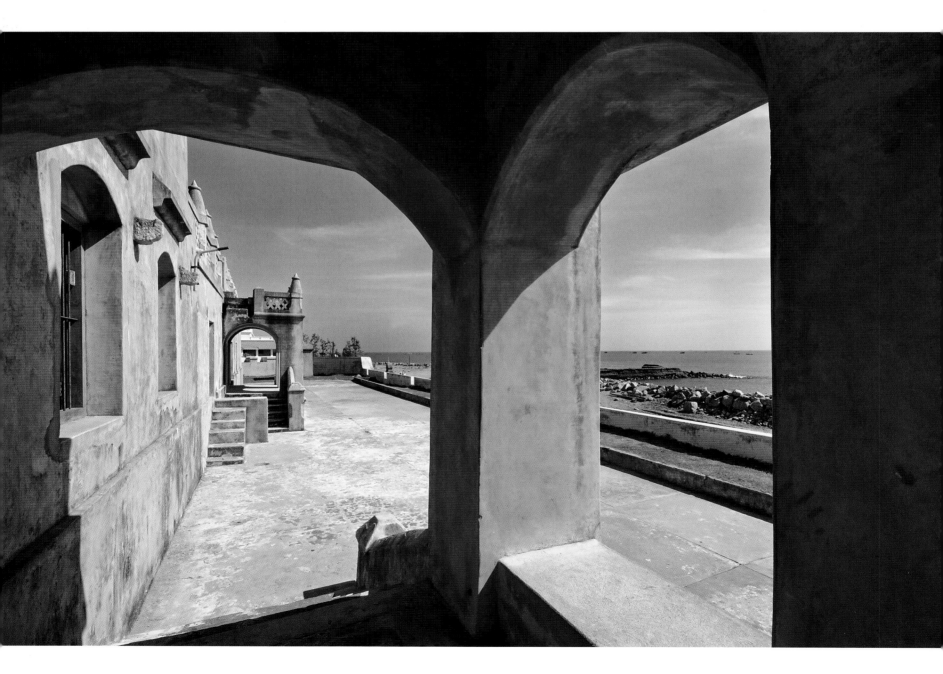

nayak and the King of Denmark. This granted them permission to erect a fortress at the village of Tarangambadi or Tranquebar, as they later called it. Theirs was a difficult venture. They were late entrants into the east coast of India and had to fight off the presence of European traders already entrenched with the Mughals. However, Tranquebar was an essential base for trade in the fabled wealth of Golconda, then at its peak. The Danes also sought to use Tranquebar as a base for trade in the Far East as they established trade in cloves and pepper with Indonesia and the coast of Thailand. They also set up ports in Masulipatnam and Pipli, all of which required to be defended. Pipli was particularly troublesome as the Danish ships were constantly looted. Nonetheless, the Danes signed trade agreements with the Mughals whose master stroke was to allow as many traders as possible and avoid monopoly; but this was short-lived. Their only sustained presence in India was to be at Serampore, along the Hooghly, where by the grace and favour of the British Empire, European aspirants were contained.

The Danish trading venture proved unviable. The company lasted less than a hundred years, during which time they took just seven ships out of Asia. They faced mutiny from within and were always under pressure from the Dutch, perhaps as an extension of pressures in Europe. In order to bolster the dwindling Danish force, Portuguese and Portuguese-Indians were hired to help garrison the fort, and they soon made up the majority of the colony's military strength. Eventually, the Danes were unable to afford paying tribute to the nayak, and he sent his army to lay siege but was unsuccessful.

In 1668, the Danish government finally sent reinforcements to India and a group of soldiers arrived a year later. With this, trade was officially resumed, and was followed by a period of prosperity. The king's emissary to the court of the nayak also resulted in Tranquebar expanding its territories by another three villages. Less than 50 years later, the Danish company was dissolved, as it had failed to acquire the independent riches of the French or the Portuguese and so of no interest to the Danish monarch. India was in disarray with the decline of the Mughal Empire, and it was in a period of realignment of power. The emergence of colonial powers, shifting from factories to fortified settlements, was not enough. The embattled war lords of India and the rapacious trading companies wanted control.

And so Dansborg Fort remains, a silent reminder of what might have been a great colony, but was effectively just a small-time East Indian trader. Inside, the fort is a stark reminder of how grim life was for seafarers of the time.

Fort St George

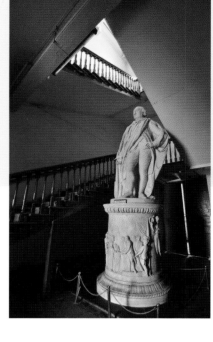

The Coromandel Coast was one of the most attractive in India even though its waters were treacherous; it was safe haven after the long voyage around Cape Comorin. It was to become one of the British Empire's most important settlements, one which established their aspirations to rule India. Fort St George was its foundation, a new settlement in 1640. Its fortifications along the seafront assured the British direct access for what was at that time a mere trading post. The British traded in spices and cheap calico and the fort was built to protect those interests.

Nearby, Madras had already been visited by the Portuguese and the Dutch, and around the 1st century AD by St Thomas, who first brought Christianity to India. Its first English settlers were Andrew Cogan and Francis Day of the John Company. They obtained a grant of land from the local ruler of the Vijayanagara Empire, the Nayak of Poonamalli. While they initially had to make do with straw huts on the beach, soon they built the fort and some houses within. The first building was the factory or fort house, enclosed within a brick and mud wall, and it took 13 years to build. As the area grew, with Armenians and Portuguese also settling here, the outer fort became necessary. At the time, the climate was pleasant and for Europeans, was healthy. Madras was a favoured place although it did not have a natural harbour. Disembarkation took place virtually on the high seas, transferring people first onto country boats, and then onto land.

The first Governor of Madras was George Foxcroft who settled in Madras in 1666. From 1639 till 1666, the head of the East India Company government in Madras were agents as befitted their position as traders. Fort St George built in 1659 was a 'white' settlement while the 'natives' lived outside in less secure enclosures. By 1682, a large masonry wall replaced the mud ramparts of the native township. At that time, lines of separation were not so sharply drawn and there was a lot of interaction, and even marriage between the British and the Indians. Indian merchants and suppliers were attracted to the settlement and encouraged to build houses with promises of exemptions from import taxes for 30 years. It is said that within the first year of the settlement, some 70 to 80 substantial houses were built to the north and south of the fort, while in the village of Madraspatnam nearly four hundred families of weavers had come to settle permanently.

In 1673, Fryers describe it as "sweet and clean", with double-storeyed houses "with beautiful porticoes and terraced walks with shade trees planted before the doors". Within a span of 60 years, Cogan and Day's fort had grown into a city housing 300,000 people. The fort's fortunes were volatile as they became the Indian focus of the Anglo-French wars, hotly contested by both sides but eventually restored to the English, who optimally used their European superiority following the Treaty of Aix-la-Chapelle, in dealing with the French in India. In 1748, Fort St George was restored to the English.

The inner fort is square in plan while the outer fort is oblong, walled on three sides, and bound by the River Elambor on one side. Following the French occupation from 1746 to 1749 when they damaged much of the built fabric, the English invested in

Right: Staircase in Clive's house

Above right: Statue of Lord Cornwallis once installed in the Rotunda, is now housed in the museum

Facing page above: Stained glass window in St Mary's Church located inside the fort

Facing page below: Corridor, first floor, Clive's house

massive reconstruction and fortification. In time, the inner wall was removed as the outer fortifications were extensively strengthened. The western front altered the course of the river, with earth infill from nearby Nari Meedu, and the northern and northeastern sections were developed. However, its present octagonal shape was created by Colonel Patrick Ross in the 1770s; two of the bastions were amalgamated into a single gigantic one and to the east, the wall was strengthened with smaller bastions. Inner and outer ravelins were sharply angled and were additions to the fortification. A moat further reinforced its position. Within the walls, there was a vaulted chamber for the troops and ammunition. Cisterns were built under the walls to hold enough water for 6,000 men over four months.

The first agents and the Governor lived inside the fort and as a result, some exceedingly handsome buildings were constructed. The architectural focus of the entire complex is the Fort Square. At the centre of the square an Ionic Rotunda was installed in 1799, with a statue of Lord Cornwallis at its centre, commemorating the defeat of Tipu Sultan, 'Tiger of Mysore', at the siege of Seringapatam. Brass cannons with tiger emblems were installed around it. In 1735, Governor Pitt constructed a handsome colonnade linking the square with the sea gate. It had a roof supported by 32 pillars of brilliant black Pallavaram stone arranged in four rows. When the French captured Madras in 1746, they took the pillars to Pondicherry. In 1761, when the British stormed Pondicherry they took the pillars back to their original location, Pitt's arcade. Here they remained, even when the arcade was walled in to create the Exchange Building. In 1910, when the new Council Chamber was built in Classical style the pillars were taken to embellish its façade. They remain, curiously resembling a grand Italian church.

In the fort, the Governor's house was his home, 'Secretariat' as well as Council Chamber. St Mary's Church was the religious centre and the first Anglican Church in India. Nearby, the Accountant General's office along with several others, present a well-planned township described by William Hodges in 1781 as follows: "*The stile of the building is generally handsome. They consist of long colonnades with open porticoes, and flat roofs and offer the eye an appearance similar to what we may conceive of a Grecian city in the age of Alexander. The clear blue and cloudless sky, the polished white buildings, the bright sandy beach and the dark green sea present a combination totally new to the eye of an Englishman.*"

Viceregal Lodge

Towards the latter half of the 19th century, a second home was becoming a characteristic part of English life in India. The development of hill stations was principally to provide for themselves relief from the searing heat of the plains; which in time grew to be the ultimate pleasure retreat, most of them exclusively for whites with a rigid social hierarchy more difficult to enforce in the plains, where business and governance tended to merge.

Lord Lawrence, the Governor General believed that it was necessary to have a summer capital, and was a great advocate of shifting the capital to the more salubrious climate of Shimla. He lobbied his government to shift the capital to Shimla on strategic grounds since it had been a safe haven during the 'mutiny'.

It had already been settled early in the 19th century by the British as a retreat during summer, with many of them building English country cottages in and around what was a tiny Himalayan village. In 1864 it became the summer capital of the British Empire in India. Rudyard Kipling in his *Tale of Two Cities* captured the entire concept of shifting a fully operational government halfway across India:

But the rulers in that City by the sea
Turned to flee
Fled with each returning spring and tide from its ills
To the hills

Lord Lawrence's achievement was soon followed by Lord Dufferin's dream of a great romantic house suitable for the stature

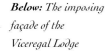
Below: *The imposing façade of the Viceregal Lodge*

of the Governor. Dufferin pursued his goals and the Viceregal Lodge was realised on a grand scale. At the same time a large number of English-style buildings were constructed in Shimla for the summer administration of the Indian Empire, transferring a bit of England to the Himalayas.

Although Henry Irwin designed the building in 1888, Dufferin personally involved himself in the details, and he and his wife visited the site almost daily, modifying it as it was built. Situated on a vast spur west of Shimla and located on a 331-acre site, it commanded the landscape for miles around. The hilltop was levelled to provide just enough land for the building and a garden. Visible from miles around, it was designed to be an unassailable symbol of Empire.

Over the portico at the main entrance is a coat of arms with inscriptions naming the architect, the executive and assistant engineers and the Earl of Dufferin, then the Viceroy, and its first occupant. Built of local gray and light blue limestone, it assumed truly grand proportions as it freely interpreted Elizabethan style with Victorian grimness, devoid of any Indian element. Irwin described it as 'English Renaissance', evoking the dark gray somnolence of a Scottish Castle.

Left: Entrance hall with wooden galleries

The great entrance hall is imposing with wooden galleries all the way round. Mullioned windows and a glass ceiling light the galleried corridors. The impressive roof rises three floors to the top of the building and is spanned by colossal wood beams and an enormous Burma teak staircase sweeps over the entrance to the upper floors. To the left, the ballroom has a sprung dance floor, which leads into the State Dining Hall, also richly panelled in wood with Elizabethan strap work and the crests of previous Viceroys.

The Council Chamber is a separate wing towards the rear and connected to the centre of the main building. The kitchen wing descends three levels along the contour of the hill. The Viceregal Lodge was amongst the first buildings to be electrified in Shimla and its kitchen and service complex is noteworthy for introducing modern conveniences. It had its own steam generator, a laundry and running hot and cold water. It was planned to the last detail with a sophisticated system for collecting and storing bath and rainwater, including two tanks under the front lawn.

The suites of the Viceroy and Vicereine located to the west of the building command a panoramic view. To the east of the main building is the public entry wing, a separate block connected by a portico. The Viceregal Lodge is situated in the quintessential English garden, almost completely protected within a rhododendron forest. To the north it descends to tennis courts and croquet lawns, catering to the whims of fine English country gentlemen. As Shimla gained in importance and as the summer capital was clearly a successful venture, the Shimla Kalka Railway was built to augment accessibility. It is one of the great engineering accomplishments of the British as it has no less than 107 tunnels and often cross chasms over precipitous viaducts. With the arrival of the railway Shimla became a bustling town as sometimes over 7,000 Europeans made the journey every summer, all of whom had to call on the Viceroy. Today it is the Institute of Advanced Studies, but now has an almost ghostly atmosphere; swathed in mist, it seems to reflect the fate of the Empire, now long gone.

Epilogue

VANISHING HERITAGE

Over the last three decades certainly, but more realistically over the last hundred plus years, the fate of the great forts and palaces of India has become increasingly vulnerable. Today governments fight to protect the heritage in a system which no longer validates traditional ownership. With the adoption of colonial systems of protection, India's massive resource of monuments went into foster care. The Archaeological Survey of India, now 150 years old, bears the responsibility of India's heritage along with State Departments of Archaeology, overall no more than 6,000 sites. But in reality much of India's heritage lies outside their protective fencing, fighting a battle against extinction.

Golconda Fort's outer fortifications are encroached upon and Court orders forbidding construction in its precinct are observed in the breach; Jaisalmer Fort has lost its plumage to rapacious hoteliers; Talbehat is slowly returning to nature, and Bandhavgarh is now almost inaccessible. Many of these, once abandoned, fell into decay and it is only in the last hundred-odd years that the painstaking process of recovery has been undertaken at some of these sites. But the battle is relentless as open cast mining threatens one and infrastructure another; remote locations, wildlife sanctuaries and sheer lack of skilled manpower make it a daunting challenge. Equally, once the monument, building or site has lost its place or relevance for its stakeholders, its future is even more uncertain.

The great forts and palaces of India once restored need to be celebrated as sentinels of India's ancient history; we need to engage with them in today's context; no longer conquered and rebuilt, but restored as the memory banks of valour, tempestuous battles; great beauty and often great cruelty. Knowing that each fort and palace provides a clue to what defines the nation today; that they are the building blocks of Bharat, there must be a paradigm shift from providing mere protection to an affirmative commitment. These sites must provide the canvas for scholarship, for a greater understanding of our history, expanding the frontiers of knowledge, and providing crucial records of our time.

New mechanisms for management must be charted. Partnership in management is essential if the forts and palaces are to become vibrant destinations. Expansion of tourism will be both challenging and constructive ensuring these sites are preserved in a new avatar, celebrating the past in the present. Indian culture requires its heritage to be infused with life to make it relevant. Each fort and palace will present a unique set of challenges, requiring unique solutions, all of which must be embraced. Ultimately restoring custodianship to the community and the stakeholders will ensure sustainability; it is a partnership waiting to happen.

Facing page: Door depicting Krishna
Leela inside Anup Mahal, Bikaner

Glossary

Agni fire, also God of Fire

Anantsayi Vishnu image of Vishnu reclining

androon inner portion of a fort

apadana square pillared hall, sometimes with porticoes on one or all sides

apsara celestial dancing girl

Arthashastra ancient Indian treatise on military strategy, statecraft and economy

ashrafi gold coin

baithak seating area

baoli stepwell

bangladar roof with curved and often drooping eaves of Bengali origin

baradari pavilion of twelve doors or pillars, generally outdoors and used in summer

batti wick lamp

begum Muslim noble lady

Bhagavata Purana Hindu literature on the ten avatars of Vishnu; Krishna in particular

bhawan house

bhoomi sacred soil or land

burj defensive tower, built as a part of the fortification but could also house pavilions

char bagh quadripartite walled garden with walkways and water channels

chattri small domed pavilion

chowk open square or court

daitya demon

dargah complex built around the shrine of a Muslim Pir or Saint

darshan practice of public audience by a king or emperor from a balcony, or viewing of the divine being

darwaza gate or door

dashavatar the ten incarnations of Vishnu

deva God

Din-e-Ilahi the new world faith conceived by Emperor Akbar that was both liberal and mystical

durbar king's public audience or court

durg fort

dwarapala guardian of the gate

farman orders of the king or palace

gaddi throne

garbagriha inner sanctum of the temple

garhi fortification or small fort

garh-mahal fort-palace

giri durg hill fort

gol circular

gopi girl who looks after cows; foremost of Krishna's devotees

gopuram gateway to a South Indian temple, often multi-storeyed

gumbaz domed mausoleum

gur mollases

gurudwara Sikh house of worship

hamam traditional bathing house

haveli residential house built around courtyard

hawa mahal palace designed with a current of air blowing through

howdah seating platform with railings on top of an elephant

jagir small territory granted by a king to his commander or general in gratitude for his services

jala durg fort secured by a water body

jali perforated screen designed for privacy

janapada strictly describes the footprint of the tribe but in usage means the land where the *jana*s settled and evolved into a state

jana tribe or clan

jauhar tradition of mass immolation, or voluntary death by women of a royal house when their men faced defeat in war

jawab answer or reply

jharokha overhanging oriel window supported by brackets

jyot sacred lamp

jyoti sacred light

kachi garhi mud fort

khandi measure of weight

khatmbandi wood craft used for ceilings in a geometric pattern from Kashmir

kiledar guardian of the fort

kudam footstep

kund tank

langar public dining hall

linga/lingam phallic representation of Lord Shiva

liwan vaulted hall

madrasa teaching college attached to a mosque

mahajanapada great republic

mahal palace

mahashila-kantaka large catapult used for hurling rocks

mahi durg mud fort

mandala diagram representing concentric energy circle

mandapa large assembly hall

mantrashala study hall

marubhoomi desert land

marusthali land of the dead

matha monastery attached to a temple

Meru Hindu mythological concept of a central world mountain

mihir sun

mihrab niche on the wall of a mosque facing Mecca

mori corridor between two fortification walls

nahar small river or stream

nara durg fort protected by able-bodied men

naubat khana drum house used to signal the arrival of the king, or other celebrations

navratna nine jewels

Nritya Mudra hand gestures, positions used in classical Indian dances

nrityashala dance hall

pachesi ancient Indain game similar to backgammon and played with cowrie shells

padipura entrance gateway of a Kerala palace

pandit Hindu gentleman of high caste and learning

pankha fan

patti leaf

phansi ghar hanging gallery or house

porte-cochère carriage entrance protruding from a building, with a canopy or roof

prasada multi-storeyed structure in a temple or palace

pujari temple priest

pumukham hall of public audience

Puranas ancient Hindu texts

rajgaddi throne of the king (Maratha)

rajwada palace of the king (Marathi)

sapta-matrika seven mother goddesses

sati ultimate sacrifice of a wife in an ancient custom of immolation on a husband's funeral pyre

sawal question

sehan courtyard

serai usually a one-sided enclosure with resting rooms for travellers

Shahenshah King of kings

shardul leogryph

Shastra ancient Hindu text

shikhara temple tower

shila stone slab

sthali sacred place

swarajya profound understanding of self-rule

takht throne (Urdu)

tal lake

talao/talav small lake or pond

Teerthankara Jain teachers

tehkhana underground chamber

tilak symbol of auspiciousness applied on the forehead

tirtha ford or place of pilgrimage

toran specific design of an arched gateway

tosha khana treasury or storehouse for wealth

vahan vehicle

vana durg forest fort

Varaha boar avatar of Vishnu

Vastu Purusha sacred concept of space and spatial quality, fundamental to the layout of a temple

vihara Buddhist monastery

wada wooden haveli usually in the western region

Yali mythological protectors of the deities in South Indian architecture

zamindar landlord

zamindari large landholding

zenana womens quarters

Acknowledgements

The research for this book has meant working through an intimidating number of books of immense scholarship. I have also attempted to draw upon the wonderful legends, which enrich every site, as it is my belief that India's cultural heritage exists in this soft zone between empirical fact and divine legend. Although much of the legend, being somewhat obscure, has not been included in this book it made the journey rich and tantalising.

I would like to record my profound gratitude to successive Directors General, officers and staff of the Archaeological Survey of India, who have been incredibly supportive over so many years that it is not possible to name any one. They have all borne my meddling with remarkable equanimity; for this I am indebted.

My grateful thanks are due to so many people who have over the last few decades shared the joy of discovering these sites and a collective passion for India's heritage. Friends, colleagues, associates and experts whom I worked with over the years came up trumps during the course of realising this book. I am especially grateful to Gaj Singhji, Mahender 'Monty' Singh, Brij Raj Singhji, Raghubir Singh, Nandini Mehtab, Kanika Devi, Richard Holkar, Geetika Kalha, Dr Aminudeen Khan, Habiba Miranda, Father Loiola, Rahul Mehrotra, Shikha Jain, Abha Narain Lambah, Annabel Lopez, and so many more who have shared my journey.

Most of all my special thanks are due to Minakshi and Kulbhushan Jain who believed in me, Alpana Khare who gave me a free hand to get on with this, Ajay Kumar and Nilakshi Banerji for research. And finally Khalid for everything.

AMITA BAIG

I would like to acknowledge the following for their help and support in putting together this book:

Mysore Palace Board, Ashok Panda of INTACH, Pondicherry, Maharaja Sawai Man Singh II Museum Trust, Maharana Mewar Charitable Trust, H.H. Maharaja of Bundi, H.H. Maharaja Sir Jiwajirao Scindia Museum, Mannu Raje Charitable Trust, H.H. Maharaja of Benaras, His Excellency Silipe Neri Ferarao, Archbishop of Goa and Daman, H.H. Usha Malhotra of Indore, Rajkumari Pragya Deb Burman, Kanwaljit Rathore in Indore, Kashi Naresh, Varanasi, Eternal Mewar, The City Palace, Udaipur, Bhupendra Singh Auwa, Jyoti Jasol, Gajendra Singh, City Palace, Udaipur, H.H. Maharaja Gaj Singh II of Jodhpur, Mehrangarh Museum Trust, Mamta K. Singh, Umaid Bhawan Palace, Jodhpur, Taj Hotels Resorts and Palaces, Harshvardhan Singh, Udaibilas, Dungarpur, Sri Brijraj Singh, Jodhpur, Maharaja Ganga Sinhji Trust for Bikaner, Mr. Upadhyay, Radha and Sabhapati, Renu Rao and the staff at Deckle Edge, Ecole Française d'Extrême-Orient, Dr. Amin-ud-din Khan, Neel and Supriti, Babu John, Shikha Jain, Bhavna and Chandrashekhar Singh, Kavita and Santosh Namby Chandran, Mr. Indulkar, Aditya Patankar, Arvind Diwan and family, Mr. Vinod, Hari Charan Pal, Mr. Maheshwarkar, the Fialho's, Elizabeth and Jaison Joseph, Ajit Rao, Shabeer Unnwala, Parag Mankeekar, Madhura Yadav, Geetika Kalha, Mr. D.P. Reddy, Harjit Singh and family, Surjit Singh and family, Conrad and Pallavi Fernandez, Asit Biswas, Pralay Dhar, Nandini Mahtab, Janhwij Sharma, Sunder Paul and Shailan Parker.

I would also like to thank the staff at the following Archaeological Survey of India locations: Agra Circle, Bangalore Circle, Bhopal Circle, Chennai Circle, Delhi Circle, Dharwad Circle, Hyderabad Circle, Jaipur Circle, Leh Circle, Lucknow Circle, Patna Circle, Shimla Circle, Directorate of Archaeology, Trivandrum, and the Director Cultural Affairs, Punjab.

JOGINDER SINGH